GEOMANCY

Published in the US by Wooden Books LLC, San Rafael, California
and in the UK by Wooden Books LTD, Glastonbury, Somerset

Library of Congress Cataloging-in-Publication Data is available.

ISBN-10: 1-952178-30-4
ISBN-13: 978-1-952178-30-6

Visit Wooden Books' web site at www.woodenbooks.com

1 3 5 7 9 8 6 4 2

Designed and typeset by Wooden Books Ltd,
Glastonbury, Somerset, UK

Printed in China on 100% FSC
approved sustainable papers by FSC
RR Donnelley Asia Printing Solutions Ltd.

GEOMANCY

EARTH GRIDS, LEY LINES, FENG SHUI, DIVINATION, DOWSING & DRAGONS

CONTENTS

Above: Fortuna, the Roman Goddess of fortune and fate, by Hans Sebald Beham, 1541. She was worshipped extensively in Italy from the earliest times and is the keeper of destiny, consulted for good fortunes and prosperity. Often depicted bearing a cornucopia of abundance, a spinner of destiny, and a ball representing the uncertainty of fortune. The ancient arts of geomancy aim to align a person or place with their best fortune and thus attract good luck.

EDITOR'S PREFACE

Geomancy, from the Greek Γεωμαντεια 'Earth Divination', is the art of atunement of a person, building or place to the subtle energies of the living Earth by means of occult techniques. One medieval technique of divination also goes by the same name (*see pages 392-395*), but in this book, as elsewhere today, the term is primarily used to cover the entire field of what has become known as 'Earth Mysteries', from the study of ley lines, dowsing and Feng Shui to the siting and alignments of ancient monuments. I became fascinated in the subject as a boy when I watched a builder use dowsing rods to find a buried water pipe. Such skills remain alive today, with acupuncturists tracking energy lines through human bodies and people sensing the vibrations of ancient temples. So what are these peculiar powers which lie within ourselves and the Earth?

This compendium of six Wooden Books aims to throw some light on to the subject. We begin with Hugh Newman's exposition of *Earth Grids*, which describes an ancient global network of geomantic structures. Next, seer Jewels Rocka introduces us to the ancient arts of *Divination*, still practiced widely all over the world. This is followed by geomancer Richard Creightmore's treatise on *Feng Shui*, arguably the oldest intact school of geomancy. Next, diviner Hamish Miller describes the history and the how-to of *Dowsing*. Then, architect Danny Sullivan, ex-editor of the *Ley Hunter* magazine, introduces us to the mysterious world of *Leys*. And finally, we present historian Joyce Hargreaves' essay on *Dragons*, the gatekeepers to the entire subject.

Welcome, dear reader, to the mysterious world of geomancy.

BOOK I

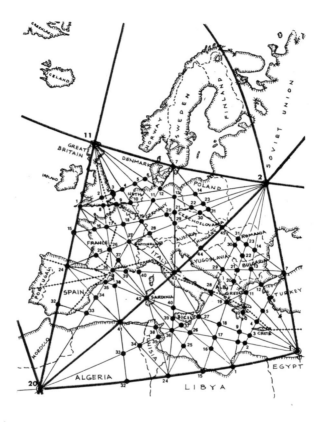

Above: European Becker-Hagens grid. Facing page: Mecca at the Golden Section of the French World Map. Golden latitudes occur at 21.25° north and south of the Equator. Mecca's latitude is 21.42° N, a mere 11.5 miles north of the Golden latitude. Golden longitudes occur 42.49° E and W of the moveable 0° meridian. Using the old 0° meridian through Paris the Golden meridian passes a mere 19 miles east of Mecca (after Martineau).

EARTH GRIDS

THE SECRET PATTERNS
OF GAIA'S SACRED SITES

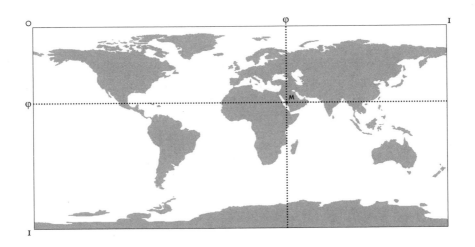

Hugh Newman

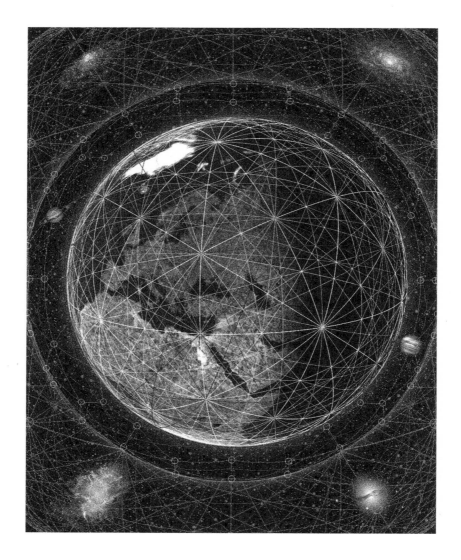

INTRODUCTION

The idea that there is, or even might be, an Earth grid seems far fetched to many people. However, travellers have always needed to know where they are on the planet and the ancient system of longitude and latitude is one such grid which we all still use today.

The use of geometry is particularly widespread in the buildings of the ancient world and modern grid researchers speculate as to whether the ancients, when siting their great temples, were aware not only of the local archaeoastronomy, but also of the relationship of their location to other important sites around the world.

Nowadays we have electricity grids, water networks, phone systems and the internet, which criss-cross and surround us all. In the ancient world, the Chinese system of medicine described meridians of energy travelling through the body with acupuncture points at its nodes, and understood the Earth as having a similar network of energy lines.

The Earth today is seen as a living organism, and in the last thirty or so years, various books and articles have proposed Earth energy grids and the placement of ancient sites upon them. Indeed, the way they are placed around the planet suggest an informed and scientific project that was shared all around the globe in prehistory.

This book unravels the short history of grid research and takes another look at the distribution of sacred sites around the planet, revealing a remarkable network of surveying and megalithic engineering that supports the ancient idea of a geometric, or 'Earth-measured' worldview, which can now be seen as a new model for Gaia.

THE EARTH

her structure, movement and natural energies

The Earth is 4.57 billion years old, and life appeared on it within one billion years of its formation. Oxygenic photosynthesis began about 2.7 billion years ago, forming the atmosphere we enjoy today. The Earth is skinned in several major layers (*opposite top*).

Earth's outer surface is divided into massive tectonic plates that migrate across the surface due to continental drift. The planet once had just one large landmass and one great ocean. Today a mid-oceanic ridge runs around the entire planet, renewing the thin sea floor. In the mid-Atlantic, this ridge constantly erupts, pushing the Americas away from Europe and Africa (*below left*). Its current pattern in some areas resembles that of a dodecahedron (*below right*).

The equatorial radius of the Earth is 3,963.19 miles, 13 miles greater than the polar radius of 3,949.90 miles; the equatorial bulge resulting from the Earth's spin. Although the Earth changes over millions of years, it has remained basically the same during human civilisation.

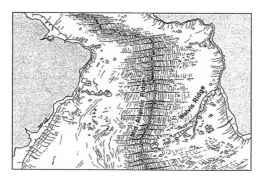

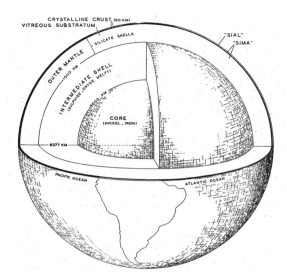

Left: *The structure of the Earth. The crust descends merely 4 miles in the oceans, and 18-40 miles on land. The slowly flowing viscous mantle has a depth of about 1,800 miles (2,900 km). The core is thought to be liquid with a solid inner centre. The Earth's magnetic field derives from convection in the outer iron-rich core, combined with stirring caused by the Earth's rotation. The inner core of the Earth also rotates slightly faster than the rest of the planet. On the surface, fault lines, earthquake epicentres, geomagnetic forces and natural electrical (telluric) currents are all part of the traditional science of geomancy, today termed 'earth energy' and central to the idea of a world grid.*

Right: *The primary fault-lines in the British Isles, along which earthquakes are most likely to occur. In the UK thunderstorms are much more frequent over areas with little or no faulting. Below: The tectonic plates which make up the Earth's crust. Opposite left: The mid–Atlantic Ridge, formed by two plates pulling apart, and the roughly dodecahedral path it follows.*

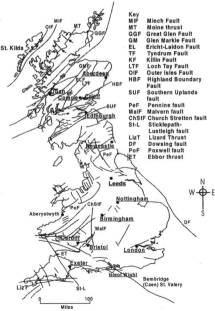

Key
MiF	Minch Fault
MT	Moine thrust
GGF	Great Glen Fault
GM	Glen Markle Fault
EL	Ericht-Laidon Fault
TF	Tyndrum Fault
KF	Killin Fault
LTF	Loch Tay Fault
OIF	Outer Isles Fault
HBF	Highland Boundary Fault
SUF	Southern Uplands fault
PeF	Pennine fault
MalF	Malvern fault
ChStF	Church Stretton fault
St-L	Sticklepath-Lustleigh fault
LizT	Lizard Thrust
DF	Dowsing fault
PoF	Poxwell fault
ET	Ebbor thrust

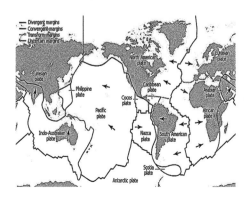

THE GEOMAGNETIC FIELD
electromagnetism and telluric energies

The Earth's magnetic field takes a daily beating when struck by gusts of solar wind, as seen in the colourful 'Northern Lights'. The system is in flux. At dawn, the magnetic field lines (*opposite top*) shrink and then surge through the land, our homes, our bodies and our brains each day. The field weakens at night then roars back to life every morning. At some natural places local geology makes this even stronger due to the effect of rocks, insulators (such as chalk) or the presence of water.

Magnetism and electrical force are two sides of the same coin. A moving electrical current generates a magnetic field, and a changing magnetic field generates electric current in anything present that will conduct it. The Earth itself is subject to the same forces—the field lines generate weak DC currents in the ground and, like all electric currents, these telluric energies travel better in some media than others. Ground containing a high level of metal or mineral-rich water conducts these natural daily currents particularly well. Drier or less metallic ground conducts it less well. When these two types of land intersect, a 'conductivity discontinuity' occurs. Interestingly, this is also where many ancient sites seem to be located and often where anomalous 'balls of light' are seen, possibly created by natural electrical charge from the sudden drop in the magnetism of the field lines.

At Stonehenge and other ancient sites, a henge cut over three feet into the ground resists this telluric energy, directing it through the entrance, building up electrical charge within the site. Is this one of the lost technologies of the ancients? Were they harnessing it worldwide into a planetary grid of energy?

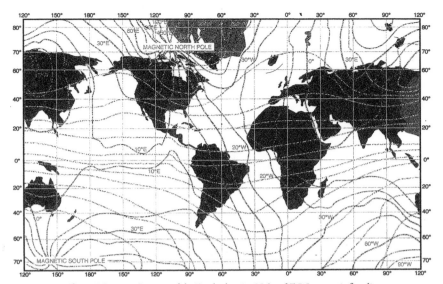

Above: Magnetic Currents of the Earth, showing N-S and E-W magnetic flow lines.

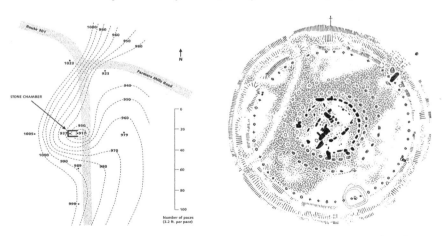

Above: Geomagnetic contour map of a Native American rock chamber in Kent Cliff, New York, showing magnetic anomaly at the doorway (J. Burke).

Above: Electrical resistivity map of Stonehenge. Darker areas show where more natural electrical current has travelled through the Earth (J. Burke).

LEYS AND DRAGON LINES
landscape alignments and lines of force

A network of landscape alignments was discovered in the 1920s by Alfred Watkins (*pages 251-255*). Alignments consisting of five or more sacred sites, whether churches, megaliths, springs or hilltops, he termed "leys" (*see Book V*). A particularly long ley was unveiled by John Michell in the late 1960s. He named it the St. Michael Line because it plotted numerous sites dedicated to St. Michael, as well taking in ancient sites such as Avebury and Glastonbury Tor. Michell noticed it also aligned to Beltane (Mayday) sunrise and Samhain (Halloween) sunset. 20 years later, Hamish Miller and Paul Broadhurst dowsed two great energy currents weaving like serpents around the St. Michael Line, never following it precisely, but meeting at major node points along it. They even found it continuing in St. Petersburg, Russia, suggesting a planetary current.

Traditions of straight alignments exist in Peru, Bolivia and in the far-East, where Feng-Shui practitioners know them as 'Dragon lines' (*pages 366-71*), while in Australia the Aborigines talk of 'Song-lines'. In 1939, Josef Heinsch noted that many ancient sites in Germany were arranged in grids over vast distances and large circular and triangular patterns exist in Britain (*opposite page*). Theories of the origin of such formations range from underground water streams, geological fault lines, spirit paths to navigational tools left by ancient alien astronauts.

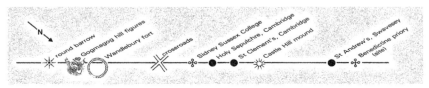

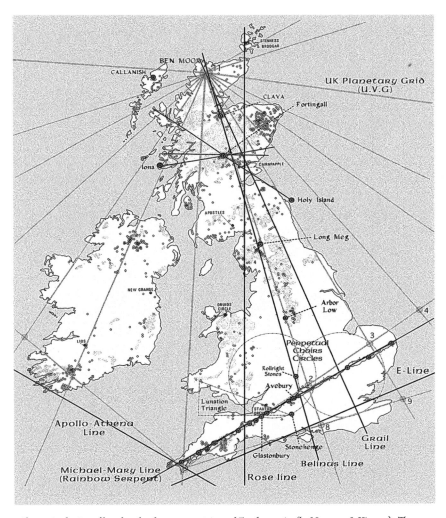

Above: A selection of long leys, landscape geometries and Earth energies (by Newman & Kirwan). The map also marks megalithic sites, 'the Lunation Triangle' (after R. Heath) and the 'Circles of Perpetual Choirs' (after J. Michell). Some of these lines neatly correspond to the Earth grid and ancient geodetic measurement systems. Shorter leys have been omitted, but as an example the 'Cambridge ley' can be seen on the left page.

Grid Beginnings
early evidence of global patterns

In his seminal 1969 book, *The View Over Atlantis*, antiquarian John Michell suggested a very ancient grid system lay across the Earth:

> *"A great scientific instrument lies sprawled over the entire surface of the globe. At some period – perhaps it was over 4,000 years ago – almost every corner of the world was visited by a group of men who came with a particular task to accomplish. With the help of some remarkable power, by which they could cut and raise enormous blocks of stone, these men erected vast astronomical instruments, circles of erect pillars, pyramids, underground tunnels, cyclopean alignments, whose course from horizon to horizon was marked by stones, mounds, and earthwork... The vast scale of prehistoric engineering is not yet generally recognised".*

Similar quotes from the distant past support this. For example *The Book of Enoch*, rediscovered in 1773 by James Bruce, is interpreted as describing a great survey of the Earth in prehistoric times:

> *"And I saw in those days how long cords were given to the Angels, and they took themselves wings and flew, and went towards the north. And I asked an Angel, saying unto him: 'Why have these taken cords and gone off?' And he said to me: 'They have gone to measure."*

Druid legends talk of twelve great 'courts' that encircle the globe, and a Hopi creation myth describes how the creator Tiowa assigned Spider Grandmother Woman to send sound and cosmic energy to the crystal at the centre of the Earth to bounce back to the surface and create 'spots of the fawn', or sacred power centres joined together by a lattice of energy. A Brule Sioux creation myth describes the Sun empowering the planets, orbits and stars to "come to the sixteen hoops", suggesting a network of great Earth circles over the planet.

A Hopi Creation Myth describes how the Creator Tiowa assigned Spider Grandmother Woman (Kokyanwuhti) as the Earth's guardian. She spat into two handfuls of Earth and created Poqanghoya and Palongwhoya (and later, Hicanavaiya, Man-Eagle, Plumed Serpent and others). The two brothers linked minds. Poqanghoya was sent to the north pole, where he gave structure and form to life. Palongwhoya went to the south pole, to say prayers and tune in to the heartbeat of Tiowa. When the two beats were in perfect harmony, a surge of life force came shooting down to the crystal at the centre of the Earth. When the sound hit the crystal, the energy shot out in all directions, channeled by the structural magic of Poqanghoya. The reflected life-energy then popped from the Earth's crust, bringing the planet to life. At some places this energy is said to be more abundant.

DYMAXION MAPS

Buckminster Fuller's cut-out globes

In the 1940s, Buckminster Fuller created several world maps in his attempts to create a visually accurate, flat rendition of a spherical globe. In 1946 he patented the *Dymaxion Projection* based on the cubeoctahedron (*opposite top*). A later 1954 version called the *Airocean World Map* used a slightly modified icosahedron (*shown below*). Each face of these polyhedra is a gnomonic projection (displaying great circles as straight lines), and on both maps the landmasses are accurately rendered, unlike other flat projections of the Earth which distort either shape, area, distance or directional measurements.

On the Mercator world map, for instance, Greenland appears to be three times its corresponding globe size, and Antarctica appears as a long thin white strip along the bottom edge of the map. Even the popular Robinson Projection, used in many schools, shows Greenland distorted to 60% larger than its corresponding globe size.

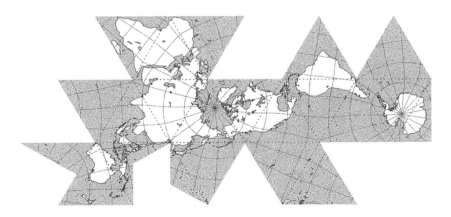

Left and above: U.S. Patent drawing of Buckminster Fuller's 'dymaxion' map of the Earth, published in 1946. Science Journal referred to this as "the first cartographic patent to issue from the US Patents office." A finite system such as a sphere can best be matched by Platonic and Archimedian solids and Fuller chose the cubeoctahedron and icosahedron for his two projections (this page and opposite respectively). Multiple rotations of the Icosahedron result in the maximum unitary sub-division of a one-radius-system resulting in 15 great circles and 120 right spherical triangles. Fuller's geometries of the Earth also became the basis of the Becker and Hagens UVG model (p.26) and Bruce Cathie's cubeoctahedron model (p.24).

THE PLATONIC SOLIDS

timeless polyhedra in ancient days

Each of the five Platonic Solids (*opposite*) is made up of faces of just one regular polygon, with all vertices lying on a sphere. Their perfect symmetry makes them an integral part of planetary grid research. The tetrahedron has four vertices and four triangular faces, the octahedron six vertices and eight triangular faces, the cube eight vertices and six square faces, the icosahedron twelve vertices and twenty triangular faces, while the dodecahedron has twenty vertices and twelve pentagonal faces. The earliest written evidence of them goes back to the era of Pythagoras and Plato [427-347 BC]. Plato writes in the *Phaedo* [110b]:

> *"The real Earth, viewed from above, resembles a ball made of twelve pieces of leather, variegated and marked out in different colours…"*.

This appears to reference a dodecahedron. It is certainly the first mention of the Earth grid. In the *Timaeus*, he also says the Demiurge used a twelve-sided form as a pattern for the World.

However, hundreds of neolithic carved stones, discovered in Northern Scotland and Europe (*see below*), perfectly resemble the Platonic solids (and date to 2000 years before Plato). Geometer Keith Critchlow believes that they could have been used to map the stars, function as navigational aids or act as props to teach students spherical geometry.

| *Octahedron* | *Icosahedron* | *Dodecahedron* | *Tetrahedron* | *Cube* |

Left:
The Tetrahedron

Below Left:
The Octahedron

Below: The Cube.

Above: Far Left: The Cube-Octahedral grid. The Tetrahedral and Cube-Octahedral system, common in crystals and widely used in architecture. It contains numerous root √2 and √3 proportions.

Left: The Icosi-Dodecahedral grid. Above left: The Icosahedron. Above right: The Dodecahedron. The Icosahedron and the Dodecahedron are each other's duals, which is to say that each is constructed from the centres of the other's faces.

Above: The Icosi-Dodecahedral system, common in viruses, pollens, plankton and other living things. Two Platonic solids embody this system, which is rich is golden section proportions.

VILE VORTICES
vanishing aircraft and time dilations

In the early 1970's Ivan T. Sanderson, a biologist and author, plotted ship and aircraft disappearances worldwide, and noticed twelve especially peculiar areas equally spaced over the globe (including the north and south pole). In these 'hot spots' magnetic anomalies, unexplained disappearances, mechanical and instument malfunctions and other energy aberrations all seemed to congregate.

One of the zones was on the western tip of the Bermuda Triangle, an infamous area off the coast of Florida, extending from Bermuda to the tip of southern Florida, and then to the Bahamas via Puerto Rico. Over 100 aircraft disappearances and about 1000 lost lives have been reported in the Bermuda Triangle since 1945.

In his 1972 article *Twelve Devil's Graveyards around the World*, Sanderson described how statistical research and modern communications technology had helped him discover other areas with similar anomolies, such as the Dragon's Triangle (or Devil's Sea) off the south-east coast of Japan. Between 1950 and 1954, nine large ships completely disappeared in this area and UFO sightings as well as magnetic anomolies have often been reported there. This area is also along the rim of the 'Ring of Fire', the highly active volcano chain of the Pacific.

When Sanderson drew the hot spots on a map, he noticed that the twelve areas were spaced equally apart and neatly formed the vertices of an icosahedron with most of them in the sea.

Sanderson was later accused of selecting data to fit his theory, but his work remains a tantalising glimpse of a planetary grid at work.

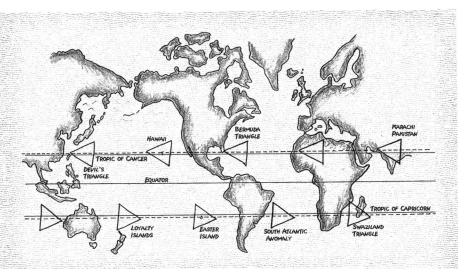

Above: The twelve "Devil's Graveyards." Ten lie on the Tropic of Cancer and the Tropic of Capricorn. The other two are at the poles. Disappearances, mechanical and instrument malfunctions and many cases of time dilations, light phenomena and magnetic variations have been reported in these areas.

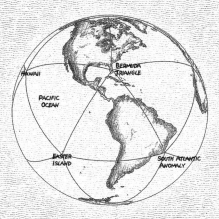

Above: A 3-D icosahedron compressed on to the Earth's surface showing the 'zones'.

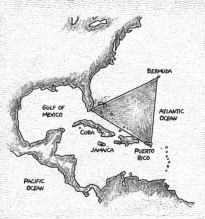

Above: The Bermuda Triangle, where aircraft and ships mysteriously disappear.

RUSSIAN DISCOVERIES
the crystal core and the dodecahedron

Around the same time as Sanderson's work, in 1973, an article was published in Moscow stating that the Earth could have started out as an angular crystal and only formed into a sphere after hundreds of millions of years. Edges of the great crystal could still be preserved within the planet with its energies still recordable on the surface.

Nikolai Goncharov, a Muscovite historian, took the idea a step further by proposing a dodecahedron aligned to the axial north/south poles and the mid-Atlantic ridge. He then mapped ancient cultures onto a globe to discover a geometric pattern. Next, with Vyacheslav Morozov, a linguist, and Valery Makarov, an electronics specialist, he published *Is the Earth a Large Crystal?* in the popular science journal of the USSR Academy of Sciences, *Chemistry and Life*. They then matched Sanderson's idea by placing an icosahedron within it.

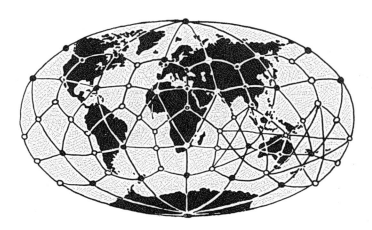

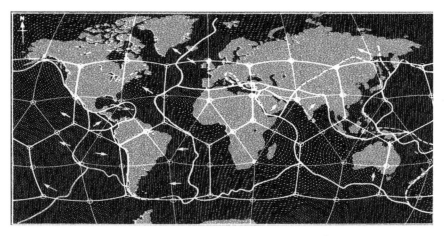

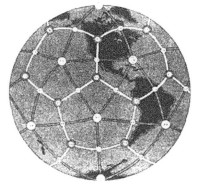

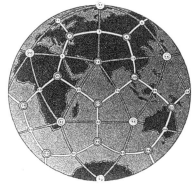

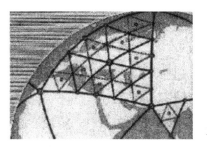

This page: Versions of the Goncharov-Morozov-Makarov
Earth-crystal grid. The lines and points match many of
the Earth's seismic fracture zones and ocean ridges, and also
worldwide atmospheric highs and lows, the paths of migratory
animals, gravitational anomalies, and the sites of many
ancient cities (after John Sinkiewicz). The geosynclinal areas
that divide these platforms go along the edges between the
triangles. Underwater mountain ridges in the oceans and the
Earth's crust breaks go along or parallel to the icosahedron ribs.

BRUCE CATHIE AND UFOS
flight paths and mysterious antenna

In New Zealand, in 1952, Captain Bruce Cathie, an airline pilot, experienced a UFO sighting that dramatically changed his life. Determined to make some sense of the phenomenon, and following the example of French ufologist Aimé Michel, he decided to look for patterns in the reported flight paths of UFOs.

By plotting onto a map the most reliable UFO sightings, including some of his own, he gradually realised there was a complete grid network over New Zealand. Working feverishly over the years which followed, he eventually discovered three grids, with north poles at Latitude 72°25'45" Longitude 89°58'59", Lat 78°25'07" Long 104°59'24" and Lat 75°32'19" Long 95°58'07". A pattern consisting of lines spaced at half-degree intervals orientated on these poles was, Cathie claimed, known to aliens and the builders of ancient sites, atomic weapons designers, antigravity and faster-than-light technologies.

To develop his theory, Cathie had seized on a strange object he termed the 'Eltanin Antenna' that had been photographed on the sea floor, 1000 miles of the coast of Cape Horn in South America. Using the coordinates of the mysterious antenna, he had drawn frenzied grid patterns on a plastic ball until the new cubeoctahedral grids correlated with his first New Zealand version. It was only years later that biologists noticed that Cathie's Eltanin Antenna looked exactly like a small deep sea sponge called Cladorhiza. The debate continues.

Shown opposite is another object which looks like a deep sea life-form. Found in Vietnam, this ancient man-made dodecahedral artifact looks remarkably like an enlarged radiolarian plankton.

Right: Grid plan over New Zealand plotting UFO sightings with half degree intervals on a slightly rotated grid of 24 nautical miles east-west grid lines and 30 nautical miles north-south parallel lines. The variation is due to the latitude being around 41° south, where longitude distances shorten towards the pole.

Below right: Cathie's cuboctahedral grid formed from two poles A and B. Below left: Cathie's 'Eltanin antenna' found 13,500ft deep, 1000 miles from Cape Horn, Chile. It was anchored upright and was, Cathie claimed, an ancient aerial planted their by an ancient civilization or beings from another world. Others believe it was a photo of a deep sea sponge called Cladorhiza.

Below centre: Gold and bronze dodecahedral figures exhibiting twelve facets and twenty "horns" have been unearthed in France and Vietnam. Vietnamese war veterans recognize them as sacred Taoist objects marking acupuncture points.

Putting it All Together

the unified vector geometry projection

In 1978, American Professors William Becker and Bethe Hagens extended the Russian model, inspired by Buckminster Fuller's geodesic domes, into a grid based on the rhombic triacontahedron (*shown opposite right*), the Archimedean dual of the icosidodecahedron. The triacontahedron has 30-diamond-shaped faces, and possesses the combined vertices of the icosahedron and the dodehedron.

Their new model, which they later titled 'The Rings of Gaia', revealed 15 great circles, 120 scalene right-triangles (with no equal sides or equal angles) and 62 node-points. The great circles divided each rhombic face into four right-triangles. Although having no interest in Earth grids, Fuller had previously noticed these triangles and recorded their internal angles in planar and spherical notations (*shown below*).

The model was eventually developed into the 'Unified Vector Geometry' (UVG) projection, connecting all of the vertices of the five Platonic solids placed inside a sphere, using Fuller's 'great circle sets' from *Synergetics II*. A total of 121 great circles appeared, increasing the number of vertices to 4,862 (*see page 376*). They proposed that the UVG grid could be a new geometrical model for Gaia.

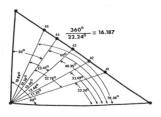 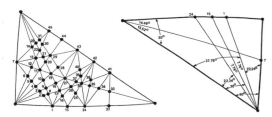

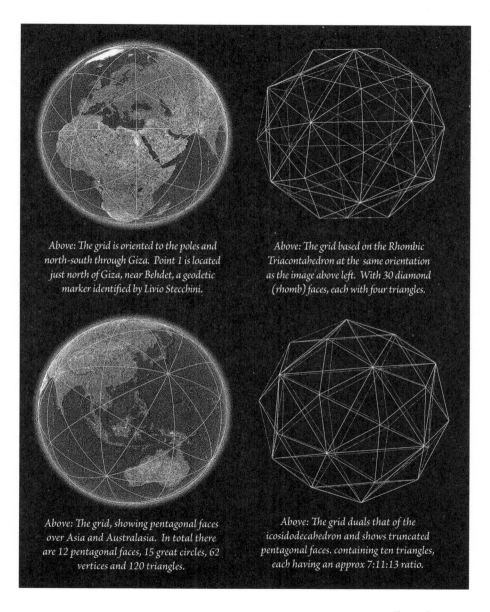

Above: The grid is oriented to the poles and north-south through Giza. Point 1 is located just north of Giza, near Behdet, a geodetic marker identified by Livio Stecchini.

Above: The grid based on the Rhombic Triacontahedron at the same orientation as the image above left. With 30 diamond (rhomb) faces, each with four triangles.

Above: The grid, showing pentagonal faces over Asia and Australasia. In total there are 12 pentagonal faces, 15 great circles, 62 vertices and 120 triangles.

Above: The grid duals that of the icosidodecahedron and shows truncated pentagonal faces. containing ten triangles, each having an approx 7:11:13 ratio.

Interesting Points
the unified vector geometry projection

The original Russian grid vertex numbering is preserved in the Becker and Hagens version shown below. Several ancient civilisations have thrived around certain grid points, but not many famous ancient sacred sites mark major vertices. Since c.2600BC the Egyptians thrived around the Giza plateau [1], as did the inhabitants of the pyramidical complex at Caral in the northwest of Peru [35].

Photographic data collected by U.S. and Russian satellites confirm a fault line from Morocco to Pakistan (points 20 to 12). There are also circular geological structures 150-200 miles in diameter located at grid points 17 (Cerro Cubabi, a highpoint just south of the Mexico/ U.S. border), 18 (Edge of continental shelf near Great Abaco Island in the Bahamas) and 20 (El Eglab, on edge of the Sahara desert, near Timbuktu). Grid points 49, southeast of Rio de Janeiro, and 27, in the Gulf of Carpentaria in northeast Australia, seem to have landmass forming around them, suggesting that these intersections could act as vortices of energy and shape the landscape over many millenia.

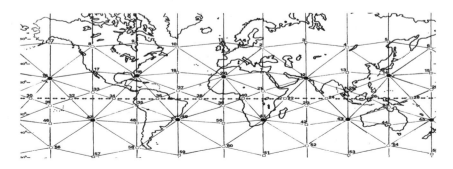

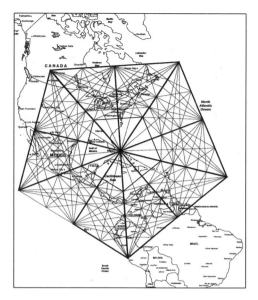

Left: Grid-points 8 and 18: Point 8 is near Buffalo Lake, Alberta, Canada. Large gas and oil reserves, major wheat farming, also with a 5000 year old 'medicine circle' near Majorville.
Grid-point 18 is the centre of a pentagonal face with intersections. Large megalithic 'roads' have been discovered in Bimini, off the coast of Florida, suggesting a previous, unknown society, who could carve and transport large stones. It is also the northern tip of the Bermuda Triangle.
Below: Grid-point 17: Near the Organ Pipe National Monument. The ancient Hohokum people built immense irrigation canals here, their civilisation lasting some 9000 years. This area marks the most sacred territory of the oldest native peoples in North America. There are small pyramids; rock art (some depicting a 'star explosion' at White Tanks) and Mt. Pinacate. Once a major drug-trafficking area, it now home to an enormous communications dish array.

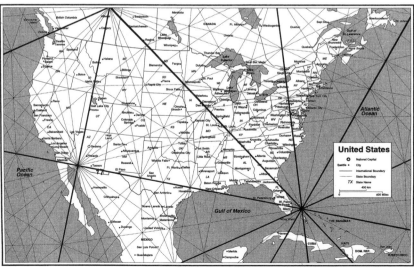

HARTMANN AND CURRY GRIDS
tools for the geopathically stressed

Geomancers have discovered several other global networks of energy. The first was discovered by Dr. Ernst Hartmann in the 1960s and runs magnetic N to S and E to W. It is a square grid spaced 5ft 5in apart, with lines 6-10 inches wide that rise vertically like invisible radioactive walls. When two lines cross, a 'Hartmann Knot' of geopathic stress occurs. Sleeping over crossings of double negative lines (which repeat at 115ft intervals) have been known to cause nervous disturbances, headaches, cramps and rheumatism. Earthquakes distort this grid and a 50% increase in radioactivity has also been recorded at crossing points.

The Curry grid was discovered by Drs. Curry and Whitman in the 1970s and runs diagonally at 45° to north. The lines repeat every 8ft SW to NE and 9ft SE to NW. They are approx 2ft wide, with double negative lines repeating every 164ft. Considered more harmful than Hartmann knots, they are linked with sleep problems, depression and other nervous reactions.

Although these two grids are scientifically unproven, in 2006 Hans Giertz, a telecommunications expert, was able to determine their existence with low frequency electromagnetic energy experiments.

Similar grids include the Broad Curry grid that is 30° off north and the 'positive' double-Curry grid that is 20° off north with very wide intervals of 410ft. Interestingly, this one is marked by megaliths, holy wells, chapels, hill forts and oak trees. In the 1980s R. Schneider discovered a grid at 45° with lines repeating every 965ft. Shaun Kirwan has discovered the 'Angel Grid', that has huge etheric lines of force and relates to the golden section ratio. No doubt more will follow!

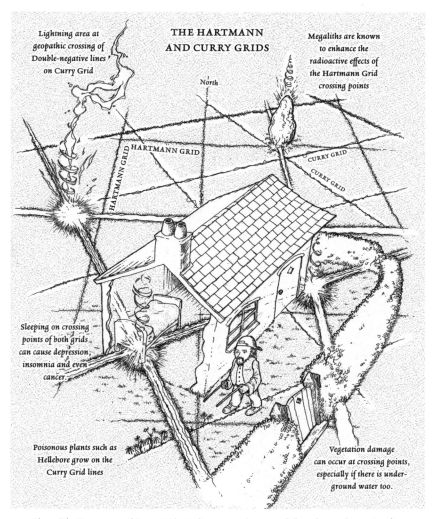

THE HARTMANN AND CURRY GRIDS

Lightning area at geopathic crossing of Double-negative lines on Curry Grid

North

Megaliths are known to enhance the radioactive effects of the Hartmann Grid crossing points

HARTMANN GRID

HARTMANN GRID

CURRY GRID

CURRY GRID

Sleeping on crossing points of both grids can cause depression, insomnia and even cancer.

Poisonous plants such as Hellebore grow on the Curry Grid lines

Vegetation damage can occur at crossing points, especially if there is underground water too.

Above: The Hartmann and Curry Grids. Both compress when stressed, depending on the severity of any trauma in the landscape. Under severe stress, such as old battle sites, the lines can be under 1ft apart. In these places the double negative knots are more frequent, and therefore more damaging to health. Geomancers say there are hundreds of grids that relate to all the different life forms and even elemental beings.

LANDSCAPE GEOMETRIES
man-made patterns on earth

Geometric grids may encircle Gaia, but looking more closely into the landscape, playful patterns turn up everywhere. For example, the capital of America, Washington DC, designed and constructed from 1791, has a layout suggesting knowledge of ancient metrology, sacred geometry and astronomy, later lost in the development of the city.

In Britain, an ancient 'national grid' of neolithic henge monuments, discovered by Robin Heath, links Arbor Low ('Stonehenge of the North'), Bryn Celli Ddu, an important burial chamber in north Wales, and Stonehenge. It displays a perfect 3:4:5 Pythagorean triangle.

Stonehenge also turns up in 'The Wessex Astrum', a landscape hexagram that is bisected by the St. Michael line. Interestingly, the line here between Stonehenge and Glastonbury is a tenth of the perimeter of the Circle of Perpetual choirs (*see page 13*). A landscape diamond (*top left*) aligns to the St. Michael axis and also to other sacred hills in the Somerset region, while a grid system and pentagonal geometry over the landscape in Rennes le Chateux in the south of France, connects churches, sacred hills and natural features (*shown below*).

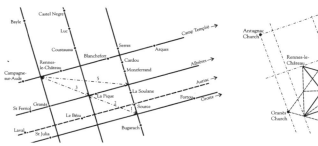

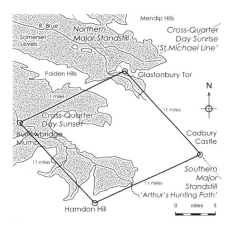

Above: The Somerset Landscape Diamond showing the St. Michael Line and major lunar standstill alignment (by N. Mann & P. Glasson, 2007)

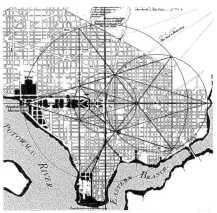

Above: Golden section geometry underlies the design of Washington DC. French architect, Pierre Charles L'Enfant Plan of 1791, Library of Congress (by N. Mann, 2006)

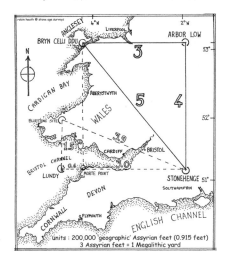

Above: A geodetic grid (by R.Heath) which links henge sites in the UK to form a Pythagorean triangle. The base line corresponds to the Lunation triangle.

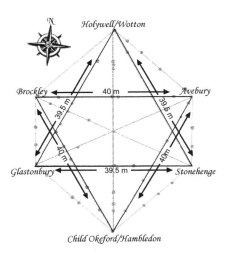

Above: The Wessex Astrum (by P. Knight, T. Perrott) showing the St. Michael axis, distances and several sacred hills on the lighter grey tone.

THE THREE STEPS OF VISHNU
triangulation of the landscape

The ancient Indian *Rigveda* is one of the oldest texts in the world, dating to around 1,500 BC. Some interpreters think it may, in its pages, describe an ancient survey:

> *"I will declare the mighty deeds of Vishnu, of him who measured out the earthly regions ... thrice setting down his footsteps, widely striding ... Him who alone with triple step hath measured this common dwelling place, long far extended ...".*

It goes on to say: *"He, like a rounded wheel, hath set in swift motion his 90 racing steeds together with the 4"*. Since 90 × 4 = 360, we may ask whether this could be a veiled reference to a full 360° triangulated terrestrial survey?

It is not only sacred sites which link up, but, as author Freddy Silva has noticed, sacred mountains and hills too (*see below and opposite*). For example, in India, Mount Kailas, the Hill of Gabbar and Maa Sharda form a beautiful triangle. And, even stranger, author John Martineau recently discovered that two of the world's largest waterfalls are exactly 90° apart (*see page 70*). Coincidence?

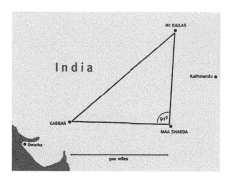
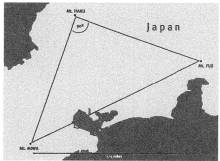

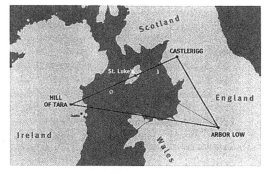

Left: A triangle linking the Hill of Tara, old home of the high-kings of Ireland, Arbor Low, a recumbent stone circle, and the impressive Castlerigg stone circle in Cumbria. A phi division between Castlerigg and the Hill of Tara lands directly on St. Luke's church, the former central 'moot' mound on the Isle of Man, also the 'geodetic centre of Britain' (see page 42).
Image after F. Silva.

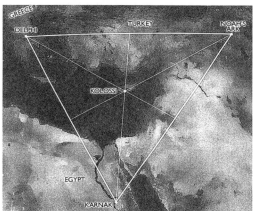

Left: An isosceles triangle linking Delphi, the Greek oracle temple, Karnak, an Egyptian oracle site and Mount Ararat, the supposed resting place of Noah's Ark. Legend states that a Dove flew 1,070 miles between Karnak and Delphi, which can be interpreted as telepathic communication. The story of Noah also contains a dove, representing 'communication'.
Image after F. Silva.

Below and opposite: The 'three steps of Vishnu,' right-angle triangles between sacred mountains in India, Japan and China. After F. Silva.

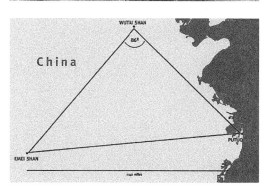

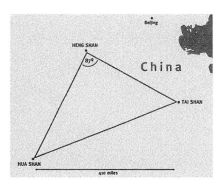

THE CENTRE OF THE WORLD
the art of surveying from a holy hill

There is good evidence to suggest that the Great Pyramid in Egypt was used as a long-distance surveying tool, and another 4,500-year old pyramid built at the same time may also have had a similar function. Silbury Hill in Wiltshire is the largest neolithic man-made hill in Europe. Once a polished white chalk cone, it could have been at the centre of a complex surveying system across southern Britain that used isosceles and Pythagorean triangles to plot out a vast grid. For twenty years, Tom Brooks, an amateur historian, plotted over 1,500 ancient sites and realised that every single one of them was equidistant to another site, using Silbury as it main point. Next, using two equal length sides, he discovered multiple isosceles triangles, many of which had 90° angles.

Sceptical mathematicians, however, have shown that Woolworths department stores also created similar great triangles across England!

Brook's system also showed how, by using notable features in the landscape, a vast spiral grid based upon his triangles formed across the countryside, enabling it to be surveyed from one area to another.

Perhaps the ancient technique of 'triangulating the landscape' was in fact known worldwide.

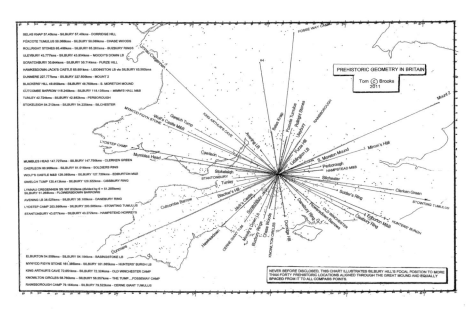

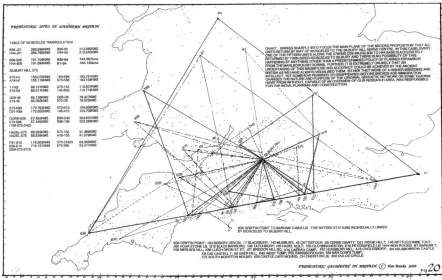

GREAT CIRCLES ON EARTH
cutting the world in two

A *great circle* is a circle on a sphere whose centre lies at the centre of that sphere, so that it cuts it into two equal hemispheres. All longitudinal meridians are great circles. The equator is the only latitudinal great circle—all other latitudes form *lesser circles* on the globe. The UVG grid is composed entirely of great Earth circles, all 121 of them.

Below is shown Jim Alison's incredible great Earth circle, viewed along its equator. This formidable alignment takes in Nazca, Machu Picchu, Tassili n Ajjer, Siwa, Giza, Ur, Angkor Wat, Easter Island and many others. As we shall see in the pages that follow, there are other reasons to take specific notice of this alignment. Were the ancients conscious of this circle? Were they recording something? Shown top is a section of a great circle proposed by Robin Heath that takes in Stonehenge, Delphi, Giza, Mecca and the Ohio Serpent Mound.

In the 1980s Glastonbury visionary Robert Coon produced an interesting planetary chakra map (*lower opposite*) with two great dragon-lines encircling the globe (he called the pair of them the 'Rainbow Serpent'). The British part of it aligns down the Michael-Mary lines (*see page 13*). The two currents do not form a perfect Earth circle but they do encircle the Earth.

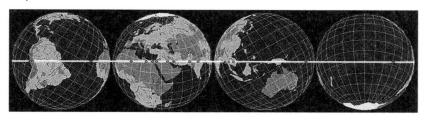

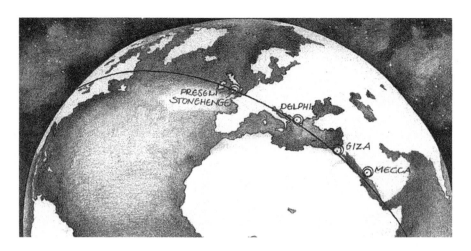

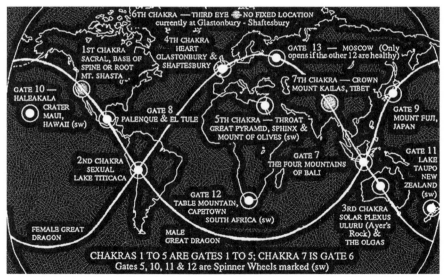

6TH CHAKRA — THIRD EYE 🌐 NO FIXED LOCATION
currently at Glastonbury - Shaftesbury

4TH CHAKRA
HEART
GLASTONBURY &
SHAFTESBURY

1ST CHAKRA
SACRAL, BASE OF
SPINE OR ROOT
MT. SHASTA

GATE 13 — MOSCOW (Only
opens if the other 12 are healthy)

7TH CHAKRA — CROWN
MOUNT KAILAS, TIBET

GATE 10 —
HALEAKALA
CRATER
MAUI,
HAWAII (sw)

GATE 8
PALENQUE & EL TULE

5TH CHAKRA — THROAT
GREAT PYRAMID, SPHINX &
MOUNT OF OLIVES (sw)

GATE 9
MOUNT FUJI,
JAPAN

GATE 11
LAKE
TAUPO
NEW
ZEALAND
(sw)

2ND CHAKRA
SEXUAL
LAKE TITICACA

GATE 7
THE FOUR MOUNTAINS
OF BALI

GATE 12
TABLE MOUNTAIN,
CAPETOWN
SOUTH AFRICA (sw)

3RD CHAKRA
SOLAR PLEXUS
ULURU (Ayer's
Rock) &
THE OLGAS

FEMALE GREAT
DRAGON

MALE
GREAT DRAGON

CHAKRAS 1 TO 5 ARE GATES 1 TO 5; CHAKRA 7 IS GATE 6
Gates 5, 10, 11 & 12 are Spinner Wheels marked (sw)

Above: Robert Coon's Rainbow Serpent travels the world from Uluru (Ayres Rock), linking 'planetary increase sites' or chakras, before meeting it back in Uluru. The Aborigines tell stories of a female snake Kuniya and her nephew Liru, who meet at Uluru. Dowsers have verified these energy lines in other parts of the world.

THE PRIME MERIDIAN
the center of the world

In October 1884, Professor Charles Piazzi Smythe, an avid Egyptologist and Astronomer Royal of Scotland, became involved in choosing the prime meridian of the Earth; zero degrees longitude.

There had already been other contenders. Paris was a possibility, but there was no fixed global agreement, so 25 countries met in Washington DC to decide on the location. At the meeting, Smythe proposed using the Great Pyramid, because great circles drawn north, south, east, and west from Giza cover more land, as opposed to ocean, than from any other place on Earth (*opposite top*). The Great Pyramid was also perfectly aligned to the cardinal points of the compass, and sited at 30° above the equator. In the end, under some pressure, 22 countries voted for Greenwich, 31° 8" 8" west of Giza.

Previously, in the late 1700s, Napoleon's surveyors had used the cardinal points of the Great Pyramid to survey Lower Egypt, using a meridian as the baseline. They discovered that this cut the Delta region into two equal portions and that lines extended from the north corners of the Pyramid precisely enclosed the entire Delta (*lower opposite*).

It has been proposed that the Great Pyramid may also represent the northern hemisphere, suggesting the Egyptians accurately knew the size of the Earth. The height and perimeter of the Great Pyramid multiplied by 43,200 yields figures very close to the modern polar radius and equatorial circumference of the Earth. 43,200 is an important metrological number, = 26 × 33 × 52. The base length of the Great Pyramid is also precisely 1/8th of a minute of a degree of the Earth's polar circumference (a minute is 1/60th of a degree).

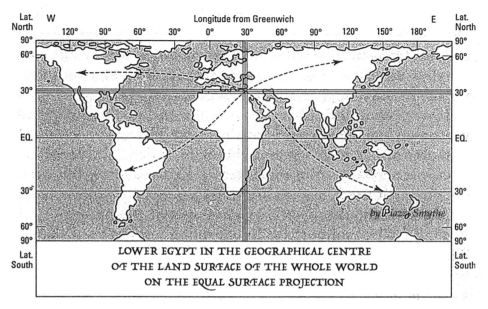

Above: Charles Piazzi Smythe's map showing the Giza Prime Meridian and landmass from Egypt.
Below left: Napoleon's survey of the Nile Delta. Below right: The Great Pyramid as Earth's northern hemisphere.

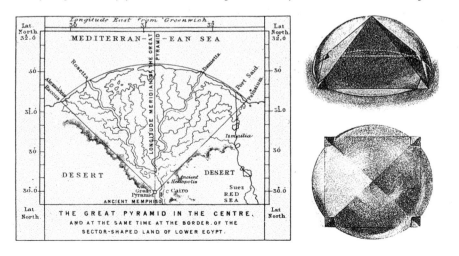

LOCATING THE CENTER
the navel of the landscape

The geodetic location of the Giza meridian echoes through other ancient cultures, who often sought to find the center of their land or society. Nordic, Greek, Celtic, and even Nazi traditions reveal a worldwide geomantic obsession with finding the exact center of the homeland. The center was seen as the birthplace of the tribe, the omphalus or "navel of the world," an axis from which the king could survey his domain, and give laws from his sacred rock. These central places, whether stone circles, earthworks, hilltops, or islets in rivers and lakes, functioned as "moot" or "ting" sites where national meetings were held "under the light of the Sun." John Michell also discovered that they were often located geographically at the center of the most northerly-southerly and easterly-westerly axes (*see examples below*).

Plato relates that the site of the symbolic center must have the physical and spiritual qualities befitting a national omphalus. Were early surveyors also priestly diviners, masters of astronomy, geodesy, and land measurement, as Caesar said of the British druids?

The two main British centers are the Isle of Man, the center of the British Isles (*see opposite*), and Meriden in Warwickshire, the center of England. The Romans named High Cross at Venonae the center because it was equidistant from Hadrian's Wall and the Isle of Wight.

Above: The main axis of the British Isles, from Duncansby Head in Scotland to Land's End in Cornwall, has its central point on the Isle of Man. The smaller circle of 100 miles in diameter, touches England, Wales, Ireland, and Scotland (from "At the Center of the World" by John Michell, 1994)

LANDSCAPE ZODIACS
heavenly signs on earth

In the 1920s Katherine Maltwood had a vision in which she perceived the signs of the zodiac overlaying the sacred landscape around Glastonbury, legendary burial place of King Arthur, and site of the first church in Europe. After plotting the figures on a map, twelve miles across, and noticing that earthworks, roads and brooks outlined the astrological signs, she published a book: *Glastonbury's Temple of the Stars*. She found that street and village names hid tell-tale and long-lost clues. The Peruvian Nazca geoglyhs were being rediscovered at the same time, also possibly representing astrological signs.

Today, there are nearly 60 recorded terrestrial zodiacs in Britain, ranging from 10 (Ongar) to 32 (Pendle) miles wide. Some have 'dogs' as an extra sign, representing Canis Major, the 'Dog Star', spiritual guardian of the zodiac. No one is sure who built them, when, or if they are naturally formed, or just figments of over-active imaginations.

The famous St. Michael line mysteriously connects several zodiacs in southern England, clipping the edges of zodiacs at Bury St. Edmunds, Nuthampstead, Glastonbury, Bodmin Moor, and one in Cornwall.

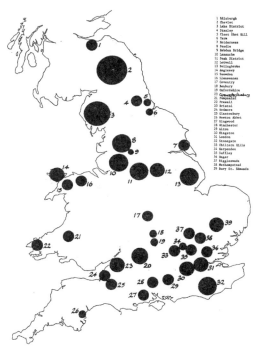

1 Edinburgh
2 Cheviot
3 Lake District
4 Stanley
5 Fleet Shot Hill
6 Yarm
7 Haldersness
8 Pendle
9 Hebden Bridge
10 Lanasche
11 Peak District
12 Letwell
13 Bolingbroke
14 Anglesey
15 Snowdon
16 Llanasanan
17 Coventry
18 Banbury
19 Oxfordshire
20 Cerne Abbas/Banbury
21 Pumpsaint
22 Preseli
23 Bristol
24 Wedmore
25 Glastonbury
26 Newton Abbot
27 Ringwood
28 Winchester
29 Alton
30 Kingston
31 London
32 Stonegate
33 Chiltern Hills
34 Harpenden
35 Cuffley
36 Ongar
37 Stagglesode
38 Nethampstead
39 Bury St. Edmunds

Above: Selected UK landscape zodiacs. Top Right: The Nuthampstead Zodiac, after Nigel Pennick (the Michael line clips the NW of the Lion near Royston). Opposite, left: The Glastonbury Zodiac. Opposite, right: The Kingston Zodiac, by Mary Caine. Below: A unicorn in the Glastonbury Zodiac touches the Lion in Somerton, where the the Lion and Unicorn coat of arms of Briatin was created. Below: The Nuthampstead Zodiac, after Pennick. Right: The Bodmin Moor zodiac.

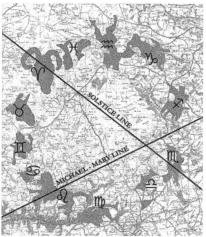

Measuring the Earth
geodesy and ancient metrology

The size and shape of the Earth has only been known for the last two centuries, but the ancients may have got there first. Measurement systems found at sites such as Stonehenge appear to be derived from an accurate understanding of the Earth's size, and builders of the ancient temples seem to have used this system to a high degree of accuracy.

In the ancient system, miles, cubits, feet and inches were all perfect sub-divisions of the Earths polar or equatorial circumference or its radius. For example, the meridian (polar) circumference is 24,883.2 miles, equal to 135,000,000 Roman feet, 63,000,000 Sacred cubits or 129,600,000 Greek feet (129,600 is the number of seconds in the 360 degrees of a circle). The values of the various ancient measures were grouped together by whole number ratios that relate to the English (geographic) foot, considered by some to be the 'root' of metrology.

The spheroid shape of the Earth means that degrees of latitude measured at the poles are longer than those at the equator. The average (mean) degree is 69.12 miles, a length quoted by Ptolemy (as 300,000 Roman remens) and which is still used officially today.

The canonical diameter of the Earth (7,920 miles) can be expressed as 8×9×10×11 miles. Likewise, the equatorial circumference (24,902.86 miles) is 360,000 × 365.242 English feet (also the number of days in a year), enabling space, time and angle to be worked out in either feet, days or degrees. The equatorial circumference relates to the meridian through the fraction 1261/1260 (*see other examples in table, right*). Various people have tried to explain how this could have been worked out in ancient times, but no definitive answer has yet come to light!

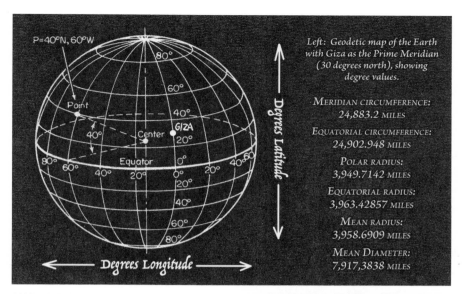

P=40°N, 60°W

80°
60°
40°
Point
40° Center GIZA
20°
Equator 0°
80° 60° 40° 20° 0° 20° 40° 60°
20°
40°
60°
80°

Degrees Latitude

← Degrees Longitude →

Left: Geodetic map of the Earth
with Giza as the Prime Meridian
(30 degrees north), showing
degree values.

MERIDIAN CIRCUMFERENCE:
24,883.2 MILES

EQUATORIAL CIRCUMFERENCE:
24,902.948 MILES

POLAR RADIUS:
3,949.7142 MILES

EQUATORIAL RADIUS:
3,963.42857 MILES

MEAN RADIUS:
3,958.6909 MILES

MEAN DIAMETER:
7,917,3838 MILES

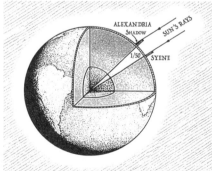

ALEXANDRIA
SHADOW SUN'S RAYS
1/50 SYENE

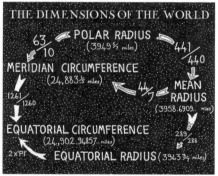

THE DIMENSIONS OF THE WORLD

63/10 POLAR RADIUS 441/440
(3949.5/7 miles)

MERIDIAN CIRCUMFERENCE
(24,883.8 miles) 4/7 MEAN
RADIUS
1261/1260 (3958.6909. miles)

EQUATORIAL CIRCUMFERENCE 289/288
(24,902.91857.. miles)

2 x PI EQUATORIAL RADIUS (3963.5/7 miles)

Above: Eratosthenes [276-195 BC] measured the size of the
polar circumference to within 180 miles by noting the angle of
a midday midsummer shadow in Alexandria. At Syene, 500
miles south, the midday midsummer Sun cast no shadow but
the angle of the shadow at Alexandria was approx 7°, or 1/50
of 360, so 50 × 500 miles gave him 25,000 miles as the Earth's
circumference (24,821 miles is the modern measurement).

Above: The principal dimensions of the Earth from the
study of ancient geodesy (courtesy Robin Heath, after John
Neal). These numbers pop up frequently in metrology.
For example, the Royal cubit identified by Petrie at the
Great Pyramid differs as 441 to 440 to a Royal cubit of
12/7 English feet. The fractional relationships seem to
have been known to the builders of ancient sacred sites.

LINE A
ancient alignments in east anglia

Just southeast of Cambridge, Wandlebury, a circular henge, sits quietly upon the Gogmagog Hills. Whilst Stonehenge, to the west, sits at Latitude 51° 10' 44" N, Wandlebury was built at 52° 09' 31" N, almost exactly one degree north. From Wandlebury, a straight ley heads south to Hatfield Forest crossing through numerous important megaliths, earthworks, henges and tumuli, at a very similar orientation to the Stonehenge-Avebury axis (see page 56).

Researcher Christian O'Brien believes this ley, now known as "Line A", was constructed to measure the polar circumference of the Earth, as it is very slightly 'curved', at the same rate as the curvature of the Earth (a 'Loxodrome'). The 52nd parallel was very important to ancient surveying, due to it being the 'mean' latitude of the world. O'Brien noted that the distance between each marker on Line A was 1430.2m, which he called a 'megalithic mile'.

In the 1920s, archaeologist Cyril Fox noted that Wandlebury could clearly be seen from Ring Hill (a site on the line) suggesting beacons may have been lit along the line to orientate the surveyors. Many of the stones on Line A are impressive sarsen stones, up to 6ft high, that were either transported from Salisbury Plain or were glacial erratics, before being placed in position by the ancient surveyor- astronomers. 11 of them have been discovered in Littlebury alone, suggesting it was the site of the only stone circle in East Anglia. Other notable stones can still be seen at Newport, Wendens Ambo, Littlebury Green, Audley End and Hatfield Forest. Was this the work of the eastern division of the astronomer-priests of the West Country?

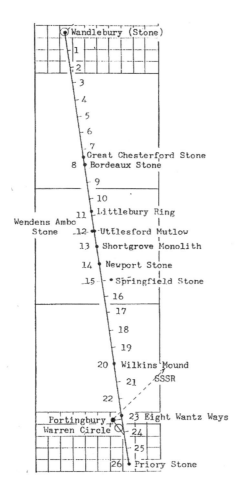

Wandlebury (Stone)

1
2
3
4
5
6
7
  Great Chesterford Stone
8 ● Bordeaux Stone
9
10
11 ● Littlebury Ring
Wendens Ambo
Stone   12 ●·Uttlesford Mutlow
13 ● Shortgrove Monolith
14 ● Newport Stone
15 - ● Springfield Stone
16
17
18
19
20 ● Wilkins Mound
21   SSSR
22
Portingbury ●   23 Eight Wantz Ways
Warren Circle ◯ 24
25
26 ● Priory Stone

Above: The Cam-Valley 'Loxodrome' constructed c. 2500 BC for the purpose of time determination, surveying and agriculture. It is an alignment of ancient megaliths, earthworks and hills in Cambridgeshire/ Essex. The slightly curving alignment matches the curvature of the Earth and could have been used to accurately calculate the polar circumference.

Above: Plan of Wandlebury Ring upon the Gogmagog Hills, SE of Cambridge, showing the passage of the approx north-south Loxodrome (left). It is surrounded by tumuli, earthworks and sits close to the ancient Icknield Way. The irregular northeast-southwest line is the famous Mary energy current discovered by Miller and Broadhurst (see pages 12-13). The northwesterly line is the 'Cambridge Ley' (see page 12).

Below: The 4 ton Leper Stone of Newport, or possibly 'leaping' stone. It toppled in the 1890s after a powerful storm, but was raised again as locals feared it would otherwise bring disaster to their community.

ANCIENT MAPS
prehistoric mariners and perplexing projections

In 1513, a Turkish admiral, Piri Re'is, produced a map with a series of grid lines, compiled from twenty old charts and eight Mappa Mundis (*opposite top right*). Used for 200 years in the Mediterranean with no improvements, it was not until the 1960s that Charles Hapgood, an American historian, solved the projections used, replotted them, and came to the extraordinary conclusion that ancient seafarers must have sailed from pole to pole. In particular, Antarctica is often shown on the maps as two islands, or a large island with a smaller peninsula (*opposite lower right*), a fact only proven by radar survey through the ice in the late 20th century. Antarctica may have been surveyed when its coasts were free of ice, suggesting a possible date earlier than 12,000 BC.

Some maps had 'portolans' on them, like grid points, radiating out either 16 or 32 spokes, and these maps also showed accurate longitude, something not rediscovered until the 1700s by John Harrison. The prime meridian of the maps passed through Alexandria in Egypt, the ancient centre of learning where Piri Re'is had found many of them.

The Di Canestris map (*opposite top left*) shows an anthropomorphic king and queen representing North Africa and Europe, defining Alexandria at its centre. Hapgood found an interesting anomaly that Hagens picked up on: a 12-node perimeter containing 28 triangles corresponding closely to the UVG grid (*opposite lower left*).

In 1866, Leonce Elie de Beaumont, a founder of geology, published a map of France, centred on Paris and based on a pentagonal format. Often dismissed as 'arcane', it is precisely 1/12 of the Earth's surface, a dodecahedral face, fitting in neatly with modern grid theory.

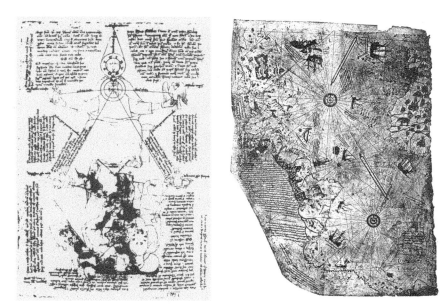

Above left: The Dicanastris Map of 1335-1337 Showing 'rhombic' geometry with four UVG grid triangles centred on Alexandria. Above ight: The Piri Re'is Map. Accumulated from 20 old charts and global maps, known as Jaferiye by Arabs in the time of Alexander the Great.

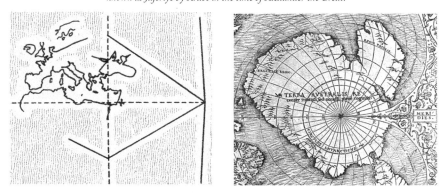

Above left: A reprojection of a detail of the Di Canestris map showing the prime meridian through Alexandria and the UVG grid triangles. Above: Antartica on the Oronteus Finaeus World Map of 1532. It was not until the mid 20th century that a modern survey was produced.

LONGITUDE HARMONICS
tuning into Giza

Many ancient sacred sites can be arranged into a coherent pattern if Alexandria (or Giza, which is southeast of it) defines the prime meridian. In 1998, author Graham Hancock developed a theory of the longitudinal distribution of sacred sites based on pentagonal geometry (*opposite top*). For example, the massive Buddhist site of Angkor Wat is at a longitude 72° east of Giza, one fifth of the way round the globe.

Hancock's ideas may be extended. The Mayan sites of Copan, in Honduras, and Chitzen Itza, in Mexico, are both within half a degree of 120° west from Giza, one third of the way around the world. Was the geographic knowledge that the West acquired with the invention of the marine chronometer already in use thousands of years ago?

Strangely, the seat of the Church of England, Canterbury, is 30° west of Giza, one twelfth of a circle.

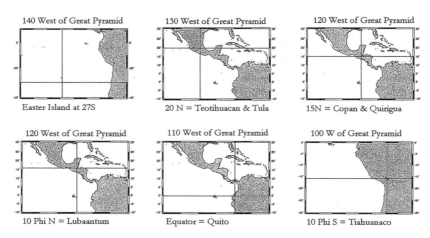

140 West of Great Pyramid	130 West of Great Pyramid	120 West of Great Pyramid
Easter Island at 27S	20 N = Teotihuacan & Tula	15N = Copan & Quirigua
120 West of Great Pyramid	110 West of Great Pyramid	100 W of Great Pyramid
10 Phi N = Lubaantum	Equator = Quito	10 Phi S = Tiahuanaco

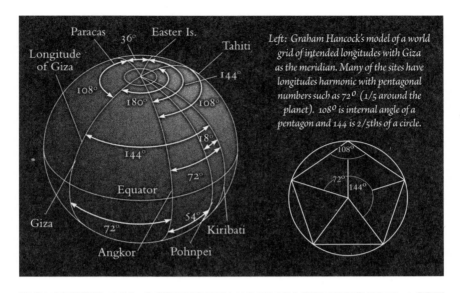

Left: Graham Hancock's model of a world grid of intended longitudes with Giza as the meridian. Many of the sites have longitudes harmonic with pentagonal numbers such as 72° (1/5 around the planet). 108° is internal angle of a pentagon and 144 is 2/5ths of a circle.

HARMONIC LONGITUDES FROM GIZA

BAALBEK, LEBANON 5° E
The worlds largest megaliths

ANGKOR WAT, CAMBODIA 72° E
Major ancient Buddhist temple

CHAVIN, PERU 108° W
Shamanic megalithic temple complex

THE PARACAS TRIDENT, PERU 108° W
Nazca-like candleabra effigy

TIAHUANACO, BOLIVIA 100° W
Pyramid temple complex

QUITO, ECUADOR 110° W
Northern Inca capital

CHICHEN ITZA AND COPAN 120° W
Major Mayan capital cities

TEOTIHUACAN, MEXICO 130° W
Ancient Toltec and Mayan city

EASTER ISLAND 140° W
Megalithic statues facing east

KIRIBATI, PACIFIC ISLANDS 144° E
Ancient megalithic ruins

HARMONIC LONGITUDES TWIXT SITES

EASTER ISLAND TO ANGKOR WAT 144°
two fifths of a circle

ANGKOR WAT TO TAHITI 108°
three tenths of a circle

ANGKOR WAT TO KIRIBATI 72°
one fifth of a circle

ANGKOR WAT TO PARACAS 180°
half a circle

PARACAS TO EASTER ISLAND 36°
one tenth of a circle

STONEHENGE TO BOSNIAN PYRAMID 19.5°
tetrahedral angle (see page 375)

BOSNIAN PYRAMID TO MACHU PICCHU 90°
a quarter of a circle

NAN MADOL, POHNPEI TO ANGKOR 54°
three twentieths of a circle

CARNAC, BRITTANY TO YONAGUNI 120°
one third of a circle

... and see appendix on page 375

Polygonal Walls

a worldwide megalithic jigsaw

In Peru, huge jigsaw-like megalithic walls exist around Cuzco and the 'Sacred Valley', and similar polygonal walls with multi-ton blocks can be found from Machu Picchu to Ollantaytambo and beyond. Garcilaso de la Vega wrote in the 1500s about Sacsayhuamán in Peru:

> *"It is indeed beyond the power of imagination to understand now these Indians, unacquainted with devices, engines, and implements, could have cut, dressed, raised, and lowered great rocks, more like lumps of hills than building stones, and set them so exactly in their places. For this reason, and because the Indians were so familiar with demons, the work is attributed to enchantment."*

It is still not clear how it was done. When the Inca tried to duplicate their predecessors' work, they lost over 3,000 lives as huge stones tumbled down hills. Even today, fringe theories hint at ancient lasers, stone-softening technologies, ET-assisted constructions and levitation.

Similar cyclopean walls also exist in Italy, along whose west coast a long-standing tradition attributes them to a people called the Pelasgi, who allegedly arrived at the end of the Bronze Age (1,200-800 BC) importing this Hittite-Mycenaean technique from Greece and Turkey.

Similar walls can be found in Turkey, at Alaca Hoyak; in Greece, at Delphi and Mycenis; in Japan, at Osaka castle; and in Saudi Arabia, where circular tombs also resemble this style. Impressive polygonal masonry may be seen in Egypt at the Osirion, Abydos; in the granite coverings for Khafre's and Menkaure's pyramids; and at the Valley and Sphinx temples at Giza, where jisgaw geometry is identically reflected on either side of passageways suggesting an architectural design to this global earthquake-proof technique, rather than random masonry.

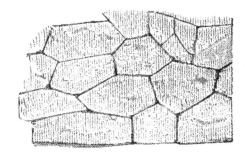

A global puzzle in stone: Top left: Typical polygonal wall from Cuzco, Peru. Top right: An example of ancient Greek cyclopean polygonal masonry from Agios Adrianos. Below, main: The manmade jigsaw of megaliths at Sacsayhuamán, Peru. Bottom left: Polygonal wall, Terracina, Italy. Bottom right: Ancient stone construction, Alatri, Italy.

LATITUDINAL HARMONICS
secret sevens and stone circles

Sacred sites were not only positioned at longitude harmonics. The massive 5,000 year-old Avebury stone circles are situated 51° 25' 43" north of the equator, exactly one seventh of a circle or 360/7° (also four sevenths of the quadrant between the equator and the north pole). The temples of Luxor (Thebes), Egypt sit at 25° 25' 43", two sevenths of the quadrant distance. Supporting this analysis, the north African historian Ibn Khaldun [1332-1406], describes how the ancient world was divided into latitudinal sevenths in his *Muqaddimah*.

Getting into more localised detail, John Michell discovered in 2004 that while the latitude of Avebury is within the 52nd parallel (between 51° and 52° N), it is strangely exactly three sevenths of the way up. Furthermore, if the 52nd paralled is divided into 28 units (*opposite top right*) then the distance between Avebury and Stonehenge equals precisely seven of those units, 17.28 miles, or one quarter of a degree at that latitude (the Rollright Stones near Oxford mark the 52° latitude). The distance between Avebury and 52° is also 39.497142 miles, exactly 1/100th of the polar radius.

Interesting latitudes also occur between ancient Greek sites. Delphi, Dodona and Delos are all exactly one degree apart and lie along the path of the Apollo-St. Michael ley, angled at 60° (*lower opposite*). The line runs from Skellig St. Michael, in Ireland, and travels for 2,500 miles to Megiddo in Israel (Armageddon).

The notable cluster of stone circles in the Shetland Islands are found at 60° (one sixth of a circle), exactly twice Giza's 30° latitude (one twelfth of a circle). Coincidence or deliberate design?

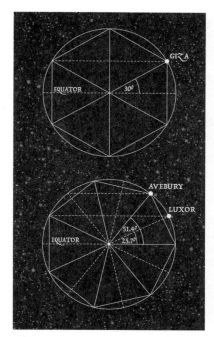

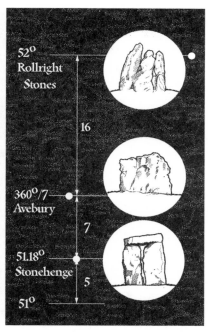

Above: Sites positioned at 6- and 7-fold divisions of Earth's quadrant (after Heath, Michell & Jacobs).

Above: More evidence of Avebury's careful positioning at 360°/7 and between the 51st and 52nd parallels.

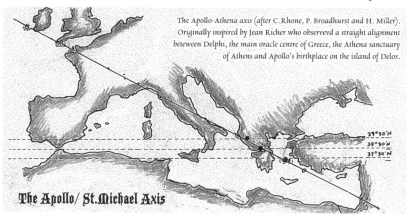

The Apollo-Athena axis (after C. Rhone, P. Broadhurst and H. Miller). Originally inspired by Jean Richer who observevd a straight alignment beteween Delphi, the main oracle centre of Greece, the Athena sanctuary of Athens and Apollo's birthplace on the island of Delos.

GLOBAL POSITIONING
lost codes of the ancients

Some ancient sites worldwide may have been built with knowledge of their exact location. Archaeocryptography, created by Carl Munck, uses the numbers of obvious features present at a site to produce the precise coordinates. For instance, the Kukulkan pyramid at Chichen Itza has 4 staircases, 4 corners, 365 steps (91 on each side plus an altar on top) and 9 terraces. These numbers multiplied together equal 52,560, a number encoded in Kukulkan's longitude west of Giza, 119° 42' 10.51620648", for $119 \times 42 \times 10.51620648 = 52,560$. Sceptics say he is just 'number crunching', selecting data to fit his results, but other commentators remain more enthusiastic.

Returning to Avebury, we find a similar 'code'. In 1996 John Martineau noticed two hidden corridors, defined by two unusual 'corners' of the henge, which align through the centres of the two inner stone circles. The angle between them is one seventh of a circle, 51° 25' 43", the precise latitude of the centre of the site. There are also exactly 72° of arc between Avebury and Chichen Itza, one fifth of the Earth's circumference.

Checking the distances and degrees between ancient sites produces some interesting results. Avebury is located 1/100th of the planetary circumference from the Hill of Tara and Newgrange, Ireland's largest megalithic structure (both 3000 BC and 249.4 miles away). The Great Pyramid to Newgrange is 1/10th of a great circle (2,487.4 miles).

The Newark earthworks in Ohio are 6,000 miles from the Great Pyramid, and distances between them and nearby earthworks encode accurate astronomical geodesy (*see lower opposite, after James Q. Jacobs*).

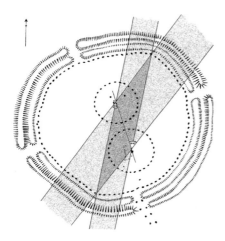

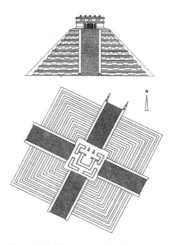

Above: The two corridors of Avebury. The angle
between them equals the latitude of the site.

Above: Kukulkan pyramid at Chichen Itza.
Latitude: 119°, 42,' 10.51620648"

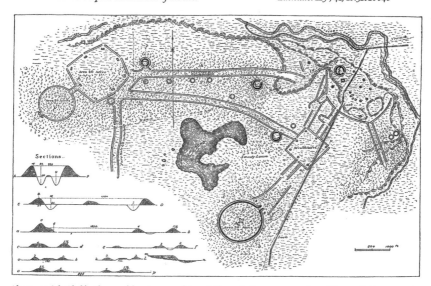

Above: 360° divided by the no. of days in a year (365.25636) equals the average number of degrees the Sun moves in a
day, 0.98561°, a distance equal to that between Marietta Square and the Newark Octagon (above).

OCTAGONS & HEXAGONS
some interesting alignments

One of the most impressive geometrical earthworks in North America is the Newark Complex in Ohio. Its vast scale has now been overtaken by the local town and a golf course, but, to put it in perspective, the Great Pyramid of Giza would easily fit within the octagon (*opposite top, and see too page 268-9*). James Q. Jacobs noticed that its orientation is 51.4° east of true north, a seventh of a circle, and also the latitude of Avebury in England (51.42°).

Geomancer Cort Lindahl followed the complex's orientation and found that its NW-SW axis points directly to the Great Pyramid, 6,008 miles away. Was it connected to both the megalith builders of England, and the pyramid builders of Egypt? Newark also encodes advanced astronomical alignments, most notably, how the octagon's eight sides encode the different aspects of the 18.6-year moon cycle (*see page 268*).

After crossing the Atlantic ocean, the line goes through Europe and hit several mounds, megaliths and temples in France, Italy, Greece and Crete, plus through the ancient Egyptian city of Alexandria. Strangely, it goes through another octagonal construction in Voletta, Italy. The Baptistery of San Giovanni was constructed in 13th century and sits within an ancient megalithic landscape once ruled by the Pelasgians and Etruscans, the architects responsible for the polygonal walls.

The temple of Jupiter at Baalbek in Lebanon also connects to the great pyramid. Featuring the largest megalithic blocks in the world, the northeast edge of Baalbek's hexagonal platform aligns precisely with the NE to SW diagonal of the great pyramid (407 miles away). Were both Newark and Baalbek specifically oriented to the great pyramid?

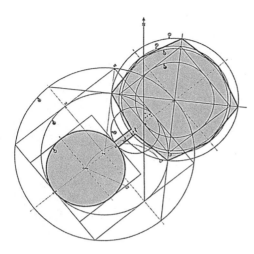

Left: The secret geometrical construction of Newark Earthworks, Ohio, USA. Its NW-SE axis points directly to the Great Pyramid in Egypt and hits several other ancient sites on the way, including Alexandria. See too pages 58-59 for more on this astonishing monument.

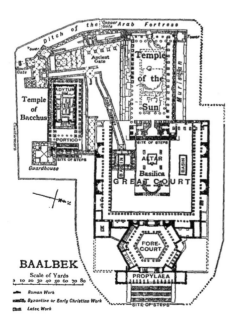

Above: Entrance to the Temple of the Sun, ancient temple complex of Baalbek, Lebanon. Left: Plan of Baalbek, showing the unusual hexagon in the east whose north-western side points directly to the Great Pyramid. Below: A single 1242 ton stone at Baalbek.

GOLDEN SECTION SITES
a web of phi

The golden section is a proportion found in pentagrams, icosahedra, dodecahedra and throughout nature. Some researchers have observed golden ratios in the distances between sacred sites thousands of miles apart, suggesting a possible ancient use of it in surveying the planet.

Jim Alison, for example, discovered in the 1990s that along his impressive great circle alignment (*see page 64*) Angkor Wat is 4,745 miles from the Great Pyramid, which is 7,677 miles from Nazca, the two distances being in the golden ratio (0.618 or 1.618), as 4,745×1.618=7,677 (*see below and top right*). Alison also found that distances (in miles) between sites hid Fibonacci sequence numbers. For example, Giza to Nazca is 7,692 miles and Nazca to Angkor is 12,446 miles (the 360th Fibonnaci number is 76,924, and the 361st is 12,446).

In the same vein, Rand Flem-Ath found that the White pyramid near Xian, China is located between the north pole and equator at 34° 26' N, which divides the quadrant into the golden ratio: 3,840 (miles from the north pole)×1.618=6,213 (miles in a quadrant). Flem-Ath also found numerous sites close to the latitude 10×1.618°, or 16° 11' north and south of the equator. Sites at these latitudes include Tiahuanaco (16° 38' N) and Lubaantum (16° 17' N), as well as those shown opposite.

Mecca's latitude is 21.420° N, 11.5 miles north of the Golden latitude.

ANGKOR WAT   GIZA   NAZCA

|— 4,745 MILES —|— 7,677 MILES —|

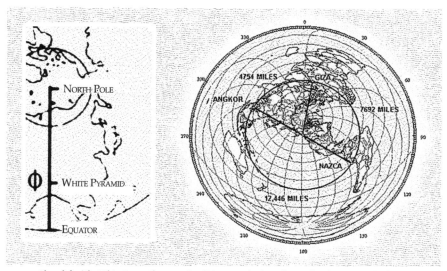

Above left : The White Pyramid sits at 34° 26' N. 3,840 miles from the North Pole, a precise Phi distance
Above right: Projection of phi distances from Jim Alisons great circle. Below: TheWhite pyramid, nr. Xian, China.

10 PHI FROM EQUATOR (16° 11'): 16°17'N · LUBAANTUM, 16° 38'N · TIAHUANACO, 16° 50'S · RAIATEA.
10 PHI POLE TO POLE (21° 15'N): 20° 40' · CHICHEN ITZA, 21° 30' · WABAR TEKTITE.
10 PHI POLE TO EQUATOR (34° 23'N): 34.00° · BAALBEK, 34°19' · EHDIN , 34° 22' · XIAN PYRAMIDS.
10 PHI EQUATOR TO POLE (55° 37'N): 55° 40' · KILWINNING (MASONIC CENTRAL), 55° 52' · ROSSLYN

Above: Various 'sacred latitudes' using different golden quadrant and hemispherical divisions.

THE SHIFTING GRID
surface slippage and the old pole

As well as studying ancient maps, Charles Hapgood (*see page 290*) made the suggestion that the Earth's crust "... much as the skin of an orange, if it were loose, might shift over the inner part of the orange all in one piece". It was already known that the inner flippings of the iron-rich core of the Earth caused magnetic pole reversals (recorded in the rock of the mid-atlantic ridge, *see page 248*). In addition to this, Hapgood radically proposed that the rigid, stony outer shell of the Earth, the lithosphere, might occasionally slide over the top of the lubricating layer, the asthenosphere. One result of this theory is that there are no 'Ice Ages' as such, instead the movement of the pole causes different areas to be covered in ice at different times.

Any movement of this sort would probably cause major worldwide devastation, and Rand Flem-Ath believes this happened between 11-12,000 years ago when the poles moved 30° to their current positions from the Hudson Bay pole (*see below*).

Albert Einstein supported Hapgood's theory, and suggested that the build-up of weight of the ice-caps could cause such a shift to occur over periods from a few thousand years to only a few days!

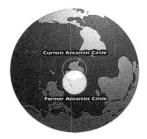

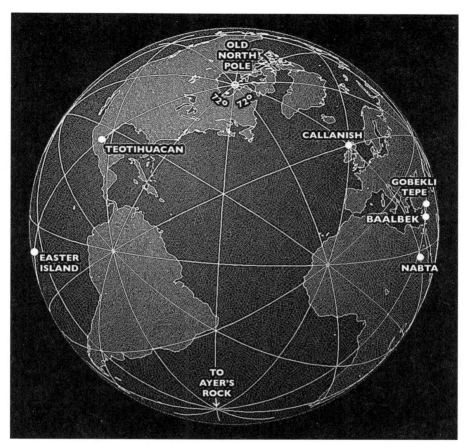

Above: A suggestive world grid, centred on the old North Pole in Hudson Bay (60°N 83°W), taking in some of the most ancient sites on the planet [produced by the author with John Martineau's World Grid Program]. Easter Island and Lhasa both sit precisely on the old equator (Lhasa on a node point). Nabta is the oldest stone circle found to date. Gobekli Tepe is the oldest city yet discovered and Baalbek has the largest megaliths in the world. Giza, Jericho, and Nazca were all at 15° N. British sites such as Stonehenge and Rosslyn also point to the old pole position (50,000-12,000 years ago). The angle between the old and new poles from Stonehenge is 46° degrees and its latitude back then was 46° N, a 46/46 site. Similarly, Rosslyn in Scotland is a 50/50 site. In fact, from the Hudson Bay pole, there are over 60 ancient sites all within half a degree of 'sacred latitudes' probably five times what we have today. Were the ancient surveyors recording the previous polar displacement and how damaging it had been, setting up a series of interrelated measuring points around the world so they could measure future slippages?

EARTH MUSIC
cymatics, sferics, tweeks and whistlers

The Earth is very noisy. It gives off a relentless symphony of countless notes imperceptible to the human ear. Seismometers can detect the Earth's 'hum', colossal mysterious ring-like oscillations or waves, that have been compared to the *aum* sound of Hindu creationism. The aurora, or 'northern lights', also emit shrieks and whistles into space (known as auroral kilometric radiation) when charged particles from the solar wind hit the Earth's magnetic field.

If humans had radio antennae as ears, we would hear lightning strikes emit a broadband pulse of radio waves. These 'sferics', 'tweeks' and 'whistlers' travel around the world by bouncing back and forth between the surface and the ionosphere, striking somewhere on the planet roughly 100 times per second, sometimes moving along magnetic flow lines. Combined with earthquakes, volcanoes, moving water and high force winds, could this symphony somehow organise the energies of the Earth into a coherent vibrating geometric grid?

The study of how sound affects matter is called 'cymatics', named after the Greek *kymatika* (matters pertaining to waves). Dr. Hans Jenny, a student of Buckminster Fuller, conducted clever experiments, in which a droplet of water containing a very fine suspension of light-coloured particles (a colloidal suspension) was vibrated at various diatonic musical frequencies. He photographed complicated geometries appearing inside the droplets, surrounded by elliptical lines connecting their nodes. High vibrations created the most complex designs, and different mediums affected the results. Jenny's work demonstrated the reality of sound forming physical phenomena.

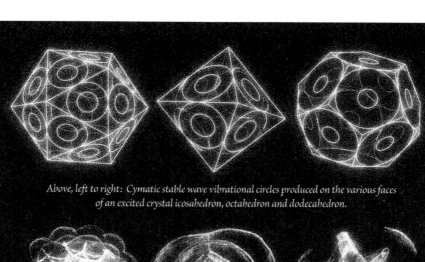

Above, left to right: Cymatic stable wave vibrational circles produced on the various faces of an excited crystal icosahedron, octahedron and dodecahedron.

Above: Cymatic forms based on Hans Jenny's photographs of light passing through vibrated water, sometimes using two tones. 3-D grid-like forms appear, with 12-, 3- and 6-fold geometry.

Above: Also redrawn from Hans Jenny's photographs. Turpentine vibrated on a film creating grid-like patterns similar to the Hartmann and Curry grids (page 270-271).

GEOMETRY ON OTHER PLANETS
energy patterns everywhere

In 1972 distinguished planetologist Dr. Robert Duncan-Enzmann suggested that tetrahedral geometry might define the locations of large scale energy upwellings on planets throughout the solar system. Tetrahedra with vertices at the poles define latitudes 19.47° above and below the equator. Olympus Mons (a Martian volcano three times larger than Mount Everest, and the highest mountain in the solar system) is found at this latitude, as is the most active volcano on Earth, Kilauea, in Hawaii. Further phenomena around 19.5° include increased solar flare activity on the surface of the Sun (*opposite top*) and the dark bands of clouds around Saturn.

There are many other examples of planetary geometries. Jupiter's great 'Red Spot' is found at 22.5°, a quarter of a quadrant distance. This is the same latitude as a similar 'great dark spot' on Neptune, accompanied by a thin band of white clouds circling the planet, which was discovered in June 1994 by NASA. The Neptune spot completely disappeared in April 1995, but it soon reappeared, this time in Neptune's northern hemisphere, again at 22.5° with identical banding! NASA noted that it was a "near-mirror image of the first spot".

In 1981, scientists were astonished to discover a stationary 'cymatic' hexagon, twice the size of the Earth, at Saturn's north pole, with multi-tiered linear clouds bands swirling around it. Uranus' moon Miranda displays huge triangular features that ressemble the faces of an icosahedron, and other polygonal areas (superimposed pentagonal and hexagonal) which seem to shape the terrain. Is it really too much to imagine energetic geometries might also exist on Earth?

Top left: Tetrahedra inside a sphere define 19.5°
latitudes above and below the equator
Above right: The Sun has increased solar flare
activity at 19.5° above and below the equator.
Centre: The Olympus Mons volcano on Mars sits
close to 19.5° north, defined by a tetrahedral vertice.
Left: The hexagonal cloud at Saturn's north pole
retains its integrity and has been visible since its
discovery in 1981 (picture courtesy NASA).

NATURAL GRIDS
waterfalls, volcanoes and mountains

There is tantalising new evidence that natural sites of major global geomantic significance, like volcanoes and waterfalls, might also be involved in grid systems. For example, two of the world's largest waterfalls, Victoria Falls in Africa and Angel Falls in Venezuela, are located precisely 90° apart, forming two vertices of an octahedron which also aligns to the pyramids of Giza (*opposite top left*). Another octahedron (*top right*), connects the world's most active volcano, Kilauea in Hawaii with two notable ancient sites, Angkor Wat and Nazca. Kilauea sits beside the world's largest volcano, Mauna Loa. Both are at 19.5° N, so relate to tetrahedral geometry (*previous page*).

Lower left are shown two great Earth circles, both passing through Kilauea and waterfalls of planetary signifiance, one of which takes in Mount Shasta in California, and the other Mount Everest. Shasta is considered sacred by some Native Americans, who say it is inhabited by the spirit chief Skell who descended from heaven to the mountain's summit. It is also a prominent site on the 'Rainbow Serpent' (*page 280*).

Finally, a newly discovered great Earth circle joins three major ancient world centres: Giza, Lhasa and the megalithic islands of Tonga. Lhasa, literally meaning 'place of the gods', is revered as the holiest place in Tibet, while on the islands of Tonga, there are hundreds of megaliths, including the Stonehenge-like trilithon of Ha'amonga. Unlike other Pacific islands, Tonga never completely lost its indigenous governance, and is the only independent monarchy still left in the vicinity. Tonga and Hawaii have both been proposed as centres of the pre-Atlantian Lemurian civilisation. The plot thickens!

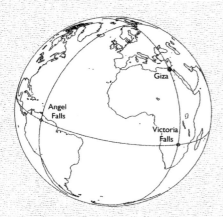

Above: Angel Falls (Kerepakupai merú), the world's highest free-falling waterfall at 3,212 ft is 90° from the Victoria Falls or Mosi-oa-Tunya (the Smoke that Thunders), the second largest (after Martineau).

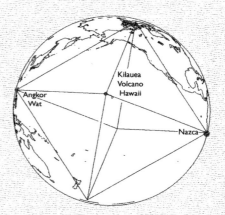

Above: Kilauea is one of five shield volcanoes that form the Islands of Hawaii. It has been active continuously since January 1983 and sits aside Mauna Loa, the worlds largest volcano.

Above: Mt. Shasta has been identified by various groups as a cosmic power point, a UFO landing spot, a Lemurian sanctury, a gateway to the fifth dimension and a source of magic crystals!

Above: A great Earth circle connects Giza, Lhasa and Tonga, three major ancient capitals that stretch back into pre-history and were considered 'sacred centres' of their cultures.

BOOK II

Above: An augur of Ancient Rome, employing Alectryomancy (p.98).

"The present moment is the only moment available to us,
and is the door to all moments" — Thich Nhat Hanh

DIVINATION

ELEMENTS OF WISDOM

Jewels Rocka

Above: Illustration by Edmond Lechevallier-Chevignard [1825-1902], showing the Greek goddess Ananke (Roman Necessitas, "necessity") as the supreme arbitrator of fate and circumstance. Holder of the cosmic spindle, she is the mother of the Moirai, the Three Fates representing destiny, fortune and inevitability; Clotho spins the thread, Lachesis measures the thread and Atropos cuts the thread.

INTRODUCTION

THE HISTORY OF DIVINATION is long and vast. Since time immemorial humans have sought to understand their place in the universe, comprehend cycles of being, interpret their relationships, find meaning in their existence, gaze into the future and see the unseen. The term comes from the Latin divinare, "to foresee" or "receive messages from the gods".

The oldest and most comprehensive writings about divination come from the *Chinese Book of Changes* the *Yi Jing* (c.1142 BC), which details a style of prophesying which evolved from even older practices of casting bones into a fire and reading patterns on their charred surfaces.

Divination methods and ritual tools have developed with time, necessity and fashion, as people sought to find the best path, guarantee their crops or secure their futures. When seeking insights into political winds of change and other kinds of weather before an important marriage or battle, a soothsayer or shaman would be consulted to read the auguries in the intestines of sacrificed animals. Today we have other tools at hand, such as polls, predictive analytics and meteorology, but divination remains stubbornly popular, especially within personality and relationship dynamics.

Humans are by nature questing creatures, always seeking knowledge of potential tomorrows. Many people, especially in times of uncertainty or vulnerability, find that connecting with the greater plan can help them feel more accepting and in control of their lives. Divination shines a guiding light on a divinely recommended line of action to secure the best possible outcomes.

The Elements of Divination
and the planes of being

There are many ancient divination tools and rituals for connecting to the divine. In this book they are grouped according to the four Aristotelian elements of western alchemy: fire, earth, air and water, plus the fifth element, ether (the binding force of nature). The five elements represent five different portals or pathways to divining the truth:

△ Fire: *Casting*. The seeker performs a ritual in the moment to draw down wisdom, knowledge and information about their concern.

▽ Earth: *Language of the Earth*. Observing physical cycles and natural patterns to gain clarity about something that is not yet manifest.

△ Air: *Mapping and Measuring*. Using theoretical constructs and known patterns to calculate relationships and investigate the character of an entity or situation to gain insight and foretell likely futures.

▽ Water: *Feeling the Vibes*. Connecting to the etheric energy of an object, situation or sensory clue to receive a picture or story.

◯ Ether: *Heaven's Gift*. The seer is given information, sometimes unbidden, from the higher planes of awareness. Messages may come from astral beings, the mental or even spiritual planes.

Many metaphysical doctrines speak of interconnected planes of being or 'states of awareness' (*illustration opposite, the Sephirotic Tree of Life, Robert Fludd, 1621*). Understanding these subtleties gives insight and focus in divination work as you connect through these states to the subject or question under investigation. These planes are, loosely speaking:

THE SPIRITUAL PLANE: That which cannot be named. The 'great mystery' of unity from which all lower planes emanate and to which they return. Communion with this plane of pure conscious awareness, the Turiya in Sanskrit, can bestow flashes of events to come.

THE MENTAL PLANE: the fundamental patterns of the cosmos whereby all lower levels have their origins. The causal plane of natural law, abstract consciousness and logic, outside of space and time. It contains the symbols, colours and blueprints for all that we experience.

THE ASTRAL PLANE: the level of consciousness and the realm of dreams and imagination. Underlying forces, principles of nature and archetypes begin to take form here. Guides, gods and cosmic beings walk these planes, as do ideas and thought forms and constructions.

THE ETHERIC PLANE: the framework of subtle energies on which all material substance is arranged. Close to matter, it exists in time and space and can affect the material world. Easily accessible for divinatory enquiry and etheric aura readings.

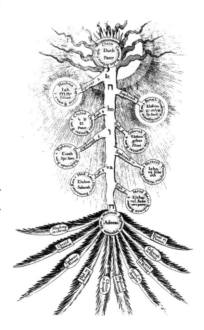

THE PHYSICAL PLANE: the state of material substance and level of manifestation, not the cause of embodiment. Everything physical is already patterned in the levels above, with the spiritual plane being the source of all being.

DIVINATORY PREPARATION
ritual for the divine

In divination, you are essentially searching for the truth. So prepare:

GROUND AND CLEAR yourself and your divinatory tools to add clarity and depth to a reading. Using dirty tools can corrupt a reading, so although you need not be squeaky clean—*"water which is too pure has no fish"*—attend to your psychic hygene. Quieten your mind, connect to the divine, and let go of pretentions and assumptions.

INVOKE SOME PROTECTION e.g. white light or guardian beings (*or see examples opposite*). Open channels attract all sorts of energy.

ASK THE RIGHT QUESTION for the chosen method of divination. Some techniques are better at eliciting a yes/no answer (e.g. dowsing), while others are better at delivering a narrative (e.g. tarot).

UNDERSTAND WHAT YOU ARE ACTUALLY ASKING. Correctly framing the question and exploring its nuances is one of the greatest skills of a seer, and is often easier to do when reading for another.

RELAX, AND LET THE "KNOWING" ARRIVE. The hallmark of a good seer is a true connection and the ability to spin a yarn or story in tune with the essence of the seeker and their question. The initial divinatory imagery which appears may suggest a quick answer, and with practice and connection the deeper message will sing to you with relevance.

Protection: Two safe ways of tuning into higher energy planes: Left: The Magician draws down power and knowledge from the universe. On his table sit symbols of the elements, a Wand (fire), Pentacle (earth), Sword (air), and Cup (water). Imagine being inside one part of the infinity sign above his head while the item being probed is in the other part. Open the crossing of the infinity figure to channel the divine and then close it quickly when enough information is gained.

Right: The High Priestess sits between the black and white pillars of the Temple of Solomon connecting heaven and earth. Solid and grounded, on her lap a scroll of esoteric wisdom, she holds her own space as she sits on her throne. When divining, imagine being between two connected pillars, then step out and open a channel with the divine, secure in the knowledge that if threatened in any way (e.g. see below) you can return to the protection of the pillars.

FIRE

divination by casting

FIRE CORRESPONDS to spirit, action, passion, desire and immediacy. In the ritual action of casting a seeker poses a question and by throwing, rolling or shaking, awakens the spirit surrounding the issue to reveal an answer. This is achieved through divine synchronicity, a coincidence between a well-cast question and a revealing outcome. Success requires a clearly formed question, posed with respect and reverence.

Divining through the element of fire is a popular technique. Originally the province of trained professional seers, it later became a popular method for dabblers and parlour games, running the risk of attracting lower astral energy, false readings and wilful misguidance.

With experience, however, a seer can learn the language of a chosen method and use the casting tools merely as a prompt to open the fire portal and access a far deeper reading.

Examples of casting systems are DICE *(p.90)*, GEOMANCY *(p.92)*, RUNES *(p.88)*, TAROT *(p.84)*, TASSEOMANCY *(see opposite)* and YI JING *(p.94)*.

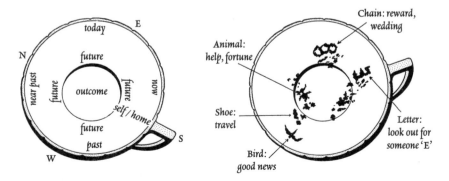

Tasseomancy is the ancient tradition of reading tea leaves, coffee grounds (Turkey) or wine lees (Rome). Bid the subject drink from a cup with a light interior while they think about their issues, until there is a little liquid left. Holding the cup in your non-dominant hand swirl it clockwise three times ensuring the liquid reaches the brim. Quickly turn the cup upside down on the saucer. Interpretation relies on creating a narrative from the association of the symbols.

Anchor: Success in business	Clumps: Busy life	Man, Woman: Love, Union
Animals: Unexpected assistance	Coffin, Bag: Illness, Trap	Oblongs: Family troubles
Arrow: Romance, Adventure	Cross: Kiss, Sorrow, Death	Question mark: Hesitancy; Caution
Bell: Unexpected news	Crown: Loyalty, Honor	Scissors: Closure, Broken bond
Birds: Freedom, Success, Good news	Cup: Reward; Fortune; Aid	Shoe: Journey, Change
Boat: Visit from a friend; Protection	Face: New people; Changes afoot	Snake: Wisdom, Enemy
Bridge: Healing, Opportunity	Finger: Look where it points	Squares: Peace, Happiness
Bush: New friends, Surprises	Fish: Good fortune from afar	Sun: Success, Power, Creativity
Chair: Unexpected Guest	Flowers, Leaf: Joy, Happiness	Sword, Dagger: Arguments, Enmity
Circle: Union, Money, Gifts	Gate, Doorway: Future success	Tower: Uncertainty, Change
Circle, broken: Delay	Hand: Open friend; closed foe	Tree: Strength, Health
Claw: Hidden Enemy	Heart: Happy, Friend, Love	Triangles: Journeys, Legacy
Clear around: Happiness	Horseshoe, Kite: Wishes come true	Waterfall: Flow, Prosperity
Clouds around: Sadness	Line, straight: Peace, Tranquility	Woodland: Beware of pitfalls
Clover: Luck, Wealth, Reward	Lines, long wavy: Loss, Frustration	Worms: Look to your health

TAROT
on the cards

No one really knows when the use of tarot cards began. Some claim that as traders passed through ancient cities speaking different languages, they created a pictorial and evocative form of divination to convey shared meaning. Both the ancient Babylonians and the priests of Egypt practiced tarot, but the first recognisable cards appeared in the French courts around 1390, while the Occult tarot deck has stayed virtually the same since the 18th century.

Encoded and depicted on tarot cards is a world of symbols and imagery carrying a great wealth of ancient occult knowledge for the dedicated student. Even a reading using only key words as a prompt for a free flowing narrative can elicit powerful insight.

An Occult tarot deck consists of 78 cards made up of 22 Major Arcana cards and 56 Minor Arcana (suit cards) representing the four elements: WANDS (fire), CUPS (water), SWORDS (air), and PENTACLES (earth). It has also spawned many different versions, designed by artists, philosophers, astrologers and others, which include images of angels, aliens, animals, trees and so on.

All decks are read in a similar way, by casting shuffled cards or those chosen randomly into a variety of spreads, to analyse different aspects of life.

Above: Asking the cards. There are many types of spreads suited to different types of questions and lengths of time. The Celtic Cross layout is one classic divinatory spread (e.g. see page 88).

Above: A three-card Tarot spread.
This simple layout can represent past/present/future or any three designated qualities. In the case shown: in the past there has been a need for truth and balance; now there is some confusion or self-deception, caution is needed; the situation will be resolved, using courage and focus.

0 THE FOOL: Taking Risks; Awareness; start on a journey or adventure.

1 THE MAGICIAN: Realising Powers; Crossroad of potential; paying attention.

2 THE HIGH PRIESTESS: Wise Woman; Psychic ability; teaching; self-discovery.

3 THE EMPRESS: Earthy Woman; Imagination; nurturing of creation; a child.

4 THE EMPEROR: A Powerful Man; Authority; taking and giving counsel.

5 THE HIEROPHANT: A High Priest; Traditional, reliable; ritual; re-evaluation.

6 THE LOVERS: A Loving Relationship; Choice that may involve sacrifice.

7 THE CHARIOT: Mastery of the Elements; Confrontation; obstacles to overcome.

8 STRENGTH: Physical and Spiritual power; Heroism; courage and self-discipline.

9 THE HERMIT: Inner Search for Wisdom; A secret revealed; withdrawal; silence.

10 WHEEL OF FORTUNE: Unexpected events; Change is inevitable, can be good fortune.

11 JUSTICE: A Balanced Virtue; Impartial Judgement; successful with law.

12 THE HANGED MAN: A New Perspective; Transformation; sacrifice to make change.

13 DEATH: Destruction and Renewal; Reincarnation; a major change.

14 TEMPERANCE: Balance and Harmony; Moderation; self-control; patience.

15 THE DEVIL: Delusion and Suffering; Bondage to others, concepts and objects.

16 THE TOWER: Breakdown of Systems; Destruction; crisis; fall from grace.

17 THE STAR: Bright Promises; Opportunity; hope; a wish come true.

18 THE MOON: Not All is What it Seems; Delusion; deceit; hidden enemies; women.

19 THE SUN: Successful and Fruitful; Expansive; creative; trusting; achievement.

20 JUDGEMENT: Improvement in All Things; Second chances; being non judgemental.

21 THE WORLD: Completion of All Things; Attainment; success; triumph; travel.

The Minor Arcana

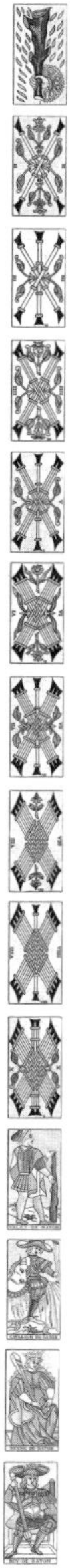

Ace of Wands (Fire): *Exciting birth of an enterprise.*

2 of Wands: *A creative opportunity.*

3 of Wands: *Patience; strong foundations laid .*

4 of Wands: *Hard work leads to celebrations.*

5 of Wands: *Opposition; plans go wrong.*

6 of Wands: *Achievement; there is more to do.*

7 of Wands: *Competition; persevere, believe.*

8 of Wands: *Long term success; hectic times; travel.*

9 of Wands: *A challenge; strength of purpose.*

10 of Wands: *Lighten your load; take a step back.*

Knight of Wands: *A curious young person; stimulating.*

Page of Wands: *Dynamic person; change; adventure.*

Queen of Wands: *Independent; enthusiastic; warm.*

King of Wands: *Inspirational leader; creative.*

Ace of Cups (Water): *New relationship; birth.*

2 of Cups: *Union; successful partnership; contact.*

3 of Cups: *Celebration; relief after difficulty.*

4 of Cups: *High expectations; resentment builds.*

5 of Cups: *Regret and sorrow; grief and acceptance.*

6 of Cups: *Something from the past; peaceful love.*

7 of Cups: *Many choices; calls to be realistic.*

8 of Cups: *A life chapter is over; walk away.*

9 of Cups: *Wishes come true; contentment; pleasure.*

10 of Cups: *Success after struggle; happy family.*

Knight of Cups: *A romantic person; spiritual journey.*

Page of Cups: *A sensitive man; quest for love; proposal.*

Queen of Cups: *A sensitive woman; tuning into emotions.*

King of Wands: *Experienced man; be open and affectionate.*

Ace of Swords (Air): *New concept; decision needed.*

2 of Swords: *Face facts and confront fears; tension grows.*

3 of Swords: *A painful realisation; arguments; betrayal.*

4 of Swords: *Rest & recuperate after a difficult situation.*

5 of Swords: *Know limitations; pushing creates conflict.*

6 of Swords: *Conflict fades; easier times ahead.*

7 of Swords: *Beware who you trust; diplomacy resolves.*

8 of Swords: *Trapped by circumstances; patience.*

9 of Swords: *Worry and anxiety; keeps fears in check.*

10 of Swords: *Difficult end of cycle; revaluate; move on.*

Knight of Swords: *A sharp young person; read the small print*

Page of Swords: *A brave assertive man; stand up for beliefs*

Queen of Swords: *Perceptive woman; knowledge is power*

King of Swords: *Powerful man; expert opinion; stay calm.*

Ace of Pentacles (Earth): *Material success; new business.*

2 of Pentacles: *Balance your time and finances.*

3 of Pentacles: *Early financial success; more to do*

4 of Pentacles: *Stuck and stagnant; reluctant to take risks*

5 of Pentacles: *See the big picture to overcome loss.*

6 of Pentacles: *An opportunity; faith rekindled; sharing.*

7 of Pentacles: *Revaluate in light of use of skills and ability.*

8 of Pentacles: *Opportunity to develop talents and new skills.*

9 of Pentacles: *Contentment through material achievements.*

10 of Pentacles: *Financial and business success; happy family*

2 of Pentacles: *A talent to develop, a small windfall.*

Page of Pentacles: *Dependable; reliable; getting bogged down*

Queen of Pentacles: *Wise business woman; Attend material comforts.*

King of Pentacles: *Top business man; count your blessings.*

RUNES
and their meanings

The RUNIC ALPHABET has been used widely in different forms for more than 2000 years in Northern Europe. Runes were used as symbols of knowledge for place names, writing, divination, healing and magic, forming sigils for luck, protection and love. The word comes from the Old Norse *runa*, 'secret' or 'whisper', and Old Irish Gaelic *run*, 'mystery'. The characters were formed of straight lines, making them suitable for burning or carving into bone, stone, tiles or wood (*see opposite*).

The runes can be drawn or cast in a variety of spreads (e.g. see below), connecting the seeker to a great lineage of divination. Consulting the runes will give answers requiring vision and interpretation.

1	2	3
Past	Present	Future

THREE RUNE SPREAD

4	2	9
Future Hidden	Best Outcome	Future Feelings

3	5	7
Present Hidden	Present	Present Feelings

8	1	6
Past Hidden	Past	Past Feelings

MAGIC SQUARE SPREAD

6 — Outcome

1	5	3
Past	Positive Influences	Future

2 — Present

4 — Other Influences

CELTIC CROSS SPREAD

ᚢ U **URUZ**
WILD OX: strength, raw
energy, changes, rebirth

ᚠ F **FEHU**
CATTLE: wealth, fulfilment,
success, abundance, fertile

ᚦ TH **THURISAZ**
GIANT: gateway, force,
conflict, wait, abundance

ᚨ A **ANSUZ**
GOD STONE: divine breath,
signs, luck, taking advice

ᚱ F **RAIDO**
WAGON: travel, journeys,
work, having perspective

ᚲ K **KANO**
BEACON: light, revelation,
inspiration, creative, vitality

ᚷ G **GEBO**
GIFT: generosity, balance,
exchanges, relationships

ᚹ W **WUNJO**
JOY: comfort, pleasure,
clarity, ecstasy, restoration

ᚺ H **HAGALAZ**
HAIL: natural forces, crisis,
destruction, trial, awakening

ᚾ N **NAUTHIZ**
NEED; delay, resistance,
restriction, self-reliance

ᛁ I **ISA**
ICE: challenge, frustration
standstill, stop and reflect

ᛃ J,Y **JERA**
YEAR: good harvest, peace
fruition, full cycle, timeliness

ᛇ EI **EIHWAZ**
YEW TREE: defence, honest
endurance, stable, reliable

ᛈ P **PERTH**
HIDDEN: secrets, initiation,
occult, women's business

ᛉ Z,R **ALGIZ**
ELK: protections, a shield,
defence, guardians, beware

ᛋ S **SOWELU**
SUN: life force, victory,
power, completion, health

ᛏ T **TEIWAZ**
TYR -Sky God: leadership,
authority, honour, justice

ᛒ B **BERKANA**
BIRCH GODDESS: fertility,
birth, growth, renewal

ᛖ E **EHWAZ**
HORSES: moving forward,
change, progress, transport

ᛗ M **MANWAZ**
HUMANITY: self or others,
social order, interaction

ᛚ L **LAGUZ**
WATER: ebb & flow, renewal,
sea, dreams, astral journeys

ᛝ G **INGUZ**
ING-EARTH GOD: gestation,
completion, rest and relief

ᛞ D **DAGUZ**
DAY: dawn, awakening,
growth, clarity, hope

ᛟ O **OTHILA**
ANCESTRAL INHERITANCE:
karma, property, values, culture

Above: The 24 runes of the Elder Futhark alphabet. A full set often includes a 25th blank rune:
WYRD—UNKNOWABLE: fate, the end is empty, as is the beginning.

DICE
shake, rattle and roll

ASTRAGALOMANCY, divination with dice, takes its name from 'astragali', knuckle bones. The practice dates back to at least 4000 BC, long before it became an obsession with the citizens of Ancient Rome. Wealthy Roman wives would gather at the Temple of the Vesta to consult the dice for their fortunes. Believing the Gods to show favour through luck, gambling on dice games became such a popular pastime that it was banned, except at festivals such as Saturnalia.

Dice divination is still used by the Roma people, and is useful for its succinct answers to tight questions, including further casts for elaboration and clarification to probe the heart of a question.

Casting with three six-sided dice is standard (although dice of 4, 8, 10, 12, 20 or 30 sides can be used).

The die may be cast on a round mat, or 12-inch chalked circle. Dice falling outside the circle can either be ignored, or render the cast null and void, or signify extra meaning.

The face values of the cast dice are added, and the sum is then reduced to a single digit (e.g. for a throw of 3:5:6, 3 + 5 + 6 = 11, and 1 + 1 = 2, so look up the reading for 2.

Relax, focus on your question and let the dice fall where they may.

ASTRAGALOMANCY

ONE DICE

Odd – Yes
Even – No

1 – Evaluate; Good luck
2 – Success depends on others
3 – Victory
4 – Disappointment
5 – Great news
6 – Uncertainty

TWO DICE

1 – Yes
2 – No
3 – Beware
4 – Reflect
5 – Good luck
6 – Certainly
7 – Have faith
8 – Be patient
9 – Absolutely
10 – Doubtful
11 – Nonsense
12 – Slight chance

THREE DICE

3 – Change for the better
4 – Disappointment
5 – Joy; Surprise; Success
6 – Bad luck; Material Loss
7 – Behind you; Scandal
8 – Tread carefully
9 – Love; Gambling; Unions
10 – Births; Opportunities
11 – Parting; Illness; Travel
12 – A message; Seek counsel
13 – Sorrow; Change
14 – New Friend; Help arrives
15 – Stay still; Beware
16 – Rewarding journey
17 – Flexibility; Advice
18 – Happiness, Success

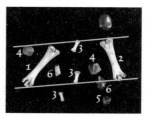

Left: SANGOMA BONES *represent human characters and the positive and negative forces influencing their lives.*

Above right: Romance and fertility are shown by the negative and positive forces lying between the man (1) and the woman (2). Positive forces - ancestor spirits (4) and eyes (6) - lie between the couple. There are also children bones (3) lying near the woman bone. A good indication of a romantic and fruitful relationship. Positive forces trump negative forces - crocodiles (5).

GEOMANCY
the earth oracle

Oracular **GEOMANCY** has been in use for millennia across Africa, Arabia, Europe and Asia. Random marks are created by throwing handfuls of earth onto the ground, or by striking sand with a stick. Patterns of odd or even numbers then generate one or two dots respectively. Performing this four times creates one of sixteen binary tetragrams (*shown opposite*) to give a reading. A full geomantic shield may be drawn up by creating four of these tetragrams which represent the four 'mothers' (*below*).

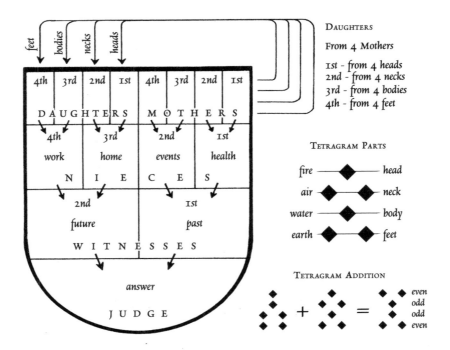

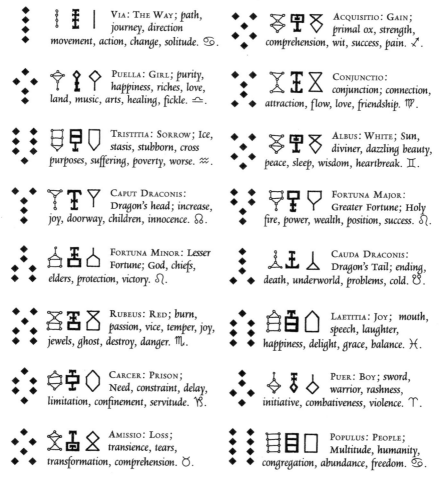

VIA: THE WAY; *path, journey, direction movement, action, change, solitude.* ♋.

ACQUISITIO: GAIN; *primal ox, strength, comprehension, wit, success, pain.* ♐.

PUELLA: GIRL; *purity, happiness, riches, love, land, music, arts, healing, fickle.* ♎.

CONJUNCTIO: *conjunction; connection, attraction, flow, love, friendship.* ♍.

TRISTITIA: SORROW; *Ice, stasis, stubborn, cross purposes, suffering, poverty, worse.* ♒.

ALBUS: WHITE; *Sun, diviner, dazzling beauty, peace, sleep, wisdom, heartbreak.* ♊.

CAPUT DRACONIS: *Dragon's head; increase, joy, doorway, children, innocence.* ☊.

FORTUNA MAJOR: *Greater Fortune; Holy fire, power, wealth, position, success.* ♌.

FORTUNA MINOR: *Lesser Fortune; God, chiefs, elders, protection, victory.* ♌.

CAUDA DRACONIS: *Dragon's Tail; ending, death, underworld, problems, cold.* ☋.

RUBEUS: RED; *burn, passion, vice, temper, joy, jewels, ghost, destroy, danger.* ♏.

LAETITIA: JOY; *mouth, speech, laughter, happiness, delight, grace, balance.* ♓.

CARCER: PRISON; *Need, constraint, delay, limitation, confinement, servitude.* ♑.

PUER: BOY; *sword, warrior, rashness, initiative, combativeness, violence.* ♈.

AMISSIO: LOSS; *transience, tears, transformation, comprehension.* ♉.

POPULUS: PEOPLE; *Multitude, humanity, congregation, abundance, freedom.* ♋.

Left: The Geomantic Shield. Four Daughters are generated from the four Mothers by adding lines, with odd sums as ◆ and even sums as ◆ ◆. In the same way, the nieces etc are generated. The First Witness is Father of the Judge and reveals past testimony. The Second Witness is Mother of the Judge and reveals future testimony. The Judge answers the original question. A 'reconciler' may also be formed by adding the judge to the first mother, to clarify the judgement. (See too page 392.)

Yi Jing
the oracle of changes

The central wisdom of the ancient Chinese **Yi Jing**, or I Ching, is that all beings and things have the capacity to adapt or change. Traditionally cast with yarrow stalks during an elaborate ritual (*see illustration below*), today the Yi Jing is more commonly cast using three identical coins, thrown six times to build a hexagram consisting of six lines:

– –	Yin; *2 tails, 1 head.*	—×—	Old Yin; *3 heads.*
——	Yang; *2 heads, 1 tail.*	—○—	Old Yang; *3 tails.*

The hexagram is compiled from the bottom up, and a commentary studied. Finally, any Old Yin and Old Yang 'changing' lines convert to their opposite to produce a second hexagram which is also studied.

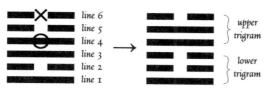

line 6
line 5
line 4
line 3
line 2
line 1

upper trigram
lower trigram

upper trigram								
lower trigram	1	34	5	26	11	9	14	43
	25	51	3	27	24	42	21	17
	6	40	29	4	7	59	64	47
	33	62	39	52	15	53	56	31
	12	16	8	23	2	20	35	45
	44	32	48	18	46	57	50	28
	13	55	63	22	36	37	30	49
	10	54	60	41	19	61	38	58

Above: Construction of a hexagram, showing how Old Yin and Old Yang 'changing lines' flip into their opposites. Right: Table for finding hexagrams in the list, below.

1. *Qian*. The Creative. Perseverance brings success.

2. *Kun*. The Receptive. Follow subtle guidance for fortune.

3. *Tun*. Sprouting. Fragility at the beginning, persevere.

4. *Meng*. Youthful Folly. Success, tempered enthusiasm.

5. *Xu*. Waiting. Good outcome with politeness and prudence.

6. *Song*. Dispute. Conflict. Compromise and take advice.

7. *Shi*. The Multitude. Troops follow responsible leader.

8. *Bi*. Alliance. Cooperation encourages others to join.

9. *Xiao Chu*. Small harvest. Restrain and attend to details.

10. *Lu*. Walking. Continuing good conduct brings success.

11. *Tai*. Greatness. Peaceful prosperity, unite in harmony.

12. *Pi*. Obstruction. Standstill resulting from selfishness.

13. *Tong Ren*. Fellowship. Group effort brings profit.

14. *Da You*. Great Possessions. Huge wealth, offer charity.

15. *Qian*. Modesty. Reverence and offerings can harmonize.

16. *Yu*. Enthusiasm. Excess, pleasure, planned movement.

17. *Sui*. Following. Experience. To rule, first learn to serve.

18. *Gu*. Correction. Decay. Work on what has been spoiled.

19. *Lin*. Approach. Forest. Advancing brings great success.

20. *Guan*. Observation. Contemplation. Looking up.

21. *Shi He*. Biting through. Chew through problems.

22. *Bi*. Adornment. Minor success with refinement.

23. *Bo*. Stripping. Vulnerability. Splitting apart. Stay at home.

24. *Fu*. Return. Turning point. Movement is advantageous.

25. *Wu Wang*. Innocence. Unexpected pestilence.

26. *Da Chu*. Great Restraint. Tame your energy. Charity.

27. *Yi*. Nourishment. Attend to comfort and security.

28. *Da Guo*. Great Excess. Measures beyond the ordinary.

29. *Kan*. Abyss. Gorge. Repeated entrapment.

30. *Li*. Radiance. The clinging net. Balanced action profits.

31. *Xian*. Influence. Wooing. Conjoining brings joyful success.

32. *Heng*. Constancy. Endure and persevere for success.

33. *Dun*. Retiring. Yielding hides assets. Modesty.

34. *Da Zhuang*. Great Maturity. Intelligent invigorating power.

35. *Jin*. Advance. Flourishing prosperous progress, caution.

36. *Ming Yi*. Obscured light. Hidden intelligence. Modesty.

37. *Jia Ren*. Family. Virtue and responsibilities all in order.

38. *Kui*. Strange. Unusual Perversion. Opposition.

39. *Jian*. Difficulty. Limping. Obstruction. Seek wise counsel.

40. *Jie*. Loosen. Untangle for deliverence. Let goals arrive.

41. *Sun*. Decrease. Sacrifice. Sincerity and inner offering.

42. *Yi*. Increase. Actions bring earthly and spiritual flowering.

43. *Quai*. Decision. Decisive breakthrough and action.

44. *Gou*. Coupling. Meeting with a powerful female.

45. *Cui*. Clustering. Gathering. Strength in numbers. Support.

46. *Sheng*. Ascending. Tender lifting. The able shall rise.

47. *Kun*. Entanglement: Siege, confinement, fatigue, distress.

48. *Jing*. The Well. Selfless service and mutual care.

49. *Ge*. Reform. Revolution. Transformation with confidence.

50. *Ding*. Cauldron. Innovation, and recruitment. Creativity.

51. *Zhen*. Arousing. Thunder. Move calmly to face a challenge.

52. *Gen*. Stilling. Movement and pausing. Self restraint.

53. *Jian*. Infiltrating. Gradual advancement by degrees.

54. *Gui Mei*. Marrying maiden. Submission to destiny.

55. *Feng*. Abundance. Excess. Maintenance of acheivements.

56. *Lu*. Travelling. Developing outwardly in adversity.

57. *Xun*. Wind. Gently enter. Unobtrusive undertakings.

58. *Dui*. Joy. Persuasion. Speaking and encouragement.

59. *Huan*. Disperse. Expand and dissolve for gain. Reunify.

60. *Jie*. Moderation. Articulate and restrict when appropriate.

61. *Zhong Fu*. Inner Sincerity. Trust radiates from the heart.

62. *Xiao Guo*. Small exceeding. Great fortune from small details.

63. *Ji Ji*. Already Completed. Amicable and gracious dealings.

64. *Wei Ji*. Not Yet Completed. No profit until the end.

EARTH

show me a sign

THE **EARTH** ELEMENT relates to the tangible world of matter, practical concerns and the senses. It gives substance to the natural rhythms by which we live, e.g. the cycles of days, moon phases and seasons. Over time these and other events, including anomalies of life and the quirks of chance, have become associated with various outcomes that can be interpreted as supportive or detrimental to a situation.

Some historic methods are too brutal or unsavoury to use today (e.g. animal sacrifice and reading entrails), while other earth associations, rooted in the customs and beliefs of a particular place and time, will have passed from common use to superstition, and then been forgotten.

Earth readings feature strongly in love divination, assessing the quality of a relationship and foretelling the nature of major social and political changes. They are often used for simple yes/no answers, e.g. pulling the petals from a daisy, saying "he loves me, he loves me not".

Earth divination includes **AEROMANCY** (*p.102*), **HYDROMANCY** (*p.103*), **OMENS** (*opposite*) and divination with **FOOD** (*p.100*) or **ANIMALS** (*p.98*).

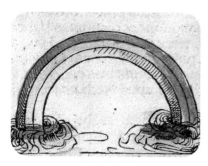

GOOD OMENS

Four-leafed clover - Meeting a sheep - Seeing a ladybird - Horseshoes in the U position - Wishbones - Bats at twilight - Walking in the rain - Gift of a beehive - Pod with nine peas - A robin flies into the house - Hearing crickets - Seeing a white butterfly - Burning your fingernail clippings - Cutting your hair during a storm - Finding a pin and hanging it on a hook - Seeing a load of hay - Seeing the New Moon over your right shoulder - Picking up a nail that was pointing towards you - Finding a pencil in the street - Keeping a piece of oyster shell in your pocket - Carrying a rabbit's foot - Sleeping on un-ironed sheets - Spilling your drink while proposing a toast - A sprig of white heather - Seeing a blue bird - A strange dog follows you home - Putting a dress on inside out - Rubbing two horseshoes together - Catching two rats in the same trap - Sneezing three times before breakfast - Meeting a chimney sweep - Well-swept doorways - Bird droppings land on you - Someone spills water behind you - Hearing the word 'rabbit' - The number 8 - Newly planted trees

BAD OMENS

An owl hoots three-times - A five-leafed clover - Peacock feathers indoors - Opening an umbrella indoors - Rooster crowing at night - Emptying ashes after dark - Bringing in eggs after dark - A hat on a bed - Giving away a wedding present - Giving scissor, knives or a clock as a present - Borrowing, lending or burning a broom - Cutting your nails on Friday - Bringing white lilac or hawthorn blossom into the house - New shoes on a chair or table - Killing a seagull, a spider or a cricket - Mending a garment while wearing it - Dropping an umbrella - An owl in daytime - Sleeping with a shelf over you - Meeting a grave digger - A button in the wrong hole - A picture falling - Breaking a glass during a toast - Dropping a glove - A ring breaking on your finger - Removing your wedding ring - Three butterflies together - Red and white flowers in the same arrangement - Putting your shirt on inside out - Walking under a ladder - Breaking a mirror - Walking over three drains - Walking over a crack - Letting a black cat cross your path - Stepping on a grate - Pointing at a rainbow

Above: An omen prophesises something yet to happen. With a question in mind simply keep your eyes open and let the cosmos supply the answer. The skill in interpreting an omen is in making the signs and symbols relevant, using symbology, signs and correspondences. Left: In many cultures, the appearance of a comet or eclipse heralds a dire warning from the gods.

Animal Behaviour
and interesting itches

Seers consider animals as pure embodiments of original spirit. Animals may therefore be closely observed to obtain valuable oracular clues.

Ailuromancy is the study of cats. In most cultures a black cat crossing your path, particularly right to left, is seen as an unfortunate sign, although it is lucky in Britain. Similarly, a cat washing its face, climbing the furniture or sleeping with its back to the fire denotes rain.

Alectryomancy is the art of fortune-telling with a chicken. A seer would scatter some corn on an alphabet drawn in a circle, and then watch the rooster peck at the grains to spell out a message.

Arachnomancy is divination using spiders. Various West African tribes observe the way spiders move small cards made from dried flat leaves which are marked with symbols and left outside their holes.

Another form of Earth divination is **Telaesthesia**. According to the Australian Aborigines of the Western Desert region, when you get an itch, pain or other body sensation it can give you information, *Punka-Punkara*, about a distant object, people or events. Equivalent systems were popular across Europe for thousands of years up to the modern period. Next time you get an itch, consult the diagram (*opposite*).

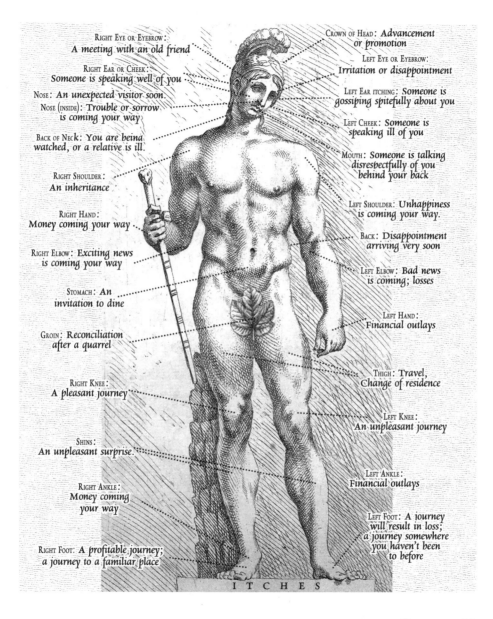

RIGHT EYE OR EYEBROW:
A meeting with an old friend

RIGHT EAR OR CHEEK:
Someone is speaking well of you

NOSE: An unexpected visitor soon.

NOSE (INSIDE): Trouble or sorrow
is coming your way

BACK OF NECK: You are being
watched, or a relative is ill.

RIGHT SHOULDER:
An inheritance

RIGHT HAND:
Money coming your way

RIGHT ELBOW: Exciting news
is coming your way

STOMACH: An
invitation to dine

GROIN: Reconciliation
after a quarrel

RIGHT KNEE:
A pleasant journey

SHINS:
An unpleasant surprise.

RIGHT ANKLE:
Money coming
your way

RIGHT FOOT: A profitable journey;
a journey to a familiar place

CROWN OF HEAD: Advancement
or promotion

LEFT EYE OR EYEBROW:
Irritation or disappointment

LEFT EAR ITCHING: Someone is
gossiping spitefully about you

LEFT CHEEK: Someone is
speaking ill of you

MOUTH: Someone is talking
disrespectfully of you
behind your back

LEFT SHOULDER: Unhappiness
is coming your way.

BACK: Disappointment
arriving very soon

LEFT ELBOW: Bad news
is coming; losses

LEFT HAND:
Financial outlays

THIGH: Travel,
Change of residence

LEFT KNEE:
An unpleasant journey

LEFT ANKLE:
Financial outlays

LEFT FOOT: A journey
will result in loss;
a journey somewhere
you haven't been
to before

I T C H E S

FORTUNES FROM FOOD
sorting good apples from bad

Holidays and feasts are popular occasions for seasonal divination.

FAVOMANCY, a spring festival divination from peas and beans, involves placing a bean in a dish of peas to be served with the main meal. The one who finds the bean in their portion gets the good luck.

KARUOMANCY, divination from nuts, is practised in Nigeria, where sixteen nuts are shaken between the hands and the pattern of odd and even numbers studied. Other traditions observe the behaviour of nuts jiggling or exploding in the embers of a fire or on a hotplate.

CROMNIMANCY was once very widespread and involves attaching names to different onions and then watching the way they each sprout.

ALEUROMANCY, performed in ancient Egypt, involves pouring flour out in small heaps and interpreting the shapes produced.

APPLES play a big role in love divination, e.g. at the Nov 1st Festival of Pomona, the Roman Goddess of orchards, when a spiral of apple peel thrown over the shoulder can reveal a letter on the ground, and apple seeds named and tossed in the fire or stuck to a face may reveal even more.

FORTUNE TELLING CAKE SET

Parties, Birthdays, Weddings, Valentine, New Years, Halloween

DIRECTION:
1. Distribute each charm in cake batter or place in cake after it is baked or bought.
2. The charms can also be drawn out of a glass or other receptacle if you do not wish to use the cake.
3. Then look at card for meaning.

TEA POT
This little teapot really does say Good Luck for some one far away.

FISH
This little fish is full of cheer. You'll soon see someone you'll love dear.

MOTORCYCLE
You'd better get used to lots of noise, for you'll have a large family of girls and boys.

RING
It isn't very hard to see that lucky in love you'll always be.

BOAT
This boat will start things humming. A happy engagement is soon forthcoming.

BANJO
Don't bother with love for pity's sake. An excellent musician you're sure to make.

BIRD CAGE
Listen to this bird whenever sad. It will make you happy and glad.

CHAIR
Don't envy others who are good looking. You'll be more popular with your cooking.

PLANE
This plane never will tarry for soon you are to marry.

HORSE RACE
Racing today is all the swing. Tomorrow you'll wear a wedding ring.

FOR PARTIES AND FESTIVE OCCASIONS OF ALL KINDS, AMUSING AND ENTERTAINING.

Above: A 1950s fortune cake set with rhyming captions. Left. 1878 Japanese senbei cooking. Chinese fortune cookies became popular in San Francisco c.1900. They contain slips of paper inscribed with different fortunes baked into dough balls.

Facing page: Apple ducking and bobbing, traditional Halloween games dating back to Roman times and the Festival of Pomona.

AEROMANCY
in the wind and the water

AEROMANCY interprets events in the sky as divine messages—winds, storms, clouds, rainbows, comets and shooting stars. Europeans once associated thunder in the east with bloodshed, while high winds at Christmas foretold the death of a king. The Etruscans and Babylonians both saw thunder and lightning as signs of foreboding. Hindus interpreted the shapes made in clouds, still a popular pastime today.

Cloud images are often very personal to the reader, with no two interpretations of shapes being the same. They give insight into the state of one's mind and can help the seer tap into the streams of future consciousness to illuminate possibilities.

Angels offer you guidance; *Babies* suggest new beginnings; *Cats* ask you to expand your psychic abilities; *Circles* mean completion; *Buildings* reveal your self-worth; *Dancers* invite you to move; *Dragons* foretell success; *Hearts* speak of love is in the air; *Horses* signal reliability and freedom; *Rabbits* are symbols of fun; *Snakes* warn of deceit or danger.

The effects of wind on everyday objects can also message a seeker, whether ringing bells, flapping flags or paper on the wind. To divine a yes or no answer, use two identical pieces of paper marked yes and no. Ask your question as you release the papers into the wind from a height. The first to flutter to the ground will give you your answer.

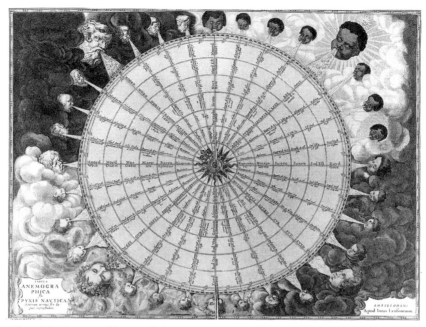

Above: *The Compass of the Winds, Jan Jansson, 1650, showing 32 different personifications of the wind, depending on where it blows from. A simple wind divination tool may be constructed with such a dial to take instant readings from the wind. The Greek poet Homer refers to four winds, Boreas (north), Eurus (east), Notos (south) and Zephyrus (west).*

Left: HYDROMANCY *involves observing the shapes, colours, patterns, and sounds of water in the sea, springs or ponds. The Pitjantjatjara people of Central Australia select a pebble and rub it under their armpit before throwing it into a waterhole. If this produces clear strong ripples it is okay to stay, but if the stone produces little or no ripples then you'd better be away.*

Above: *The Chinese Emperor was given his morning reading via a singing bowl. The water was vibrated by rubbing the handles and the ripples were then studied.*

AIR
mapping and measuring

THE ELEMENT OF **AIR** is associated with thought, logic, communication, theories and systematic knowledge. Divination through this portal is analytical. Theoretical constructs are used to calculate and interpret cycles and relationships, to analyse the character or nature of an entity or situation and to predict likely futures based on predictable cycles, patterns and correspondences. These techniques lend themselves to deep analysis of situations, character and personality and the election of favourable timings or locations.

From the 18th century, emerging scientific concepts in astronomy, medicine, physics, chemistry and philosophy undermined these ancient systems. Nevertheless, an interest in many of them persists to this day and has evolved, e.g. modern computers have made the arduous task of mapping and calculating cycles much easier. The many books, websites and workshops on these subjects is evidence of the continuing interest in such structured analysis of our existence.

Divinatory tools and tables are used to map and measure cycles and correspondences in disciplines such ASTROLOGY (*p.108*), PALMISTRY (*p.107*), PHYSIOGNOMY (*p.106*), NINE STAR KI (*p.106*), SELENOMANCY (*p.110*) and NUMEROLOGY (*opposite*).

SIMPLE ENGLISH			VALUE	GREEK	HEBREW	ARABIC	COMPLEX ENGLISH
a	j	s	1	A α alpha	א aleph	ا 'alif	A
b	k	t	2	B β beta	ב bet	بـ ba	B
c	l	u	3	Γ γ gamma	ג gimmel	ج jim	C
d	m	v	4	Δ δ delta	ד dalet	د dal	D
e	n	w	5	E ε epsilon	ה he	ه ha	E
f	o	x	6	F ϛ digamma	ו vov	و waw	F
g	p	y	7	Z ζ zeta	ז zayin	ز za	G
h	q	z	8	H η eta	ח het	ح ha	H
i	r		9	Θ θ theta	ט tet	ط ta	I
			10	I ι iota	י yod	ي ya	J
			20	K κ kappa	כ kof	كـ kaf	K
			30	Λ λ lambda	ל lamed	ل lam	L
			40	M μ mu	מ mem	مـ mim	M
			50	N ν nu	נ nun	ن nun	N
			60	Ξ ξ ksi	ס samekh	ص س sin/sad	O
			70	O o omicron	ע ayin	ع 'ayn	P
			80	Π π pi	פ pé	ف fa	Q
			90	Q ϙ qoppa	צ tsade	ض ص sad/dad	R
			100	P ρ rho	ק quf	ق qaf	S
			200	Σ σ sigma	ר resh	ر ra	T
			300	T τ tau	ש shin	س ش shin/sin	U
			400	Υ υ upsilon	ת tav	ت ta	V
			500	Φ φ phi	ך kof	ث tha	W
			600	X χ chi	ם mem	خ kha	X
			700	Ψ ψ psi	ן nun	ذ dhal	Y
			800	Ω ω omega	ף pé	ض ظ dad/dha	Z
			900	ϡ san	ץ tsade	ظ غ dha/ghayn	
			1000			ش غ ghayn/shin	

Left: GEMATRIA Table. In the ancient world, letters stood for numbers, so every word was also a number. Many ancient texts (e.g. the Kabbalah, the Bible and the Quran) encode secret meanings using the interplay between letters and numbers (e.g. Jesus, ΙΗΣΟΥΣ, is 888).

For your "Life Path Number" add the numbers in your birth date until they reduce to one of the 11 numbers below (e.g. 22.10.1991 → 2+2+1+1+9+9+1= 25 → 2+5 =7.

For your "Character Number" add the numbers of the letters in your name using the Simple English table top left. Also analyse addresses, pet names and other key words in your life.

NUMEROLOGY - THE MEANING OF NUMBERS

ELEVEN NUMBERS ARE USED: 1–9, 11 & 22.

1 - BEGINNINGS: *leader, pioneer, innovator*

2 - PARTNERSHIP: *perfectionist, teamwork, mediator*

3 - GROWTH: *optimistic, versatile, good humoured*

4 – STABILITY: *determined, practical, conservative*

5 – SOCIAL: *creative, traveller, charming*

6 – LOVE: *affectionate, successful, indulgent*

7 – SPIRITUAL: *intuitive, sensitive, aloof*

8 – SECURITY: *hard-working, ambitious, organiser*

9 – DYNAMIC: *visionary, impatient, independence*

11 – STRENGTH: *idealistic, inspired, communicator*

22 – PERFECTION: *capable, talented, wise*

PHYSIOGNOMY
palmistry and moleoscopy

PHYSIOGNOMY is the art of assessing someone's character or disposition from their appearance, especially their face It is a fundamental facet of Chinese medicine and fortune-telling. The ancient Greek physician Hippocrates [460-370 BC] described how the excess or deficiency of any the four humours, which were believed to regulate the human body, could be read in someone's face (*see below*).

MOLEOSCOPY was also described by Hippocrates, although it predates both the Ancient Greek and Chinese cultures. The placement and quality of moles on the body enable a reading of character and fortune (*see table opposite*). It became hugely popular during the 16th and 17th centuries when elaborate maps and interpretations were developed, linking the position of moles on the body with astrology.

PHELGMATIC   CHOLERIC   SANGUINE   MELANCHOLIC

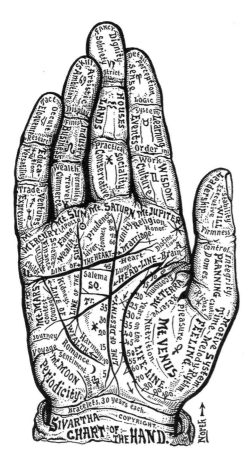

SIVARTHA CHART OF THE HAND.
COPYRIGHT.

APPEARANCE OF MOLES

ROUND Good character * ANGULAR Bad character * OVAL Bad luck * OBLONG Prosperity * RAISED Good fortune * GETTING LIGHTER Luck improving * BECOMING DARKER Trouble * HONEY/RED Good luck * BLACK Bad luck * TWO NEARBY Two marriages; affairs * TWO, SYMMETRICAL Dual nature

MOLES ON THE FACE

MIDDLE OF FOREHEAD Prosperous; bad temper/cruel * LEFT TEMPLE Spendthrift, headstrong * RIGHT TEMPLE Capable * EYEBROW Persevering, happy * RIGHT EYEBROW Active & successful * OUTER CORNER EYE Honest, reliable, needy * EAR Wealth & fame, reckless * LEFT CHEEK Serious, studious, struggling * RIGHT CHEEK Successful * TIP OF NOSE Sincere friend, hardworking * BRIDGE OF NOSE Lust, extravagance * LEFT OF NOSE Changeable, untrustworthy * RIGHT OF NOSE Traveller, active * NOSTRILS Wanderer * LIPS Ambitious, greedy * LOWER LIP Quiet, studious, fortunate later * CHIN Conscientious, practical, adaptable, affectionate * LEFT LOWER JAW Critical * RIGHT LOWER JAW Danger from fire or water

MOLES ON THE BODY

THROAT Artistic, successful * FRONT OF NECK Unexpected good fortune * SIDE OF NECK Temperamental * BACK OF NECK Desires a simple life * SHOULDER Sensible, industrious * LEFT SHOULDER Easy going * RIGHT SHOULDER Prudent, discreet * SHOULDER BLADES Restrictions * LEFT ARMPIT Fortune from work * RIGHT ARMPIT Struggles against odds * RIGHT ARM Difficult early life, happy old age * LEFT ARM Courteous, industrious * ELBOW Talented, struggler, adventurer * HAND Talented, successful * WRIST frugal * RIGHT WRIST Frugal, ingenious, dependable, successful * LEFT WRIST Ingenious, artistic * FINGER Dishonest, exaggerator, unrealistic * CHEST Lazy, quarrelsome * RIGHT BREAST Lazy, intemperate * LEFT BREAST Active, energetic, fortunate * NIPPLE Fickle, unfaithful RIGHT RIBS Insensitive, cowardly * LEFT RIBS Lazy, humorous * NAVEL Great fortune * ABDOMEN Voracious, intemperate * BACK Unreliable, untrustworthy * BUTTOCKS Lack of ambition, complacent * GENITALS Sex addict * HIP Resourceful, valiant, amorous * LOINS Dishonest * RIGHT THIGH Wealth, happy marriage * LEFT THIGH Warm natured * RIGHT KNEE Friendly * LEFT KNEE Rash, extravagant, ill tempered * RIGHT LEG Energetic, persevering * LEFT LEG Lazy * ANKLE Kind, humorous * HEEL Active, easily makes enemies & loses friends * RIGHT FOOT Traveller * LEFT FOOT Introspective, gloomy, sedentary * INSTEP Athletic, quarrelsome

Above: A 1898 palmistry chart by Sivartha Alesha. Palmistry, or CHIROMANCY, *reads lines in the palm of a person's hand as telling their life story. It is a practice found all over the world. Alexander the Great [356-323BC] famously studied the palms of his officers to gain insight into their characters.*

Right: A moleoscopy table, giving analysis of mole locations for luck and character.

ASTROLOGY

shining a light

ASTROLOGY is the study of how the sun, moon and planets influence life on Earth. The Sun, the Moon and planets move along the path of the *ecliptic* in front of the twelve constellations of the *zodiac*. Early astronomers predicted planetary movements via complex tables and astrolabes. Astrologers interpreted their meaning. There are many styles and applications of astrology including: the election of auspicious timing for weddings, inaugurations, battles, operations etc.; political analysis; cartography and the fortunes of location; prediction; horary divination of a chart constructed for a question; natal astrology involving the analysis of a person's birth chart or horoscope to interpret their character and destiny.

A horoscope, from the Greek *hora* (time) and *skopos* (observer) is a map of the positions of the sun, moon and planets as observed from a particular place on earth at a particular time. The planets, originally thought of as gods and goddesses, each radiate specific types of energy, the signs of the zodiac representing different modes of expressing those energies and the houses (segments of sky) representing the spheres of life where these energies play out. Astrologers synthesise the unique pattern of the heavens at the birth of a person, enterprise or event to interpret their character, destiny and fortune (*see opposite and below*).

THE TWELVE HOUSES

1ST: *The body, the identity*	7TH: *Relationships and partner*
2ND: *Personal resources and self worth*	8TH: *Sex and death*
3RD: *Environment, neighbours and siblings*	9TH: *Travel and higher education*
4TH: *Home and security*	10TH: *Career and status*
5TH: *Children and creative expression*	11TH: *Friends, hopes and wishes*
6TH: *Work, health and service*	12TH: *Self undoing, institutions*

THE ASPECTS

☌ 0°: CONJUNCTION
∠ 45°: SEMISQUARE, *buggy*
✱ 60°: SEXTILE, *positive*
⬠ 72°: QUINT, *grow*

90°: SQUARE, *stressful* □
120°: TRINE, *harmony* △
135°: SESQUI, *careful* ⊡
144°: BIQUINT, *fizz* ⯐
180°: OPPOSITION ☍

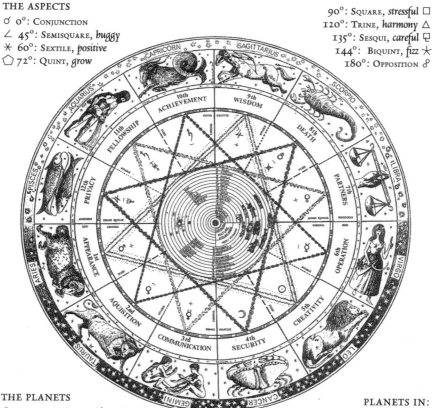

THE PLANETS

☉ SUN: *True inner self, vitality*
☽ MOON: *Responsive self, emotions*
☿ MERCURY: *Communication*
♀ VENUS: *Relationships and pleasure*
♂ MARS: *Aggression and energy*
♃ JUPITER: *Growth, benevolence and grace*
♄ SATURN: *Restriction, duty and learning*
♅ URANUS: *Freedom and breakthroughs*
♆ NEPTUNE: *Dissolution and mysticism*
♇ PLUTO: *Destruction and regeneration*
☊ NORTH MOON'S NODE: *Life's purpose*
☋ SOUTH MOON'S NODE: *Life's gifts*

PLANETS IN:

ARIES *are assertive and impatient* ♈
TAURUS *are retentive, patient and acquisitive* ♉
GEMINI *are intellectual, quick and superficial* ♊
CANCER *are sensitive, clingy and protective* ♋
LEO *are bold, warm, creative and showy* ♌
VIRGO *are shy, self-analytic and helpful* ♍
LIBRA *are charming, balanced and fair* ♎
SCORPIO *are secretive and intense* ♏
SAGITTARIUS *are active and expansive* ♐
CAPRICORN *are ambitious and conservative* ♑
AQUARIUS *are humanitarian and independent* ♒
PISCES *are selfless and sensitive* ♓

Selenomancy
by the light of the moon

SELENOMANCY is divination by the appearance and phases of the Moon. Ancient markings on bones and cave walls show that lunar cycles were being recorded as far back as 25,000 BC. Timing activities according to the Moon invites supportive energy for that endeavour, indeed gardening using the moon cycles is still widely practiced.

The Moon passes through each of the twelve signs of the zodiac every lunar month as it orbits the Earth. The phase of the Moon (*below*), the position of the Moon in the zodiac (*opposite*) plus important planetary transits and aspects all inform detailed forecasts of auspicious timings for contracts, weddings, purchases and periods of inactivity.

New Moon	First Quarter Moon	Full Moon	Final Quarter Moon	New Moon

1ST QUARTER	2ND QUARTER	3RD QUARTER	4TH QUARTER

NEW	CRESCENT	1st Q	WAX. GIBBOUS	FULL	WAN. GIBBOUS	4th Q	BALSAMIC
338°-22°	23°-67°	68°-112°	113°-157°	158°-202°	203°-247°	248°-292°	293°-337°
beginnings	inspiration	action crisis	enthusiasm	power	reassessment	conscience	justice
instinct	clarity	balance	growth	completion	wisdom	contemplation	enemies
health	romance	motivation	building	magic	destruction	endings	obstacles
improve	planning	courage	dancing	change	protection	ancestors	removal
creative	firming up	friendship	acquisition	love	stress	prayer	separation
lettuce	cabbage	peas	tomatoes	onions	potatoes	weeding	digging
endive	spinach	beans	peppers	squash	berries	pests	rest

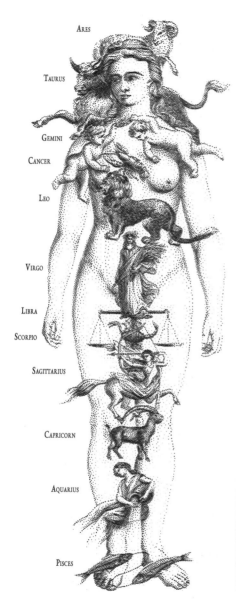

ARES
TAURUS
GEMINI
CANCER
LEO
VIRGO
LIBRA
SCORPIO
SAGITTARIUS
CAPRICORN
AQUARIUS
PISCES

Left; The signs of the zodiac assigned to different parts of the human body. The Moon rules Cancer, the crab, shown over the heart. For centuries, this concept was used to plan the timing of operations. For example, Aries is associated with the head, so Moon in Aries is not a good time to have brain surgery. Any day in which the Moon is void (makes no aspect to another body before leaving a zodiac sign) is also not ideal. Surgery is avoided when the Moon is in a mutable sign (Virgo, Gemini, Pisces or Sagittarius) and encouraged in fixed signs (Taurus, Leo, Scorpio or Aquarius). Operations are best five days before or after the new Moon, with fluids at their lowest ebb and less chance of swelling, and avoided five days before or after a full Moon when bodily fluids are at their highest with risk of swelling, haemorrhaging and wounds that won't heal.

NINE STAR KI

Japanese astrology

NINE STAR KI is a system of Japanese astrological cosmology derived from the eight trigrams of the Chinese *Yi Jing* (*see page 94*). It is a system for determining one's natal element, using the Chinese five elements, and from that making predictions regarding travel, personality, health, relationship and environmental dynamics.

Chinese astronomers believed that Polaris, Vega and the seven stars of the Ursa Major system—the nine stars of Nine Star Ki—cause a slight 9-year fluctuation in the Earth's electromagnetic field. As the energy flow changes from year to year, one of the five elements becomes accentuated, giving rise to fire, earth, metal, water and wood years repeating in a 9-year cycle. This cycle is similarly reflected in smaller and larger increments, with cycles of nine, in months, days and hours.

水	土	木	木	土	金	金	土	火
1-WATER	2-EARTH	3-WOOD	4-WOOD	5-EARTH	6-METAL	7-METAL	8-EARTH	9-FIRE
1954	1953	1952	1951	1950	1949	1948	1947	1946
1963	1962	1961	1960	1959	1958	1957	1956	1955
1972	1971	1970	1969	1968	1967	1966	1965	1964
1981	1980	1979	1978	1977	1976	1975	1974	1973
1990	1989	1988	1987	1986	1985	1984	1983	1982
1999	1998	1997	1996	1995	1994	1993	1992	1991
2008	2007	2006	2005	2004	2003	2002	2001	2000
2017	2016	2015	2014	2013	2012	2011	2010	2009
2026	2025	2024	2023	2022	2021	2020	2019	2018
2035	2034	2033	2032	2031	2030	2029	2028	2027
2044	2043	2042	2041	2040	2039	2038	2037	2036

9 - FIRE - EXPANSION

PASSIONATE. *clarity, charismatic, radiant, active, outgoing, clear opinions, sharp minds, can be lonely, vision, determined, impulsive, can be inconsiderate, impatient, thoughtless, self-confident.*

8 - EARTH - MOUNTAIN

STRONG. *Self reliant, can become isolated or stubborn, optimistic, spiritual quality, grace, stillness, proud, haughty, tenacious, may seem obstinate, gentle hearts, like adventure, tend to be possessive.*

7 - METAL - LAKE

JOYFUL. *Aware of aesthetics, sensitivity to life, easy talking, entertainers, social personalities, nervous, sometimes insincere, open and frank, practical, changeable, optimistic, may be bossy, good with money.*

6 - METAL - HEAVEN

CREATIVE. *Resilient, thinkers, efficient and highly organised minds, self-control, honest, direct, leadership, may be arrogant and dictatorial, not social, noble attitudes, not good at compromise, can offend.*

5 - EARTH - PRIMAL POWER

GREAT CONTROLLER. *Creative / destructive balance. At the centre of things, leaders, social, well respected, may be egotistical, confidence, vitality, bold, can have difficult early family life, tenacious.*

4 - WOOD - WIND

MOVEMENT. *Changeable. Independent, determined, generalists, desire for freedom & justice, indecisive, not practical, gentle, turbulent emotions, strength, impulsive, inspire confidence, giving nature.*

3 - WOOD - THUNDER

EXPLOSIVE. *Vibrant, sometimes threatening, poetic, idealistic, impulsive, bold, quick minds, easily frustrated, action oriented, can be rash, sensitive, determination, open and honest, self orientated, many projects.*

2 - EARTH - EARTH

RECEPTIVE. *Nurturers, quiet person of action, diligent, constant, hard working, conservative, relationships important, secure, thoughtful, can be perfectionists, supportive, service, like acknowledgment.*

1 - WATER - WATER

DANGER. *Gentle surface, strong inside, secretive, sensitive, deep thinkers, dreamers, easy going, good listeners, diplomatic, independent, adaptable, communicator, can be indecisive and lacking in clear direction.*

Above: Interpretations for each of the nine stars in Japanese Nine Star Ki.

Left: The Chinese Five Element system. In Nine Star Ki these elements are further expressed as being either Yin (black), Yang (white) or neutral (grey).

Facing page: Look up your year number. The Chinese solar year starts on February 4 or 5, so if you were born before that date you need to subtract one from your year of birth.

WATER

feeling the vibes

WATER, THE ELEMENT OF THE SUBCONSCIOUS, is flowing, emotional, yielding, deep and penetrating. Foresight comes from tuning into the "etheric planes" and reading the energy signatures from objects, people, places, situations or sensory clues. This may come as snippets of knowing, sensed via the awakened third "eye of consciousness".

Divination through the water portal involves merging with the feeling of things rather than mental constructs. Unlike air and earth, the skill here is relaxing, letting go and using senses that may be beyond the rational. Development of this art is a very useful divinatory skill.

Even those professing no skills in the psychic arts can sense vibrations, feel the emotional undercurrent in a situation or place and perhaps see ghosts or auras. Being able to read the vibes of a being, object, place or situation will alert you to its health, wellbeing and suitability.

This can be applied even in mundane settings, such as choosing a seat at a restaurant, buying an antique, trusting a salesperson or assessing the health of a pet.

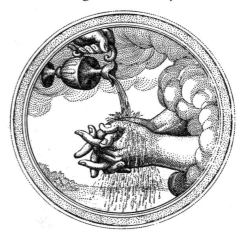

Water element divination includes DOWSING (*opposite*), ANTHOMANCY (*p.118*), PSYCHOMETRY (*p.116*), and SCRYING (*p.120*).

Above: DOWSING. *A dowser looking for water or minerals using a traditional forked hazel branch. Dowsing uses subconscious senses to discover water, pipes, cables, lost pets, misplaced keys, food additives, the sex of an unborn babe, medical issues, earth energy lines and more.*

All sorts of things can serve as dowsing tools: L-rods (above) made from copper or an adapted wire coat hanger, a forked hazel branch (top), high-tech carbon fibre bobbers or a pendulum (right). L-rods have the advantage of working well for directional questions, such as "find me a clean earth energy spot in the back garden to place my bench." Your rods will show you the direction and then cross when you reach the spot.

To begin dowsing you need to establish a base line for responses. Put your device in a 'neutral position'. For a pendulum that is swinging gently back and forward. Ask to be shown a "yes" response (often a clockwise swing). Do the same for 'no'. Repeat the procedure a few times. Different dowsers have their own responses. Once you have established a system, your responses will stay the same for all similar devices.

Psychometry
reading imprints

The vibrations or imprinted energy emanating from an object can at times be almost tangible. A focused reading such as **PSYCHOMETRY** can reveal information about previous owners or the use of an object. A seer may be able to pick up on the personality of the person linked with the item, their emotions and other factors—past, present and future.

A reader may receive information as a vision, emotion or subtle change of point of view. Any object can hold vibrations, but something personal that has been in close contact with the person, such as jewellery, is the most effective for reading. The energy of a building or space can also reveal information about former occupants and their activities.

With the object in front of you, put yourself in a meditative state, clearing yourself of any emotions and idle thoughts. Imagine yourself flooded with light before engaging with the object. Pick up the object and pay attention to your impressions, asking questions if needed.

Practice by tuning into an old piece of jewellery or clothing that you haven't worn for a while. See if it evokes memories and feelings. Or tune into an old door knocker in a junk shop to read if it belonged to a happy home. Modify your technique for distant readings. Use a photo of a place or person, touch a front door, or simply immerse yourself in the vibration of a space.

ANTHROMANCY
flower reading

ANTHOMANCY, or flower psychometry, appears widely in folklore. It is common knowledge, for example, that roses are the flower of love and beauty, that rosemary is for remembrance and lilies are for death.

One only reads flowers for another. The seeker must be drawn to the flower they choose, pick it freshly, hold it and tune into it for a minute or two. The seer, then receiving the flower, should steady themselves and link with the vibration of the flower. Describe what you feel as you move your fingers along the stem and onto the flower.

Leaves and flowers branching off of the main stem indicate diverging or competing interests and distractions, drives, hobbies, friends, family or work. Smooth stems suggest happiness, balance and understanding. A knot or bump on the stem warns of trouble, and isolation. Bigger lumps and breaks point to unresolved issues, relationships or addiction. Weak stems suggest sensitivity, fragility, anxiety and depression.

Notice how many flowers there are and examine their condition. Flower buds indicate patience and that which is yet to come, new opportunities in mundane matters such as money and work. A single large bloom represents an expansive nature, restless but open hearted and kind. Symmetrical flowers are chosen by people who like a sense of order, profuse blooms by those who love comfort and luxury, small flowers by homebodies and tiny single flowers by spiritual types.

CHART OF FLOWER MEANINGS

ACACIA: Stability
APRICOT: Fruitfulness
AGAPANTHUS: Love
ANEMONE: Death
ASPIDISTRA: Fortitude
AZALEA: Passion
BAMBOO: Youth
BLUEBELL: Humility
BUDDLEIA: Profusion
CARNATION: Love
CHAENOMELES: Resolution
CHERRY: Fruitfulness
CHINA ASTERS: Fire
CAMELLIA: Evergreen
CHRYSANTHEMUM: Resolution

CORNFLOWER: Relationships
CYCLAMEN: Resignation
CYPRESS: Nobility
DAFFODIL: Hope & Contentment
DAISY: Loyalty & Innocence
DELPHINIUM: Consolidation
EUONYMUS: Modesty
FORGET-ME-NOT: Remembrance
FORSYTHIA: Vigour
GARDENIA: Loveliness
GERANIUM: Peacefulness
GLADIOLI: Severed ties
HIBISCUS: Profusion
HOLLYHOCK: Fertility
HYDRANGEA: Achievement

HYPERICUM: Profusion
INCARVILLEA: Flamboyance
IVY: Friendship
JADE: Wealth
JASMINE: Friendship
JONQUIL: Desire
JUNIPER: Tolerance
KERRIA: Individualism
LILAC: Virility
LILIES: Death
MAGNOLIA: Fragrance
NANDINA: Holiness
NARCISSUS: Rejuvenation
NOMOCHARIS: Tranquillity
OLEANDER: Everlasting love
ORANGE: Wealth
ORCHID: Endurance
OSMANTHUS: Evergreen
PEACH: Friendship
PEAR: Longevity
PELARGONIUM: Determination
PEONY: Wealth
PETUNIA: Anger
PINE: Longevity
PLUM: Youthfulness
POMEGRANATE: Fertility
POPPY: Eternal sleep
PRIMROSE: Youth
PRIMULA: Fire
PYRACANTHA: Vigour
RHODODENDRON: Delicacy
RODGERSIA: Profusion
ROSE: Beauty
SAXIFRAGA: Heavenly
SORBUS: Achievement

SPIRAEA: Marriage
SUNFLOWER: Follower
SWEETPEA: Pleasure & departure
SYRINGA: Fragrance
THUJA: Longevity
TIGER LILY: Wealth
TULIP: Love & devotion
VIOLET: Mourning
VIRGINIA CREEPER: Tenacity
WATER LILY: Fortitude
WEIGELA: Profusion
WILLOW: Grace
WISTERIA: Beauty

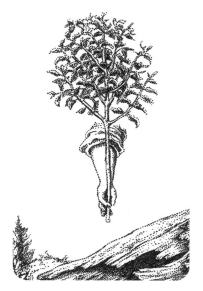

SCRYING
mirror mirror

To **SCRY** is to connect with the divine by gazing into a reflective surface. The earliest forms involved water; the Egyptians gazed into a pool of ink; the Babylonians gazed into various liquids in sacred bowls; the Hindus used bowls of molasses; ancient Greeks lowered mirrors into sacred wells and springs; the Chinese used polished bronze mirrors; witches used blackened mirrors or polished onyx; Nostradamus used a brass bowl of water resting on a tripod and a looking glass.

Today the most popular form of scrying is **CRYSTALLOMANCY**, scrying with crystal balls. Some people use a lamen, an ornate circular table standing inside a magic circle, both inscribed with mystical names.

Use a sphere of about 4 inches (100mm) diameter made of beryl or quartz. Keep it wrapped, away from sunlight (moonlight is okay) and extremes of hot and cold. Ensure it is not handled by others.

Use a north-facing room with just enough light to read by. Place the crystal on the table or hold it in your hand, with a black cloth behind. Remove all distractions and gaze into the crystal. It should slowly fill with a milky hue, then go black before images are gradually revealed.

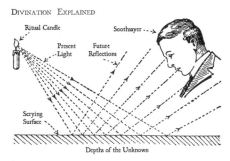

DIVINATION EXPLAINED

Ritual Candle

Soothsayer

Present Light

Future Reflections

Scrying Surface

Depths of the Unknown

INTERPRETING SYMBOLS

ANCHOR: Safety, hope
BEETLE: Long life
BIRD: A message
CROWN: Glory, responsibility
EYE: Good fortune, also symbol of evil
FRIEND: Fertility, beneficial but hidden
FRUIT: Children, success
GLOBE: Travel, correspondance
HEART PIERCED BY DAGGER: Suffering
LIGHTHOUSE: Danger ahead, but hope
MASK: Deceit, tragedy
SCALES: Justice, even-handedness, or not
SKULL: Death, wisdom
SNAKE: Health, knowledge, temptation
STAR: Success, but be careful
SWORDS: A quarrel
WATER LILLY: Creativity

INTERPRETING CLOUDS

WHITE: Good fortune
BLACK: Ill fortune
VIOLET, GREEN OR BLUE: Joy
RED, ORANGE OR YELLOW: Danger
ASCENDING CLOUDS: Yes to your question
DESCENDING CLOUDS: No to your question
CLOUDS MOVING TO RIGHT: Spirits present
CLOUDS MOVING LEFT: Spirits have departed

INTERPRETING EVENTS

AT FRONT OF CRYSTAL: Relates to the
present or immediate future
AT BACK OF CRYSTAL: Relates to the
remote past or distant future
TO YOUR LEFT: Events are real
TO YOUR RIGHT: Events are symbolic

Above: Interpreting your scrying results.
Left: 1920s poster.   Facing page: Left:
Divination explained, after Craig Conley.
Right: Scrying, Lustige Blätter, 1902.

ETHER
Heaven's gift

ETHER IS THE FORCE that ties together the other elements and all that is. It is beyond action, manifestation, thinking and feeling. The insights that arrive via ether may be unbidden and even unwelcome, such as dreams, premonitions and precognition. Some people are gifted with the ability to consciously draw from other planes of awareness, but this is a skill that can also be developed through focus, practice and training.

Connecting with the ethers is a pursuit shared by many different cultures and within shamanic practices, where seers achieve heightened states in rituals involving trancing, ecstatic dance, drumming and the use of entheogenic herbs, such as ayahuasca and mushrooms.

Divination using the ethers includes PSYCHISM (CLAIRVOYANCE, CLAIRAUDIENCE and CLAIRSENTIENCE, *opposite*), ASTRAL PALACE (*p.125*), AURA READING (*p.126*), CHANNELLING (*p.128*), DREAM WALKING (*p.124*) and VISION QUESTS (*p.130*).

Left: Siberian Shaman with drum. Below: PSYCHISM, or second sight, includes CLAIRVOYANCE, the power to see what is hidden, CLAIRAUDIENCE, hearing what is normally inaudible, and CLAIRSENTIENCE, a kind of super-feeling super-empathy.

We live surrounded by a vast sea of ether to which we are mostly insensitive. Second sight is the ability to extend consciousness beyond the five senses into the vibrations of the other planes.

Etheric perception intensifes colours, feelings and hearing. Walls can become transparent. You may glimpse coloured clouds, pathways to other landscapes and dimensions and even the magnetic field of etheric energy that surrounds humans, animals, trees and rocks.

You may meet nature spirits and elementals: fairies, plant spirits and gnomes; as well as other energetic constructs and thought forms from the astral realms who can pop in and out at specific times and locations in the more visible form of etheric matter: ghosts, entities, ghouls and other denizens of the lower astral, either haunting places or people, or just passing through after a death.

ONEIROMANCY
a dream within a dream

Dream divination has been a source of prophecy widely practised by all cultures. In dreams we walk the astral and causal planes and can tap into what Carl Jung [1875–1961] called the collective unconscious.

PSYCHIC DREAMING takes many forms: VISITATION DREAMS where a message is received, EMPATHY DREAMS which precipitate change, PRECOGNITIVE and WARNING DREAMS and TEACHING DREAMS.

Some people know they are dreaming. LUCID DREAMING allows a dreamer to direct their dream and consult with mages, guides, etc. Practice REALITY TESTING (*see caption opposite*) to dream more lucidly.

DREAM WALKING incubates dreams targeted to a specific question. Before dropping off to sleep, mentally run through the day's events in reverse order. Then ask your question and go to sleep with it on your mind. Remember to keep writing equipment by your bed.

Left: Drawing by Florence Harrison, 1910.
Below: Woodcut by Gwen Raverat, 1910.
Opposite: Drawing by Miriam English, 1977.

One pathway to the astral planes is to imagine an ASTRAL PALACE or garden. Begin with a guided meditation (see p.130), then give it more structure and life. Persistent creative thoughts will form a corresponding astral body, so as you add more details, your Palace will become more and more substantial. You can visit it at will and use it as a source of wisdom, knowledge and prophesy, inviting guides to work with you there. Use it as a gateway to access other astral lands and experiences.

'SHE·SLEEPS· ·A·CHARMED· SLEEP·

Facing Page: Awake into a lucid dream using REALITY TESTING. While awake, click your fingers and read some text while trying to pass your hand through a table or door. When dreaming it's easy to pass your hand through a door but hard to click and read text. Practie often while you are awake to remind yourself to repeat it when asleep, when it will act as a trigger to propel you into a lucid state. You can also pop a dream sachet of mugwort, lavender, hops, chamomile, lemon balm, rosemary, cloves or lemon verbena under your pillow to help. Set an alarm to wake you 5-6 hours after bedtime and then let yourself go back to sleep, straight into a cycle of REM dreaming.

AURA READING
seeing double

We are, in essence, an unfolding dance of cosmic dust. The aura is an energy phenomenon in an interwoven and complex network, which sustains, protects and informs our physical self, while connecting us to the great cosmic loom. It offers an excellent window to our mental, physical and spiritual wellbeing.

Although the basic structure of the aura is relatively fixed (*see opposite*) it is highly sensitive to emotional, physiological, social and environmental factors, and contains a chronicle of one's entire life.

To read an aura, place your subject in front of an off-white wall in natural indirect lighting. Stand about 10ft (3m) away and focus on a point on their forehead. Now expand your awareness to your peripheral vision while still looking at the point.

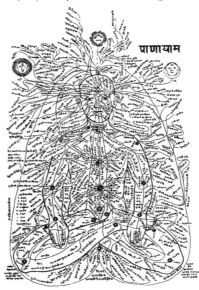

Allow your focus to become soft. A white energetic halo will pop into view around the subject. Look beyond this and the details of the aura will come into view.

Colour and vibrancy are two of the most noticeable qualities of the human aura, and each has a story to tell (*see opposite*). Psychic impressions and insights into health and emotional issues may also appear while reading the aura.

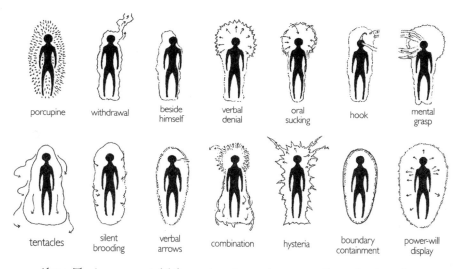

| porcupine | withdrawal | beside himself | verbal denial | oral sucking | hook | mental grasp |

| tentacles | silent brooding | verbal arrows | combination | hysteria | boundary containment | power-will display |

Above: The Aura as a varied defense system. A person's aura can tell you a lot about them. Facing page: The subtle body involves meridian lines and chakra centres which power the aura.

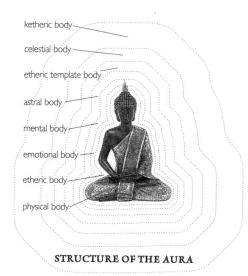

ketheric body

celestial body

etheric template body

astral body

mental body

emotional body

etheric body

physical body

STRUCTURE OF THE AURA

COLOURS IN THE AURA

YELLOW: *intelligent, dependable, sociable*

LIGHT BLUE: *balance, insightful, optimism*

DEEP BLUE: *sharp intellect, self-discipline*

BRIGHT GREEN: *healing, caring, enlightened*

DULL GREEN: *inner turmoil, pessimism, envy*

IRIDESCENT GREEN: *psychic, magic workers*

PINK: *youth, idealism, longevity*

BROWN: *practical, independent (also smoke)*

PURPLE: *creative, philosophical, intelligent*

ORANGE: *achievers, extroverts, competitive*

DULL ORANGE: *impatient, egotistic, unstable*

RED: *anger, aggression, violence*

GREY: *Forewarns crisis, adversity or illness*

CHANNELLING
is there anybody out there?

Channelling is a technique for contacting spirits of the dead, guides and angelic beings. Channellers enter an altered state of awareness and open themselves to receive messages like a relay centre for otherworldly messages. Others, who work with spirit, such as shamans, pagans, psychics and mediums, may receive auditory, empathic or visual messages. Similar practices, including séances (*below*), mediumship (*lower, opposite*), automatic writing (*opposite, top right*) and drawing, are allied techniques for pulling in spirit messages. All such techniques have different traditions and rituals but essentially share the same process.

As the astral planes are populated by all types of beings, it is important to be aware of protection protocols (*see page 80*) before attempting to communicate with these realms. When spirit beings initiate contact with you it is wise to be wary, as they may have dubious agendas and a poor quality of information.

Top left: Parlour games using the Ouija board became very popular in the late 19th and early 20th century. Think of a question, write it down and relax your body and mind allowing the writing to flow spontaneously.

Facing page: Victorian holiday entertainments and parties would often include a séance to communicate with the dead – a form of NECROMANCY.

Top right: Automatic writing allows a seer to produce words without consciouslessly writing. It has a long tradition In China, where it is known as Fuji, or spirit writing.

Left: Alphonse Mucha, from Le Pater (1889). Some seers work in a mild trance state while others need an elaborate ritual to enter a deeper trance. Following a request for contact with a spirit being, contact may feel like an sense of love, the presence of a wise being or a vision of serendipity.

Vision Quest
into the mystic realms

A **VISION QUEST** is a rite of passage, a journey of self-discovery into the spirit realms for healing, connecting with life purpose and stepping into one's own power. The aim is to seek divine revelation and connect with your higher self, guides, totems and allies. Traditionally, a quest might include cleansing rituals, fasting, energy raising activities, meditation practices and the use of entheogenic herbs, undertaken in a group with experienced guides in a natural setting.

There are many ways to make the journey. You may find a teacher, participate in a working group, climb a mountain or simply dedicate time to contemplate in the stillness of a natural environment or a sacred space. The way you frame your journey will colour your experience. The form of the ritual facilitates the "heroic step" through the open door and onto the spirit path that connects you to your own mystical dimensions. Undertake your own quest using these guidelines:

Clear your mind ◊ Visualise a symbol for your quest emblazoned on a double door in front of you ◊ See the doors open and see the realm beyond ◊ Walk through the doors and follow the spirit path before you ◊ Observe every detail of your journey, noting all landscapes and beings you encounter ◊ Accept any gifts or wisdoms offered with gratitude ◊ When you are to return, go back the way you came, through the doors and back into your physical body.

BOOK III

FENG SHUI

SECRETS OF CHINESE GEOMANCY

Richard Creightmore

Above: Si Xiang, the Four Celestial Spirits.
From top left: Eastern Green Dragon; Southern Vermilion Bird;
Northern Dark Tortoise; Western White Tiger.
Page iv: Green Dragon bearing the Twelve Earthly Branches.
Pages 134 & 136: Buddhist Temple, and circular motif, both showing Perfect Form.

INTRODUCTION

Feng Shui, literally "wind water," is the study of people's relationship with their living environment. Geomancy means "to divine the Earth." Feng Shui encompasses the entire spectrum of Chinese geomantic practices and includes in its full scope the landscape design of dwellings, work-places, villages, cities, palaces, temples and graves. It is rooted in Daoist and Confucian philosophy and practicality.

The term Kan Yu predates the term Feng Shui; Kan represents Heaven and by extension higher areas, and Yu Earth and lower areas of land. It is a fundamental precept of ancient Chinese philosophy that humanity is the intermediary between Heaven and Earth, and thrives when it learns to balance these two forces. A Kan Yu practitioner works ceremonially with the spirits of Earth and Heaven, and is expert in astrology, architecture, economics, geography, hydrology, landscape design, interior design, medicine, sociology, structural engineering and town planning. A related term is Xiang Di, the practical geographical appraisal of the landscape, involving hunting, agriculture, travel and warfare as well as building dwellings and towns. Most ancient sites in China were located on raised grounds near rivers, where fish and water could be obtained without danger of flooding. The common-sense practice of Xiang Di helped the ancients to select the best sites for settlement, and provided the basic principles of subsequent good Feng Shui practice.

This book presents a comprehensive and practical distillation of the essential elements of this venerable tradition. Feng Shui is at once an earth science, a magical tradition and an aesthetic art.

HISTORY
the development of geomantic ideas

During the Zhou Dynasty [1046-256BC] a dwelling's fortune was often determined by Zhen Pu—divination by SCAPULIMANCY (using the shoulder blades of an ox). In the Warring States period [475-221 BC], use of the Yi Jing (I Ching) became popular, and Daoism, Confucianism, and the theories of Yin and Yang, Wu Xing (Five Elements) and Ba Gua (Eight trigrams) began to take shape.

By the time of the Han Dynasty [206 BC-220 AD] written records of Feng Shui consultations appear. The first use of the term Feng Shui is attributed to Guo Pu of the Jin Dynasty [265-420 AD], who wrote in the Zang Zhu (Book of Burial):

> *"The dead should take advantage of the Sheng Qi. The wind will disperse the Qi and the water will contain it. The ancients said that one should try to gather the Qi so that it will not disperse. The aim is to keep it flowing but contained. Hence it is called Feng Shui."*

Feng Shui thus means the art of understanding movement and stillness in the land:

> *"Without water Qi disperses when there is wind, with water Qi stills and wind disappears… It follows that the best sites are those with water, then follow sites that are sheltered from the wind."* – Fan Yu Bing

Since the Song Dynasty [960-1279], two main schools of Feng Shui have evolved: the *Xing Shi Pai* or *Forms School*, based on the subjective observation of the physical world, and the *Li Qi Pai* or *Compass School*, based on the objective observation of the subtle and intangible world using the *Luopan* or Feng Shui Compass. Both are used together in practice to determine the auspiciousness of a site.

Above: Emperor Da Yu, a Kan Yu expert
and water diviner, with dowsing instrument.

Left: Traditional divination using a tortoise
carapace and yarrow stalks.

Above: Calculating the equinox, March 21st
or Sept 21st, using a gnomon.

Left: Early style of divination by heating a
tortoiseshell or ox scapula in the fire and
reading the cracks.

THREE GIFTS AND FIVE LUCKS
between heaven and earth

The fundamental triad of Daoist metaphysical philosophy is of the *Three Gifts (San Cai)*—Heaven *(Tian)*, Earth *(Di)* and *Humankind (Ren)*. These encompass all aspects of Feng Shui, and are often found symbolised in tripartite architectural plans and forms. The Temple of Heaven in Beijing has three principal buildings, each with an altar to one of the Three Gifts *(e.g., the Imperial Vault of Heaven, opposite top)*.

Also central to Daoist philosophy are the *Five Lucks*. In order of importance these represent five variables in the human experience of life. *Destiny (Ming)*, includes the concepts of destiny inherited from ancestry and also the Ming of a site—every site has its timely rightful owner. *Luck (Yun, timing)* distinguishes between the luck every human creates and the luck over which one has no control. *Feng Shui* is centrally concerned with the external environment and how it can reflect the internal environment (and vice versa), and thus is one of the Eight Limbs of traditional Chinese Medicine (it is a basic tenet that an alteration to the external form of a home will cause an internal shift within its inhabitants, so a Feng Shui cure can affect the other four Lucks, including Destiny). *Virtue (Yin De)* represents good deeds and service to others. Finally, *Knowledge (Du Shu)* represents education and self-cultivation.

Daoist philosophy perceives a unity in which every being, living and dead, is connected, and most strongly within a family lineage, so the destinies of descendants are influenced by ancestors' graves *(e.g., Ming Imperial tombs centre opposite)* and the destinies of ancestors by the provision of good house sites for their descendants.

		Astronomy
		Astrology
	Cosmic Qi	Moon & Stars
		The "Yi Jing"
		Time & Cycles
Heavenly Qi		
		Rain
		Sunlight
	Weather Qi	Heat & Cold
		Wind
		Seasons
		Tides
		Mountains
		Valleys & Plains
	Topographical Qi	Rivers and Streams
		Magnetic Fields
		Di Mai (Earth Meridians)
Earthly Qi		
		Orientations
		Dwellings
	Environmental Qi	Manmade Objects
		Form and Space
		Colour & Sound
		Furniture Layout
		Political
		Cultural
	Social Qi	Social Contacts
		Neighbours
		Family + Relatives
Human Qi		Partner
		Memories
		Ideals & Visions
	Personal Qi	Personality
		Sensitivity
		Vital Qi

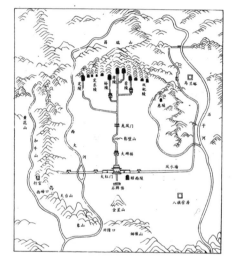

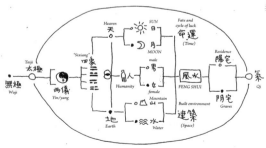

"The Dao gave birth to One, One gave birth to Two, Two gave birth to Three, Three gave birth to the ten thousand things." Dao De Jing, Ch.2.
Dao, or "the way", is understood as a pantheistic composite of, and the intrinsic order within all things.

QI
breaths of life

The life-breath of Dao is *Qi* ("chi"), often translated as "energy" though more precisely "breaths of life". *Qi* is understood as permeating Heaven and Earth, all things living and transforming because of *Qi*. *Sheng Qi* (creative, fertile *Qi*) is the harmonious expression of *Yin* and *Yang*, the physical phenomenon of vitality; it is *Qi* in motion constantly in all things. In contrast, *Sha Qi* is harmful environmental *Qi* which can range from noxious earth radiations and other physical phenomena (*see pages 174-76*) to subtle psychological and astrological threats. The aim of Feng Shui is to seek the time, space and direction of healthy *Sheng Qi* and avoid or transform unhealthy *Sha Qi*.

> *"Feng Shui values Qi of the mountains and rivers as they are the backbones of the Earth. Mountains congeal because of Qi, Qi becomes obvious because of mountains"*
> – Jiufeng Zhao, Di Li Wu Jue.

The geographical aspect of life energy is termed *Di Qi* or Earth Energy, and places that are congenial for plant growth and human habitation have good *Di Qi*. Biological health is subtly influenced by rock and soil quality, dampness, the Earth's magnetic fields, and radiations from minerals, geological faults and underground streams.

Qi Yun (*Qi Timing*) is the state and passage of *Qi* in time and space, derived from *Xiang Di* (appraisal of land) and Astrology (consideration of timing): Earth rotates and Heavenly *Qi* (weather) follows it; Heaven moves and Earth *Qi* is affected. A piece of land with good Feng Shui will not always remain so: timely use of the site is important. Similarly not everyone can benefit from a good site as each has its rightful owner, according to their personal astrology.

Left: A Dragon-shaped mountain, a very beneficial simulacrum. Centre: Accumulated Qi, the ideal configuration of topographical features, mountains and rivers around the Long Xue, or Dragon's Lair, the most favorable site. Right: "Hidden Qi is Qi that is intact."

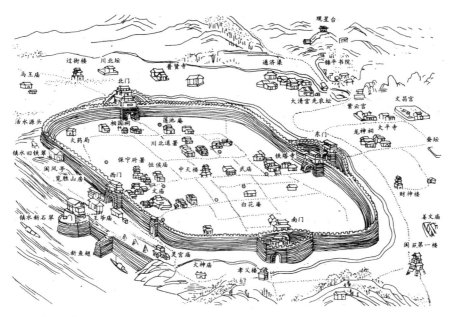

Above: The Qi Cang is an area where Qi converges and congregates, a discrete and precious space like a jewel box, within which Yin Qi and Yang Qi can interact and harmonize.

SHAN SHUI

mountains and water

Qi circulates throughout the earth in varying ways depending on local geodesic forces and topography. The *Long Mai* or *Dragon Meridian* is a current of concentrated Earth *Qi* that emanates the valuable *Long Qi* or *Dragon's Breath*. Long undulating mountain chains are thus seen as major *Mountain Dragons*, and large rivers as major *Water Dragons*. Majestic mountains embody *Yang Qi* (the higher the land the stronger its *Qi*), while meandering water is *Yin Qi* (the deeper the water, the bigger its *Qi*). Dragons link all features in the landscape, and are considered the most important. Where the Dragon *Qi* is big, a capital city may develop; where it is small, only a town will thrive. The Dragon trunk becomes cities and towns, and its feet become villages.

Heavenly Qi descends from above into Mountain Dragons below, following the spines of their ranges, and flowing through their ridges, branches and formations like arteries. As it flows it either scatters and dissipates or is held and condensed by *Water Qi*, for *Shan* (mountain) is like a host and *Shui* (water) its guest. When *Qi* circulates through landforms, landscape entities are thereby given life.

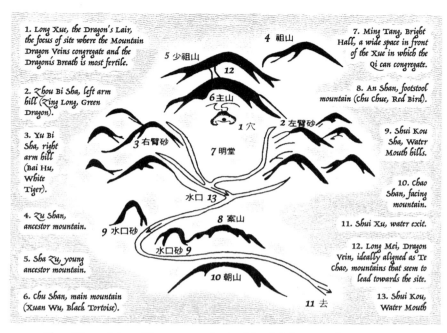

1. Long Xue, the Dragon's Lair, the focus of site where the Mountain Dragon Veins congregate and the Dragon's Breath is most fertile.

2. Zhou Bi Sha, left arm hill (Zing Long, Green Dragon).

3. Yu Bi Sha, right arm hill (Bai Hu, White Tiger).

4. Zu Shan, ancestor mountain.

5. Sha Zu, young ancestor mountain.

6. Chu Shan, main mountain (Xuan Wu, Black Tortoise).

7. Ming Tang, Bright Hall, a wide space in front of the Xue in which the Qi can congregate.

8. An Shan, footstool mountain (chu Chue, Red Bird).

9. Shui Kou Sha, Water Mouth hills.

10. Chao Shan, facing mountain.

11. Shui Xu, water exit.

12. Long Mei, Dragon Vein, ideally aligned as Te Chao, mountains that seem to lead towards the site.

13. Shui Kou, Water Mouth

5 少祖山　　4 祖山
12
6 主山
1 穴　　2 左臂砂
3 右臂砂
7 明堂
水口 13
9 水口砂　　8 案山
水口砂 9
10 朝山
11 去

Above: Nomenclature of features around a site. Below left: Location of prosperous cities.
Below right: Principal Mountain and Water Dragons of China. Opposite left: Scattered
Dragon veins, the ranges have no systematic pattern. Opposite right: An inlet with mountains
gradually sloping into the sea, gathering the Qi of both Mountain and Water Dragons.

SHAN LONG
where Mountain Dragons roam

Mountain Dragon ranges are traditionally rated by the strength of their central *spine* and branches. Ideally, they *"should seem to be arriving from the distance in a never-ending manner"*. Nestled beneath them, the best site for settlement is the *Long Xue,* or *Dragon's Lair,* located where the greatest number of beneficent Mountain Dragon veins congregate, and where the Dragon's breath is most fertile.

The end of the mountain range nearest any potential site is termed the *Head of the Dragon,* and the furthest end its *Tail.* The *Qi* can run forward or backward from the site according to the formation of the limbs. Gentle beginnings and endings of ranges are sought over abrupt ones as they allow space for the Dragon to develop, and for the *Qi* to gather where the *Mountain Long* merges into the plain. Cutting through a Mountain Dragon spine, e.g., for a road or rail cutting, can have a disastrous effect on the flow of *Qi,* and similarly damming a river can choke a Water Dragon. Facing and footstool mountains serve to contain the *Ming Tang* (*see page 148*) and can balance excess *Yang* from high mountains to the rear.

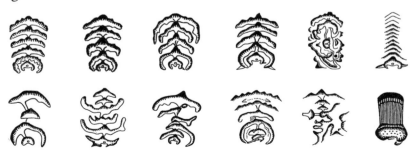

Convergence of Dragon's Breath at various Xue (marked as circles).

Barren, broken, rocky, excessive or solitary mountains destroy luck.

Mature Journeying Mountain Dragon nourishing the Xue (marked as circles).

Coherent Mountain Dragon veins surrounding the Xue.

SHUI LONG
there be Water Dragons

The *Ming Tang* is the open area in front of the *Xue*, ideally containing a river and fertile flood plain, in which the *Qi* can congregate and prosperity accumulate. The point where the water flows into the *Ming Tang* is known as the *Shui Kou* or *water mouth*, and the bigger the *Shui Kou* the greater the wealth it will encourage. Long, deep, slow, meandering watercourses are most conducive to the accumulation of Water Dragon *Qi*, particularly if they wind around seeming to embrace, and especially if they pool in front of the site. Water should be seen to linger as it flows away, with its exit point invisible from the site.

> *"With mountain one desires solidity. With water one desires clarity and stillness. The meandering of the emergent water compels high rank, abundance and wealth. If the mountain passes the water so that it winds, there will be a myriad of descendants. If the mountain causes the departure of water to be straight, one will be the servant of others or live with relatives because of straitened circumstances. If water passes from east to west, there will be endless wealth."* – Qing Wu, Burial Classic.

Sites on the outside of a bend or facing an oncoming current are at risk of inundation and therefore inauspicious, as are sites beside straight or fast-flowing streams which can conduct the *Qi* away from the site too rapidly. Joining streams are desirable as *Qi* concentrates. These Water Dragon precepts also apply to roads and paths.

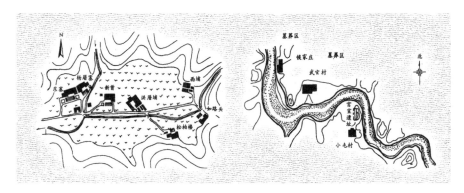

Above: Streams flowing east to west are favoured as they link the Dragon and Tiger, following the Sun. The best sites above are in the upper right of the left map and the centre of the right map. "The ideal site is nestled among watercourses protected in the belly of the Dragon" (Shui Long Jing).

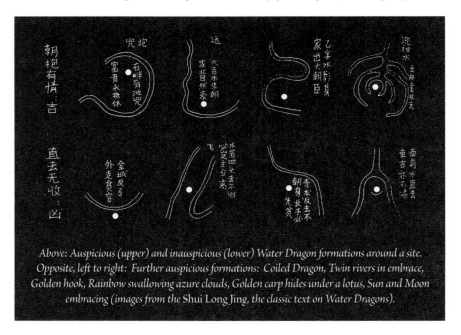

Above: Auspicious (upper) and inauspicious (lower) Water Dragon formations around a site. Opposite, left to right: Further auspicious formations: Coiled Dragon, Twin rivers in embrace, Golden hook, Rainbow swallowing azure clouds, Golden carp hides under a lotus, Sun and Moon embracing (images from the Shui Long Jing, the classic text on Water Dragons).

YIN YANG
defining each other

All Feng Shui is based on the balance of 陰 *Yin* and 陽 *Yang* in the environment. Even the ideograms are fundamentally rooted in the landscape, *Yang* meaning "the sunny side of the mountain" and *Yin* "the shady side". Healthy *Sheng Qi (see page 142)* accumulates best where *Yin* and *Yang* occur in a 40%–60% proportion.

    Yin and *Yang* symbolize unity through the interaction of bipolar forces, essentially passive and active. Almost everything has a *Yin Yang* twin, for example night and day, Earth and Heaven, moon and sun, female and male, and death and birth. *Yin* and *Yang* qualities always exist in relation to each other, and are often further divided, elevation into high and low, and low into slightly raised (*Yang*) and flat (*Yin*). *Yin* and *Yang* also control and balance each other (if *Yang* is excessive then *Yin* will be weak and vice versa), and they create and transform into each other, this constant flux being the source of all change.

    As *Yin* "-- " and *Yang* "— " revolve they produce two sons and two daughters: the *Si Xiang ("sir shang")*, or *Four Celestial Spirits*:

    ⚏ *Shao (young) Yang* is east, spring, the green Dragon, the fixed stars, daylight, corporeality, rotation, unity in multiplicity, the Prince.

    ⚌ *Tai (old) Yang* is south, the red Phoenix, summer, heat, the sun, the eyes, duality or origin, the nature of things, the Monarch.

    ⚍ *Shao Yin* is west, autumn, the white Tiger, the planets, night, materiality, inertia, succession, multiplicity in unity, the Duke.

    ⚎ *Tai Yin* is north, winter, the dark Tortoise, the moon, the occult, passion, equality, the attributes of things, the Emperor ruling Earth.

YIN	YANG
EARTH	HEAVEN
MOON	SUN
DEPARTING	ARRIVING
STILLNESS	MOVEMENT
SLOW	FAST
NORTH	SOUTH
WEST	EAST
NIGHT	DAY
WET	DRY
DEAD	LIVE
WATER	FIRE
VALLEY	MOUNTAIN
INTERIOR	EXTERIOR
COLD	HOT
DECREASE	INCREASE
WINTER	SUMMER
AUTUMN	SPRING
EVEN	ODD
BLACK	WHITE
RECEPTIVE	CREATIVE
FEMALE	MALE

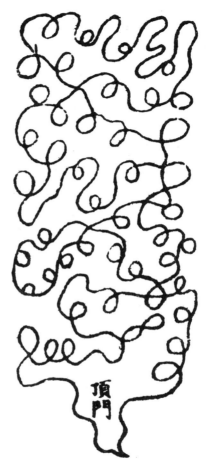

頂門

Above: Daoist meditation diagram:
The Blessed Union of Yin and Yang.
Top left: The Tai Ji, the Daoist Yin Yang
symbol, the circle representing the whole,
divided into Yin (black) and Yang (white),
each containing the seed of the other.

SI XIANG
the four Celestial Spirits

The *Four Spirits* simultaneously represent the four quarters of the ecliptic (or zodiac) and the topographic space around the *Xue*.

To the north the dark Tortoise (or black Turtle) represents the protective mountain wall behind the *Xue* whose strength is reflected in the prevailing health and social harmony of the residence where the earth *Qi* pools. To the south, the red Phoenix (or vermilion sparrow/pheasant) indicates the frontal area where the *Qi* is con-tained by the Phoenix (or water) wall. The open movement of *Qi* here reflects in prosperity through the healthy flow of Heavenly and Human *Qi* into the front door.

Traditionally this fundamental model is oriented with the Tortoise in the north, deriving from the practical benefits in China of facing sunshine from the south while being shielded from the cold winds of the north. However, this template can also be applied equally whatever the orientation of the landscape around a site. For example, in the case of a house with its back to a western mountain, the Tortoise is seen in the west, the Dragon in the north, the Tiger in the south, and the Phoenix and *Ming Tang* to the east.

The scheme may be similarly applied at other scales. In the urban landscape large surrounding buildings can substitute for mountain ranges. In domestic and commercial architecture the design may be represented in the shape of the built form within the plot. For example, in a bedroom the head of the bed should be against the most solid (Tortoise) wall of a room while facing the most active (Phoenix) wall, probably the one with the entrance or windows.

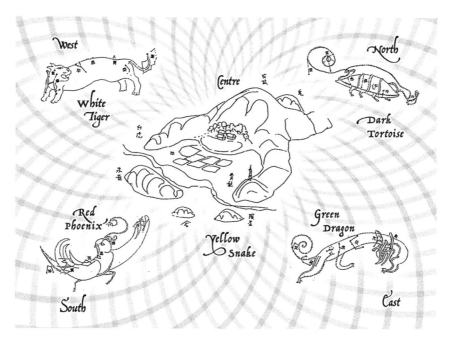

West

North

Centre

White
Tiger

Dark
Tortoise

Red
Phoenix

Green
Dragon

Yellow
Snake

South

East

"In front there is a Red Bird followed by a slow moving Tortoise
at the rear, to the left is the Azure Dragon
and to the right a White Tiger"– from the Li Ji (Book of Rites).
The centre is represented by a Yellow Snake.

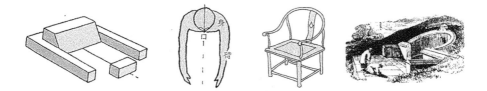

Above: Si Xiang principles visible in (from left to right): A traditional Chinese house,
a fundamental Qi Gong posture, an armchair, and a Chinese grave.
Central in all is the Ming Tang (or Bright Hall) in which the Qi can gather.

SI XIANG IN THE LANDSCAPE
animals all around

According to Feng Shui, the ideal formation around a site consists of a dark Tortoise, a strong high mountain range, behind but not too close, balanced by a red Phoenix, a lower range of hills or a single footstool hill in front. Meanwhile, to each side, the Yang Qing (azure or blue-green) Dragon and Yin white Tiger should meet in dynamic equilibrium. Specifically, the Dragon hill formation to the east should be craggy with a sense of movement, in contrast to the hills in the west which should be lower, rounder and more compact, much like a crouching Tiger.

Finding the Dragon is the key to finding the *Xue*. The Dragon is seen as dry and potent, its lines harsh and straight, its strength activating the earth, vitalizing the soil and reanimating minerals for plants. The true green Dragon is a hill to the northeast, east or southeast, rising above the others with a sharp slope to its summit while on the other side it falls away more gently.

Where there is a true Dragon there is always a Tiger, for they are inseparable. The white Tiger current is moist and subtle, its lines soft, rounded and undulating. The realm of the Tiger lies in the foothills and lowlands, providing the fertile substance of the earth. A site's Dragon and Tiger will reflect in its male and female residents respectively, and the site is especially auspicious if the two embrace.

Above left: Dragon and Tiger flirting. Above right: Dragon and Tiger embracing.
Below: Ideal Si Xiang formations, left to right, good, variant and best.
Opposite left: Ideal Tortoise, Phoenix, Dragon and Tiger formations,
each cradling a site, improving left to right.

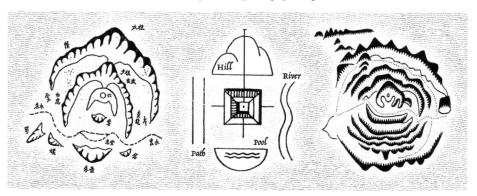

DWELLING ORIENTATION
aligning earth and heaven

Chinese geomancers identify three kinds of *Na* (receiving) *Qi* for a building: Earth *Qi*, Human *Qi*, and Heaven *Qi*. The *Sitting position* or back wall of the house relates to Earth, health, and relationships, and should be at a favorable orientation to the most propitious Mountain Dragon vein. The orientation opposite is the *Facing position*, which relates to Heaven, prosperity, vitality and creative expression. The front door is best placed here, as the most important *Qi Kou* (*Qi* mouth) or portal for external environmental and Human *Qi* entering a building. This face ideally has the most active view and best connection with the wider local environment, where *Sheng Qi* influences are greatest.

Houses are best sited with the front garden lower than the back, with a hill or trees behind and a good *Ming Tang* and river or road in front. In mountainous areas emphasis is placed on Mountain Dragons while on plains Water Dragons are considered more important. In urban landscapes large buildings can be treated as mountains, and roads as rivers. If even one of the *Si Xiang* is well represented in the landscape, the site is auspicious. Having all four is excellent.

With basic orientation within the landscape established, the *Luopan* or Feng Shui compass is then used to fine-tune the orien-tation of a dwelling, integrating considerations of both the Earthly *Forms School* (*pages 68-83*) and the Heavenly *Compass School* (*pages 84-99*). The Compass School developed later than the Forms School as practitioners sought more objective measurements of *Qi*, and precise degrees of direction of Forms School features can be mapped using a Luopan for their *Qi* quality and effect.

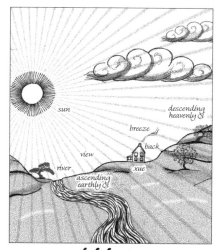

Ideal elevation

Si Xiang around a tomb

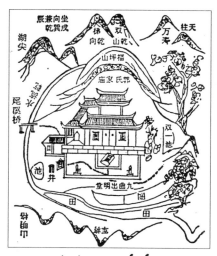

Si Xiang around a house

Si Xiang around a town

DAOIST COSMOLOGY
Chinese whispers

The Compass School of Feng Shui is founded in the root precepts of Daoist cosmology. This begins with *Wu Qi* (Nothingness), also described as *Wen Hom* (the Mystery of the Void), the source of all.

Tai Ji is the Great Pole from which everything hangs, depends and revolves. *Tai Ji* is perceived as existing in space at the centre of any dwelling, and as *Tian Chi* (the Heavenly Pool) in the centre of the Luopan where the magnetic needle moves.

Tian is the universal spark, the central point or primal Heavenly force in which there is no time and space, and from which the *Four Emanations*, *Yuan*, *Heng*, *Li* and *Zhen*, then arise, creating time and space.

Yuan is the creative force, rising in the direction of *Heng* and rooted in *Zhen*. *Heng* is the ever-penetrating conscious force, which permeates and enlivens all matter.

Li is the beneficial gathering force, the consequence of the continuation of the cycle. *Zhen* is the primal invariable and determining force; gathered from the *Qi* of *Li* it feeds the energy of *Yuan*. The text of the *Yi Jing* (*Book of Changes*, earliest written version c. 350 BC) begins with their invocation:

"Yuan Heng Li Zhen; the Origin, a Sacrificial Offering, Profit the Divination." – Yi Jing

The Mystery expresses itself in the *Seven Form Forces* (the *Three Gifts* plus the *Four Emanations*) as the Sun (*Yang*), Moon (*Yin*), and five Elementary planets, Mars (*Fire*), Mercury (*Water*), Jupiter (*Wood*), Venus (*Metal*) and Saturn (*Earth*). Four meditation diagrams from the *Dao Zang*, Daoist Canon [c. 400], are shown opposite.

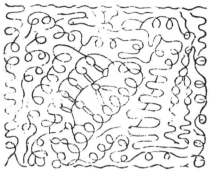

Earth—the Dark Earth of the Great Float, the
Floating Island of the Immortals.

Heaven—the Space Song of the Blue Sky, the
Sound of Jade falling from Heaven.

The Pattern of Change—the intercourse
between the Jade Sovereign (Heaven) and
Primordial Darkness (Earth) reveals the
action of the Dao.

The Diagram of the Talisman
—"Fu" (Happiness)—
hung to ward off bad luck
and attract good.

HO TU AND LO SHU
the sage faces south

The *Ho Tu* describes the state of *Qi* in the spiritual plane of Early Heaven. A gift to the Daoist sage Fu Xi, it appeared on the back of a Yellow River Dragon-horse in 2943 BC, and is usually written in green. The centre manifests in a vertical line, then a horizontal line, and the Elements give birth to one another in a clockwise progression moving out from the centre. The Element and trigram ascriptions of the numbers (*see page 170*) are used in surveying a site, reading the Luopan (*see page 174*) and deciding spiritual cures. Note that south is traditionally placed at the top in Chinese cosmological diagrams.

The Lo Shu magic square was revealed to Emperor Da Yu in 2205 BC, inscribed on the back of a tortoise which came out of the river Lo. The Nine Palaces provide a map of the flow of benevolent and malevolent Qi through time and space, on any scale, forming the basis for the numerology of Later Heaven, the material plane. Each sector of space is assigned a number representing a Star of the Big Dipper constellation and its associated qualities. The Nine Star numbers rotate around the Lo Shu in sequence to reveal changing influences in different Palaces over time (*see page 38*). Each Palace is also assigned an Element (*pages 164-7*), as well as two trigrams (*pages 168-71*). The Nine Palaces, Star numbers, Elements and trigrams are used extensively in secular building and interior design.

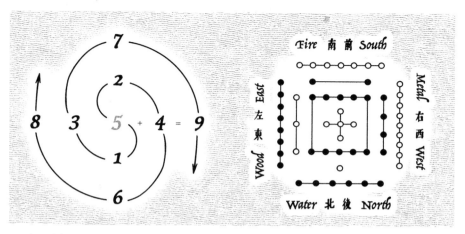

Above: The Ho Tu magic square, oriented with south at the top, the numbers creating the Elements. The first ten numbers are ascribed to the five directions and the five elements in a creation sequence with the first four numbers representing the Four Emanations (Yuan, Heng, Li and Zhen) and the next six the Five Elements, with 5 and 10 as Earth in the centre.

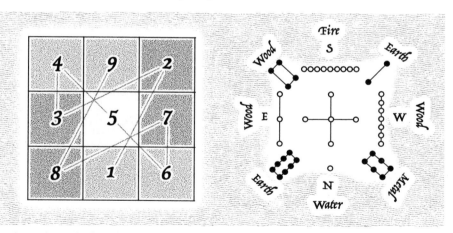

Above: The Lo Shu (magic square of Saturn). All columns, rows and diagonals add to 15 with even Yin numbers in the corners alternating with odd Yang ones, and Earth again central. The sequence moves through 9 palaces (the sigil of Saturn), representing Qi crystallizing into form and matter.
Opposite, left to right: Ho Tu Dragon Horse; early Ho Tu; Fu Xi; Early Lo Shu; River Lo Tortoise.

FIVE ELEMENTS
creating and destroying

The *Wu Xing* or *Five Elements* of traditional Chinese metaphysics are more accurately seen as phases of transformation. *Huo* Fire; *Tu* Earth; *Jin* Metal; *Shui* Water; and *Mu* Wood (or Tree) are arranged in two ways, first as the fourfold *Early Heaven* cycle of the *Si Xiang* and *Ho Tu* with Earth in the middle (*previous page*), and second as the pentagonal *Later Heaven* arrangement related to the *Lo Shu* with Earth in the position of late summer (*shown opposite*).

> *"Five elements refers to water, fire, wood, metal and earth. Water is moisture below, Fire is heat rising, Wood is right and wrong, Metal is change and Earth is farming"*
> – Zang Zhu (Book of Burial), ascribed to Guo Po [276-324 AD].

In the *Sheng* or creative cycle (*the outer circuit opposite*) each Element creates and nourishes the next: Wood feeds Fire, Fire yields ashes of Earth, Earth condenses into crystalline Metal, Metal melts into Water, and Water nourishes Wood. Thus five distinct phases from birth to death are described—creation, gestation, maturation, completion and resting. Also present within the pentagram is the balancing *Ko* or control cycle. Here Fire melts Metal, Metal cuts Wood, Wood weakens Earth, Earth contains Water and Water destroys Fire.

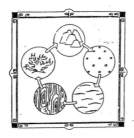 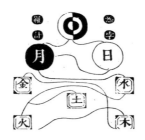 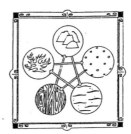

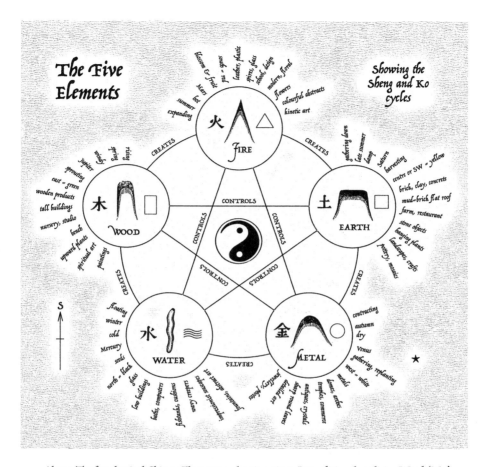

The Five Elements

Showing the Sheng and Ko cycles

FIRE 火 △
CREATES — CREATES
blossom & fruit · fibres, glass · leather, plastic · modern, floral · flowers · colourful abstracts · kinetic art
Mars · hot · summer · expanding

WOOD 木 □
rising · spring · windy · Jupiter · sprouting · east = green · wooden products · tall buildings · nursery, studio · bench · upward plants · spiritual art · painting

EARTH 土 □
gathering down · late summer · damp · Saturn · harvesting · centre or SW = yellow · brick, clay, concrete · mud-brick flat roof · farm, restaurant · stone objects · hanging plants · landscapes, crafts · pottery, mosaics

CONTROLS · CONTROLS · CONTROLS · CONTROLS · CONTROLS · CONTROLS

WATER 水 〰
floating · winter · cold · Mercury · seeds · north = black · glass · low buildings · baths, computers · fishtanks, cushions · wavy covers · impressionist, abstract · formless absorbent art

METAL 金 ○
contracting · autumn · dry · Venus · gathering replanting · west = white · metals · domes, arches · trophies, commerce · crystals · sharp metal forms · wealth art · pottery, photos

CREATES

S ↑

★

Above: The five classical Chinese Elements and assignations. In traditional medicine Wood (Mu) rules the liver, gall bladder, tendons, nerves, nails & eyes; Fire (Huo) rules the heart, pericardium, small intestine, arteries & tongue; Earth (Tu) rules the spleen, pancreas, stomach, muscles, lips & mouth; Metal (Jin) rules the lungs, large intestine, skin, body hair & nose; and Water (Shui) rules the kidneys, bladder, reproductive organs, bones & ears. The five Emotions are assigned as Joy-Fire, Worry-Earth, Grief-Metal, Fear-Water & Anger-Wood; and the five notes in the Pentatonic Scale Do-Earth, Re-Metal, Mi-Wood, So-Fire & La-Water, as are moves in martial arts, strokes in calligraphy, etc. Opposite: Sheng Cycle; Birth of five Elements; Ko Cycle.

ELEMENTS IN THE LANDSCAPE
nourishing and clashing patterns

The presence of two or more Elements in a situation creates various dynamic patterns. Similar Elements (e.g., an Earth structure in an Earth environment) will be mutually supportive, while elements with others preceding or following them in the Sheng cycle will be harmonious (so, for example, it is considered very auspicious to have three mountain peaks around a site that suggest Wood, Fire and Earth). Likewise, a Water building in a Wood environment will drain itself to benefit the community, and a commercial building with a triangular Fire motif will be nourished by, and therefore drain, the Wood forms of neighboring rectangular buildings. However, when Elements are present with others preceding or following them on the Ko cycle, clashing disharmonious Qi is created, so a Wood building in a Metal environment will be oppressed, while an Earth structure in a Water area will bring business success at the expense of respect.

When a structure is affected by an Element that is harmful to it, or is of mixed Elements, a harmonizing or controlling Element may be introduced using shape, colour, substance or symbol at an appropriate scale. Thus for a Metal Element threatening a Wood house, Water will drain the Metal and nourish the Wood on the *Sheng* cycle (e.g., a water feature). As another example, a Metal house in a Fire environment will benefit from the introduction of Water (to control Fire) and Earth (to drain Fire and nourish Metal), possibly using a rockery and pond (*see pages 382–383*).

Use the diagram on the previous page to help find imaginative solutions to rebalancing the elements around you.

THE **WHITE TIGER** (CENTRE) BEARS THE **FIVE ELEMENTS**

CLOCKWISE FROM TOP: THE SHARP ANGLES OF **FIRE**; THE FLAT PLAINS OF **EARTH**; THE ROUNDED SHAPES OF **METAL**; THE FLOWING LINES OF **WATER**; TOWERING FORMS OF **WOOD**.

BA GUA
the eight trigrams

As *Yin* and *Yang* generate the *Si Xiang*, so each of the four Celestial Spirits further divide into a son and daughter to create the *Ba Gua* or eight *trigrams (below left)*. *Shao Yang* ⚎ gives rise to *Zhen* ☳ and *Li* ☲, *Tai Yang* ⚌ to *Dui* ☱ and *Qian* ☰, *Shao Yin* ⚍ to *Xun* ☴ and *Kan* ☵, and *Tai Yin* ⚏ to *Gen* ☶ and *Kun* ☷.

While the origins of the names for the eight trigrams are lost in history (although they hint at a possible pan-Celtic derivation) their meanings are derived from the images they suggest (*opposite*). In accordance with the Three Gifts (*see page 140*) the top line of a trigram relates to Heaven and the future, the middle line to Humankind and the present, and the bottom line to Earth and the past.

As we shall see on the next page, both the positions of the eight trigrams in the *Early* and *Later Heaven* wheels and their Elemental assignations are related to the *Ho Tu* and *Lo Shu* magic squares. The external environment of a house is read primarily in the *Early Heaven Ba Gua*, and the internal environment in the *Later Heaven Ba Gua*, each shining through and balancing the other.

Qian (chien) is HEAVEN, its three solid Yang lines symbolising the essential spirit from which all else is manifest: strength, power, creativity, authority, time, duration, immaterial.

Kun is EARTH, its three broken Yin lines open to receive heaven's blessings are the soil receives nourishment from the sun and rain: yielding, receptive, passivity, surrender, space, extension, material.

Zhen (chen) is THUNDER, the trigram shows a solid powerful rising force, dispersing harmlessly: arousing, movement, activity, growth, natural shock, exciting, impetus, stimulation, volition, impulse, vitality.

Xun (Sun) is WIND, which has no root but carries a powerful force over the ground: small efforts, gentle effects, work, flexibility, penetrating, sensitivity, responsivity, intuition, assimilation, pervasiveness.

Kan is WATER, which appears clear and open, but has substance in the middle: mysterious, profound, meaningful, dangerous, difficult, dark, formless, uncertainty, emotion, Eros, Lunar forces.

Li is FIRE, the image of a flame, with solid form on the outside but empty in the middle: illuminating, intelligence, dependence, attachment, bright, formed, clarity, discrimination, Logos, Solar forces.

Gen (Ken) is MOUNTAIN, the image of space in a container, a solid surface pushed up by the earth below: stillness, resting, meditation, equaninity, solidity, immobility, heaviness, concentration.

Dui (Tui) is LAKE, the trigram open on the surface with mass below, like a body of water reflecting the Moon: openness, pleaseure, satisfaction, excess, bouyancy, lightness, joyful, observatio, intuitive vision, volatility.

Fu Xi & Wen Wang Ba Gua
early and late heaven arrangements

The *Fu Xi* or *Xian Tian* (*Early Heaven*) arrangement (*upper opposite*) of the *Ba Gua* derives from the *Ho Tu* (*see page 160*), with opposite trigrams facing across the centre. Firm Heaven balances yielding Earth; gentle Wind balances arousing Thunder; mysterious Water balances illuminating Fire; still Mountain balances joyful Lake. This sequence depicts the timeless Heavenly order and is emphasised in outdoor, temple and tomb designs, locating form, function and symbol in space and time, and for diagnosing problems.

The more widely used *Wen Wang* or *Hou Tian* (*Later Heaven*) *Ba Gua* sequence (*lower opposite*) describes the practical application of the trigrams to Earth *Qi* via the cycle of seasons. It is emphasised in residential and commercial design. The Nine Palaces of the *Lo Shu* ascribe the trigrams to eight directions on any scale (city, house or room), indicating the best rooms for specific functions or family members, with the central Palace as the *Tai Ji*, the vertical axis between Heaven and Earth, reflecting the household's spiritual health.

Ba Gua directions from the centre of the house indicate problems and remedies, e.g., a *Sha* form (*see page 176*) to the south augurs headaches and authority problems, particularly for the father (*Early Heaven Qian*), and eye and reputation (fame) problems, especially for the middle daughter (*Later Heaven Li*). Doorways, extensions, windows, mirrors, talismans, plant and animal symbols, *Lo Shu* numbers and Five Element cures such as pictures, colour, and ornaments can be used to enhance or remedy *Ba Gua* directions. A useful skill here is to notice metaphors suggested by forms and images around you.

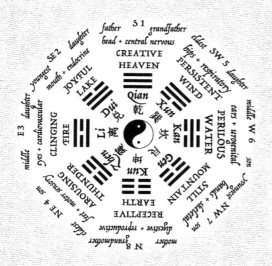

S 1

father grandfather
head + central nervous

eldest SW 5 daughter
lips + respiratory

CREATIVE
HEAVEN

Qian 乾

PERSISTENT
WIND

Xun 巽

middle W 6 son
ears + urogenital

PERILOUS
WATER

Kan 坎

youngest NW 7 son
hands + skeletal

STILL
MOUNTAIN

Gen 艮

N 8
grandmother mother
digestive + reproductive

RECEPTIVE
EARTH

Kun 坤

eldest NE 4 son
feet + motor sensory

AROUSING
THUNDER

Zhen 震

middle E 3 daughter
eyes + cardiovascular

CLINGING
FIRE

Li 離

youngest SE 2 daughter
mouth + endocrine

JOYFUL
LAKE

Dui 兌

Left and above: The sacred Early Heaven Fu Xi Ba Gua: The universe is revealed as the wheel rotates. "Heaven and Earth anchor the positions. Vapour flows between mountain and lake. Thunder and wind nourish each other. Fire and water do not conflict" (Yi Jing).

Right: The secular Later Heaven Wen Wang Ba Gua (outwardly facing version above): Two duck figures (conjugal bliss) in the SW of a house or room will enhance relationships. A water feature (feeds Wood) southeast aids prosperity.

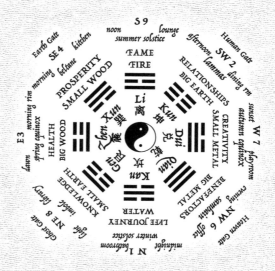

S 9

noon lounge
summer solstice

Earth Gate
SE 4
morning rim morning beltane kitchen

PROSPERITY
SMALL WOOD

Xun 巽

Human Gate
SW 2
afternoon dining rm lammas

RELATIONSHIPS
BIG EARTH

Kun 坤

sunset W 7
autumn equinox playroom

CREATIVITY
SMALL METAL

Dui 兌

Heaven Gate
NW 6
evening office samhain

BENEFACTORS
BIG METAL

Qian 乾

N 1
midnight bathroom
winter solstice

LIFE JOURNEY
WATER

Kan 坎

Ghost Gate
NE 8
light imbolc

KNOWLEDGE
SMALL EARTH

Gen 艮

E 3
dawn morning rising light

HEALTH
BIG WOOD

Zhen 震

FAME
FIRE

Li 離

YI JING
the book of changes

According to tradition it was Zhou Wen Wang (King Wen) who first combined the *Ba Gua* to form and name the sixty-four hexagrams in the *Gua Ci* [c.1142 BC], in the early days of the Zhou Dynasty. One of his sons, Zhou Gong Dan, later wrote the *Yao Ci*, a commentary on each of the lines, 384 in all (also the number of days in 13 moons).

The *Zhou Yi Jing* is used in both *Early* and *Later Heaven* sequences, and both can appear on a *Luopan* compass (*see page 98*). Site, building and door orientations are traditionally interpreted according to the hexagram and *Yao* (line) located in the respective compass direction from the centre of the property or doorway. Auspicious or inauspicious omens are then discovered in the text of the *Yi Jing*, the meaning of each *Gua* (symbol) being derived from the attributes and relationships of its two component trigrams (*see pages 386-387*). Specific hexagrams can define plan and elevation in palace, building and garden design.

The oracle may also be consulted by a ritual sequence of either dividing yarrow stalks or casting coins, in order to gain insight into questions of location and timing. Building the hexagram from the bottom, for each line three coins can be thrown, one or three heads indicating an unbroken *Yang* line, one or three tails a broken *Yin* line.

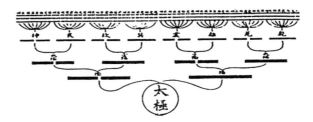

Above left: The sixty-four hexagrams are each built from two Ba Gua trigrams.
Right: The evolution of Tai Ji to Yin Yang, Si Xiang, Ba Gua and the hexagrams.

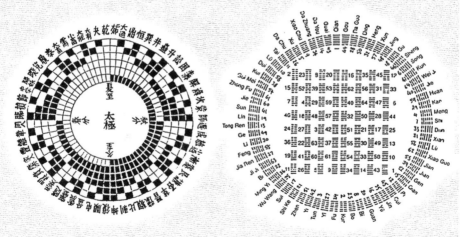

Above left: A similar scheme to above top right.
Above right: The positions of the sixty-four Gua in Heaven (circle) and on Earth (square), with 1 Qian due south at the top.

THE LUOPAN
the geomancer's compass

Luo means all-encompassing net, *Pan* means plate, and the first known Luopan or Feng Shui compass with directional characters (*centre left below*) dates to the Warring States Period [475-221 BC].

A modern Luopan consists of a rotating circular plate set in a square base overlaid with sighting crosshairs. The device is placed carefully, level and raised, at the *Tian Xin*, Heavenly Heart, or centre of a building or site with the base aligned to the walls (*below left*). The disk is rotated until the magnetic needle aligns with the line and dots in the central Tian Qi or Heaven Pool (*see opposite top*). Bearings to interior and surrounding features such as doorways, windows, gates, garden features, mountains, roads and waterways are then judged by characteristics read off appropriate rings on the rotated plate (*pages 385-386*). For example, the Ho Tu ordered trigrams of the Early Heaven Ba Gua (*the ring around the Tian Qi in both diagrams opposite*) might be applied to external features, and the *Lo Shu* glyphs of the Later Heaven *Ba Gua* (*the next ring out, lower opposite*) to interior design. Thus a house sitting in (with its back to) the northeast is in Early Heaven *Zhen Gua*, Later Heaven *Gen Gua* (*Lo Shu Star 8*), and faces southwest, Early Heaven *Xun Gua*, Later Heaven *Kun Gua* (*Lo Shu Star 2*).

Left: San He (Triple Harmony) Luopan, emphasizing three different 24 Mountain rings (Earth plate for Ba Gua, Mountain Dragons and facing/sitting axis, Human plate for footstool hills and local built environment, and Heaven plate for reading Water Dragons and stars). The outer two plates are rotated by 7.5° in each direction, reflecting the notion that Human Qi comes after Earth Qi, while faster Heaven Qi arrives early. (See pages 385-386.)

Right: San Yuan (Triple Era) Luopan, emphasizing Nine Star and Yi Jing rings (see pages 387 and 386). The Nine Stars refer both to the nine stars of the Big Dipper (Plow) and the Nine Palaces of the Lo Shu (see page 87). Also shown are the 64 hexagrams of the Yi Jing (pages 386-387). Most rings detailing Daoist and Confucian calendrical and metaphysical cycles were added after the Tang Dynasty [618-907AD].

Opposite: i. How to read a Luopan from a dwelling's centre. ii. The Si Nan Luopan (c. 300 BC) with its fabled lodestone spoon (now thought to be an archaeological error). The square bronze divination plate shows the 8 trigrams, 10 Stems, 12 Branches and 28 Lunar Mansions. iii. Han Dynasty (206 BC-220 AD) Liu Ren divination plate. iv. How to read a Luopan for door orientation.

UNDERGROUND ENERGIES
subterranean Water Dragons

According to classical Feng Shui, various man-made and landscape features can cause troubling geopathic stress problems for a site. The Ming Dynasty [1368-1644] text *Shui Peng Ba Zhen Fa* (*Eight Needles of the Water Compass Method*) gives a protocol for divining underground streams, cavities, geological faults, mineral deposits, old wells, tombs, abattoirs and battlefields. An even earlier text states:

> *"In the subterranean regions there are alternate layers of earth and rock and flowing spring waters. These strata rest upon thousands of vapors (Qi) which are distributed in tens of thousands of branches, veins and threadlike openings...The body of the earth is like that of a human being..."* – Chen Su Xiao [d.1332].

Underground meridians are regularly disturbed by excavations for building foundations, quarries, mines, and embankments and cuttings for roads and railways. In China offerings are traditionally made to the local landscape spirits before such works are undertaken. Traumatic blockage of *Long Mai* and the resulting stagnation in the flows of *Qi* generally give rise to toxic *Sha Qi*, poisonous energy which rises especially from underground water meridians. This can have major health implications for those living directly above.

Ideally places with such influences should be avoided or designed to minimize their effects. Alternatively, protective charms may be used to shield a residence, or *Earth Acupuncture* can be employed to release landscape trauma and restore the healthy flow of *Qi* to injured underground Water Dragons. This may involve the temporary or permanent insertion of wood, metal or stone needles into nodes on the meridian pathways to heal and harmonize the disturbed *Qi*.

Above: Pagodas, like huge acupuncture needles, may be sited to control dangerous visible and underground Water Dragons. Regular ceremonies also maintain the spiritual hygiene of an area.

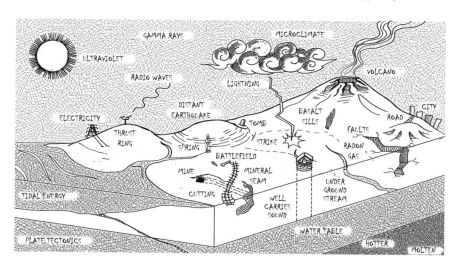

Above: Hidden and visible geopathic Sha. "No dwelling shall be built until the earth diviners have confirmed the intended building site to be free of earth demons" — Emperor Da Yu [2205-2197 BC].

SHA QI
hostile forces, causes and cures

The term *Sha*, literally "poison," covers a range of hostile environmental influences. Straight lines such as roads, fences, power cables or sharp corners that point at a dwelling are considered unfortunate, as they aim *Sha Qi* towards the front door and can carry malevolent spirits. The only straight lines found in the classical landscape are leys incorporated into temple and palace design, with a series of gatehouse pagodas to step down and cleanse the *Qi* as it approaches the site. Roads and paths, like most natural forms, are best when curving and meandering. The outsides of bends in rivers and roads; T-junctions, forks, and the entrances to valleys; wind tunnels between buildings and bridgeheads are all considered dangerous and therefore inauspicious, as are ugly or threatening local features, especially if facing the front door or main room.

Feng Shui solutions may be *Ru Shi*, physical changes (*e.g., see lower opposite*) including moving the location or orientation of a door, or they can be *Chu Shi*, psychological and transcendental changes, such as installing a mirror, animal symbol or talisman. Shown below (*left*) is a *Sha*-averting stone facing a bridge. The stone which blocks the *Sha* is inscribed *Shi Gan Tang*—"the stone dares to resist."

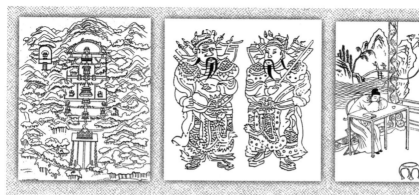

Left: Taoist temple design harnessing the Heavenly Qi of a ley line. Centre: The talismanic Door Gods Shen Du and Yu Lie are often placed to guard the portal against demons especially from the potentially dangerous northeast. Right: Seeking to avoid Sha Qi altogether.

Left: Nasty Sha Qi. Right: Cures include removal of the threatening feature, protective walls and vegetation, a concave or Ba Gua mirror to deflect, a fountain or pond to absorb, a pair of guardian stone lions at the portal, and a round object ("completeness") in front of the house.

HOUSE AND PLOT SHAPES
living in squares and triangles

Many dwellings in China have a circular pond within a rectangular courtyard, or a circular door in the garden (*see pages 182–83*), thus creating a union of the Heavenly circle and the Earthly square. The ideal plot shape is square (representing the Earth element which supports humans) or rectangular (representing the Wood element which supports growth), oriented with the sides facing the cardinal directions. The dwelling should have the same orientation and be located in the centre, with the same precepts regarding plot shape applying also to house and room shape. Missing corners suggest *Ba Gua* shortcomings and will direct *Sha Qi* towards the dwelling from the internal corner.

Triangular plots (representing the Fire element) are inauspicious as the sharp corners tend to trap stagnant *Qi,* yielding thick *Predecessor Qi,* the presence of the past in the atmosphere of place, a vibrational imprint of previous activities and inhabitants, which may include *Gui* or spirits. Irregular plots belong to the Water element (which supports Wood) and can be good or bad depending on the shape. They are to be avoided if the form and slope direct *Qi* away from the building, or if areas of the house stagnate outside the flow of *Qi.*

Cures for sick shapes often involve introducing landscape enhancements to represent the elements of missing trigrams, or by creating separate well-shaped garden areas within the whole. Terracing can help contain the *Qi* on steep slopes, especially if the back of the plot is lower than the front, in which case the house might well be better reoriented with the main door facing downhill.

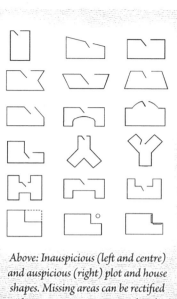

Above: Roof profiles are uplifted to invoke Heaven. Corners and ridges may display sculptures of protective magical animals, such as the Chinese Dragon, which has elements of nine different animals.

Above: Inauspicious (left and centre) and auspicious (right) plot and house shapes. Missing areas can be rectified with an extension, or improved with a tree, light or mirrors (lowest row).

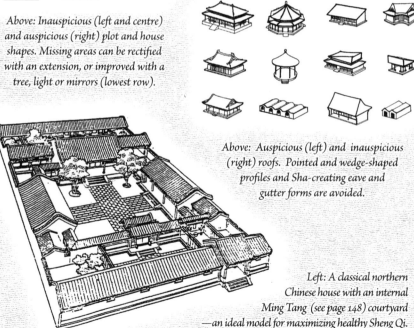

Above: Auspicious (left) and inauspicious (right) roofs. Pointed and wedge-shaped profiles and Sha-creating eave and gutter forms are avoided.

Left: A classical northern Chinese house with an internal Ming Tang (see page 148) courtyard —an ideal model for maximizing healthy Sheng Qi.

INTERIOR DESIGN PRECEPTS
containment and flow

The entrance to a house is like its mouth, leading to the business and public living areas, while the kitchen and family living areas are its heart and the bedrooms and bathrooms the private parts. The design of a house should reflect this progression from public to private space, with a clearly defined frontage, the front door not opening directly onto the kitchen, stairs or toilet. The placement of doors, windows and furniture should allow the flow of *Qi* to meander and circulate, avoiding long straight lines. If the front and back doors or gates are in a straight line, or the windows in the main rooms opposite each other, the *Qi* will leak and prosperity will not congregate.

Beds, desks and sofas should be arranged following the principles of *Si Xiang* (*see page 152*) to provide a sense of enclosure. Bathrooms and toilets should never be in the central *Tai Ji* area, nor over the front door or stove. Partially offset doors can generate irritability, while irregular plans often create *Scattered Qi* and pockets of *Sha*, which can be cured with round objects, e.g., rugs or tables. *Cutting Qi* from sharp internal corners can be masked with plants or fabric, and *Oppressive Qi* from beams lightened with corbels, flutes, feathers or a canopy. Mirrors raise *Yang Qi,* expand space, amplify whatever they reflect, but impair sleep when installed over a bed.

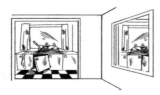

Some Feng Shui guidelines. What to do and what not to do. Check the diagrams then check your home.

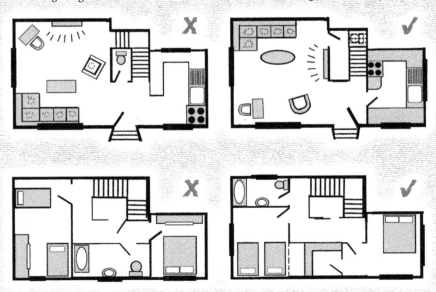

CLASSICAL GARDEN DESIGN

heaven on earth

Classical Chinese garden design is rooted in *Yin Yang* theory, as a crafted harmony of Earth and Heaven. The dots in the *Tai Ji* symbol suggest the inclusion of the sky within the design, smaller gardens within bigger gardens, and the impression of unlimited space within a compact space. Compositions balance naturalistic landscaping with symmetrical buildings, using hills and rockeries, watercourses and ponds, bridges and corridors, pavilions and paths, walls and lattice windows, trees and shrubs, lawns and flowers, ornaments and poetic calligraphy, birdsong and music, animal life and human ceremony.

Circles and curves suggest Heaven, and squares and straight lines Earth. A square lawn can be combined with a circular entrance door (a moon gate), or a circular pavilion placed near a square pond.

Above: Happy Garden, Suzhou, Jiangsu Province, China [19th century]. Each garden has a founding theme and one climax feature. We walk and stand seeing a series of views, from differing elevations, some framed by pavilions, some borrowed from outside the garden, avoiding a full view of the whole garden at once, until we reach the focus and then depart through increasingly serene vistas.

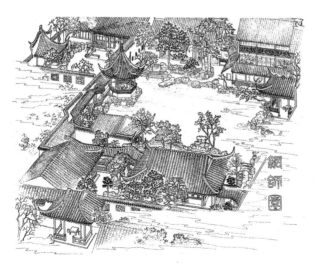

Left: Retired Fisherman's Garden, Suzhou, Jiangsu Province, China [1140, rebuilt 1750]. It combines movement & stillness, substantial & insubstantial, with symbolisms suggested by plants and simulacra and juxtapositions of design raising ambiguities and insights. Both Early and Later Heaven Ba Gua directions influence garden design.

Opposite: Rockery garden within Lingering Here Garden, also Suzhou [built 1593].

BOOK IV

*Dowser locating a metal seam for mining purposes,
from* Practica Minerale *by Marco Antonio della Fratta,
Bologna, Italy, 1678.*

DOWSING

A JOURNEY BEYOND OUR FIVE SENSES

Hamish Miller

with illustrations by Jean Hands

Introduction

The delight about dowsing is that everybody can. Some better than others, but it usually depends on how much practice you put in. Like playing golf, a piano or making love you seem to get better the more you do it.

The old dictionary definition was uncompromising: "*... the use of pendulum or rods to find water or minerals ...*", but happily in recent years there has been a considerable breakthrough in the appreciation of dowsing ability. A more informed establishment recognising the increased scope and importance of the art has redefined it as "*... the use of apparently paranormal powers to make discoveries*".

So dowsing has undergone a paradigm shift from the useful but relatively mundane science of finding water sources, lumps of metal and old drains to the realms of a spiritual search into the mysteries of human consciousness and its relationship with the Earth.

There is a practical, exciting journey waiting for everyone interested in the skill. It can lead by progressive expansion of thought to perceptions far beyond the normal restrictions of our five senses.

Better to start simply, learn the use of the various tools, find the one which suits you best, and grow slowly.

HISTORY
thousands of years of dowsing

Around 450 BC the 'father of history' Herodotus the Greek reported the use of wooden Y-forks for the finding of water while he was roving around Scythia north of the Black Sea. This is the first written evidence of true dowsing, although there are references to similar functions in ancient Chinese literature. Earlier cave drawings may depict dowsing implements of various shapes but it's difficult to believe that these outlines are anything to do with dowsing. A silver coin struck in 936 AD clearly shows a wee man with a forked stick in action above mine workings.

Martin Luther outrageously pronounced that it was "Devil's Work" in the early 16th century (*see below*) and as a result the art was fiercely opposed by religious establishments for centuries. Fortunately the knowledge was preserved and passed on quietly by people who lives were closely connected to the earth.

About the same time, a German mineralogist and metallurgist called Georgius Agricola published *De Re Metallica*, a treatise which included precise details of dowsing techniques in mining (*opposite top*). It aroused considerable interest in the industry throughout Europe although Agricola himself, still acutely conscious of the association of the art to the occult, hedged his bets by admonishing prospective miners "not to make use of the enchanted twig".

This page: Miners using magical dowsing rods to discover hidden veins of ore, from De Re Metallica *by Georgius Agricola, 1566. Facing page: The Dowser Unmasked, frontispiece from* Das Entlarvete Idolum, *by T. Albinus, 1704.*

DEVELOPMENT
by royal command

Elizabeth I of England first got wind of the valuable 'forked stick' methods of finding metal ores through Agricola's work and introduced German miners to help develop England's resources. They brought their knowledge of dowsing with them, and by 1660 Charles II, recognising the importance of the art to the financial success of the mining industry, demanded to know everything about the operation of the *'Baguette Divinitoire'* ... splendid name for a dowsing rod.

In 1693 Pierre de Lorrain, Abbé de Vallemont caused consternation in religious circles and Paris society by publishing his *Occult Physics* which included detailed illustrations of dowsing techniques (*lower opposite*). It was promptly put on the prohibited list by the Inquisition, and he was probably one of the first authors to create a bestseller by having his book banned. His work triggered a vigorous pro-and-anti debate in the world of scientists and religious leaders, leading to a proliferation of scientific tests on the abilities of dowsers over the next century.

In museums round the world there are some fine examples of seventeenth and eighteenth century artwork, including silver drinking mugs, paintings and Meissen pottery, which figure little men with Y-rods akimbo looking for minerals. The burgeoning mining industry was a major contributor to the development of dowsing and the art thrived under the increasing pressure to find more and more mineral and water sources.

Above: European dowsers hard at work, surveying a line of underground mineral seams, from Speculum Metallurgiae Politissimum by Balthazar Rössler, 1700. Below and opposite: Early French illustrations of dowsers employing 'La Baguette Divinitoire'.

Pioneers

an emerging science

In eighteenth century France, Germany and Italy, the use of 'wands', 'sceptres', 'bobbing-sticks', 'rods', 'pendulums' and 'forks' by various 'twitchers', 'deusers', 'twiggers', 'dowsers', and 'water-witchers' to find all sorts of things became fair game for scientists and priests to investigate, and for the public to have fun with. A plethora of essays and publications by Lebrun, Menestrier, Zeidler, Albinus and Thouvenal fired broadsides at each other for and against the mysterious art.

Barthelemy Bleton, a brilliant natural water-witcher, working with the Bishop of Grenoble (author of the 'Bishop's Rule' for finding the depth of water) became the focus of Thouvenal's attempt to associate dowsing with electrical effects, but physicists could find no simple explanation of his talents.

Further work in Italy with the elegant Pennet, who constantly confounded observers by achieving remarkably accurate results (*shown aloft below*), still failed to persuade the authorities that dowsing was a talent worthy of serious debate. On the contrary it seemed that as 'absolute proof' in scientific terms was not readily available it was easier to accept the French astronomer Lalande's arrogant dismissal of all dowsing as trickery. He put dowsing rods in the same category as 'flying ships' declaring that "it is impossible for a man to raise himself from the ground". A year later the Montgolfier brothers were off in their first balloon.

LE SOURCIER

PRACTITIONERS
excitement reborn

In the late eighteenth century William Cookworthy of Plymouth, England gave the art a shot in the arm by chronicling the undeniable talents of the Cornish mining dowsers. They had earned their reputation purely by the accurate results they had produced for that very tough industry, and had begun to be rewarded accordingly.

For a time local people who 'could just do it' were used to find water sources, but gradually some eminent Victorian British and Irish geologists became aware of the growing water needs of industry and the larger estates. One of the greatest practitioners of all time was Wiltshire's John Mullins. The legendary stories of his successes probably did more to make dowsing acceptable in the right circles than any contemporary academic papers.

In 1912 the mighty *Metallica* was translated from Latin to English by *Mining Magazine* in London, sparking a fresh interest for many lateral thinkers of all disciplines. Then, in 1969, Guy Underwood's *The Patterns of the Past* broke new ground by exploring in meticulous detail the energies of sacred sites and their connections with water (*illustrations opposite*).

In 1976 Tom Lethbridge's *The Power of the Pendulum* explored other realities and in 1978 their work and the perceptions of John Michell inspired Tom Graves to write *Needles of Stone*, a dowsing book which introduced far-reaching concepts of our relationship with earth and cosmic energies.

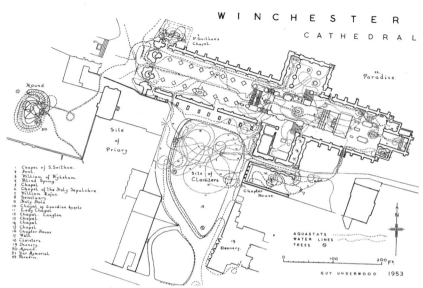

WINCHESTER

CATHEDRAL

Paradise

Mound

Site
of
Priory

Site of
Cloisters

Chapter
House

Deanery

1 Chapel of S.Swithun.
2 Font.
3 William of Wykeham
4 Blind Spring
5 Chapel
6 Chapel of the Holy Sepulchre
7 William Rufus
8 Sanctuary
9 Holy Hole
10 Chapel of Guardian Angels
11 Lady Chapel
12 Chapel. Langton
13 Chapel.
14 Chapel.
15 Chapel.
16 Chapter House
17 Well.
18 Cloisters
19 Deanery.
20 Mound.
21 War Memorial.
22 Paradise.

AQUASTATS
WATER LINES
TREES

100   200 Ft.

GUY UNDERWOOD   1953

*Three surveys by Guy Underwood, showing:
i. aquastats in Winchester Cathedral, ii. Trees
leaning over water lines, and iii. the effect of
the Moon on the energies at Woodhenge.*

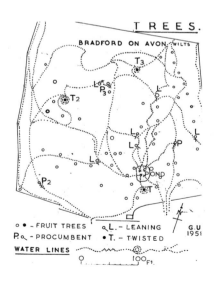

T R E E S.

BRADFORD ON AVON WILTS

T3

P3

T2

L

L

L

P

L

POND

T

P2

o • – FRUIT TREES   L. – LEANING
P. – PROCUMBENT   • T. – TWISTED

G.U
1951

WATER LINES

0   100 Ft.

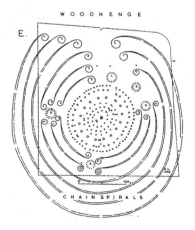

WOODHENGE

E.

CHAIN SPIRALS

PROTAGONISTS
blazing the trail

In the last few decades an international array of dowsers have applied their talents to an expanding range of dowsing disciplines.

Terry Ross from Vermont could find water for villages in Mexico by instructing a surrogate dowser over the telephone, and wrote that dowsing could lead ultimately to "co-creation with nature".

Bill Lewis of Wales had an awesome talent for finding objects in all parts of the world without leaving his home.

Roger Brown from Australia accurately recorded complex manifestations of earth energy field changes for a hundred-mile radius around Adelaide.

Russian specialists like Professor A. I. Pluzhnikkov could pinpoint mineral resources and archeological remains, and paranormal expert Neklessa developed a unique combination of pairs of scientists and mystics working together using advanced dowsing techniques to investigate the reasons for the failure of historic civilisations.

Many 'doodlebuggers' across the USA are fine-tuned to locate obscure oil deposits, while Elizabeth Sulivan of Wales is recognised by the authorities as an expert on the location of humans and animals by map dowsing.

Colin Bloy in Spain initiated a sophisticated form of the dowsing process in the delicate art of healing, additionally applying it to the energy centres or 'haras' of towns and villages to improve the quality of life of people living there.

The list is endless and confirms a global interest in the art.

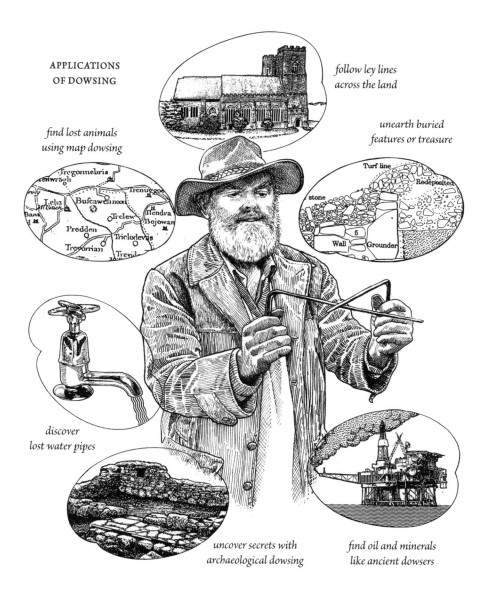

APPLICATIONS
OF DOWSING

follow ley lines
across the land

find lost animals
using map dowsing

unearth buried
features or treasure

discover
lost water pipes

uncover secrets with
archaeological dowsing

find oil and minerals
like ancient dowsers

TOOLS
as long as they work

There are almost as many variations of tools as there are competent dowsers. Some are ingenious and some downright hilarious - a Californian one made from bent wire in the form of a continuous Greek Key pattern was five feet long and had to have a piece of broderie anglaise on the end.

It doesn't matter in the least, as long as it works. To work it has to be a comfortable link between the mind of the dowser and the target, the tool acting as an amplifier of the dowser's reactions.

Most people learn with one of three types, angle-rods, pendulums and Y-rods, but some prefer a form of 'bobber' or a wire loop. Y-rods were originally preferred because they could be conveniently cut from a hedge near the site where they were to be used, while bobbing sticks at this time were usually thin, sometimes shaped, slightly-curved branches. The Romans used pendulums, and rods developed later as metal became available.

Some practiced dowsers use their hands, with fingers moving in unison like a bunch of little L rods, or with their thumbs throbbing on forefingers. New materials such as carbon fibre have allowed dowsers to create imaginative, lightweight, sensitive and discreet tools to help them in their searches.

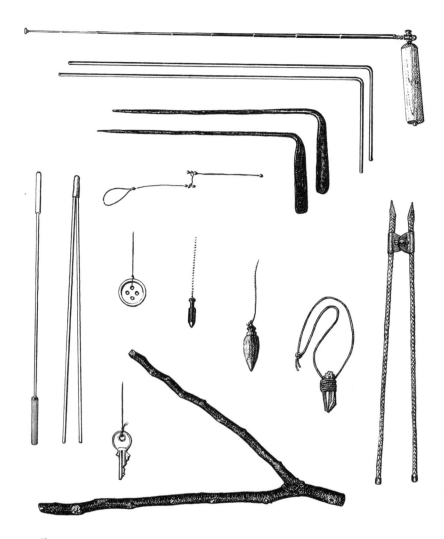

Choose your weapon: telescopic rod by Alan Heiss folds to pocket size and extends to 25";
Hand-forged bespoke rods in iron from Hamish; Guy Underwood's tricky wire loop device;
'Y' rods in discreet carbon fibre 8" long; Copper-hinged horse whips!

Making & Holding Tools
rods, pendulums and Y-rods

Rods can be bent from welding or brazing rod or chopped coat-hangers. Leave about 4-5 inches for the handle and crop wee bits off the long end until the balance feels good. Hold them level about fifteen inches apart in front of you in each hand like the Sundance Kid and relax.

Pendulums consist of something flexible tied to a weight. The 'cord' can be thread, string, chain, or plaited hair from your partner. You should have some rapport with the weight, like a favourite old ring, locket or miniature bottle of Lagavulin. Crystals are fine if you are careful but they sometimes have memories which can confuse your results.

Hold the cord about six inches above the weight at first to get used to its movement. It will start wobbling about even when your hand is still.

Y-rods can be cut from a willow or hazel in the shape of a fork, or split from a single branch, or made from carbon fibre or wire rods fixed together at one end. These have to be tensioned to work (*see opposite*). Bobbers can be whippy sticks or wires with springs and knobs, like the one below.

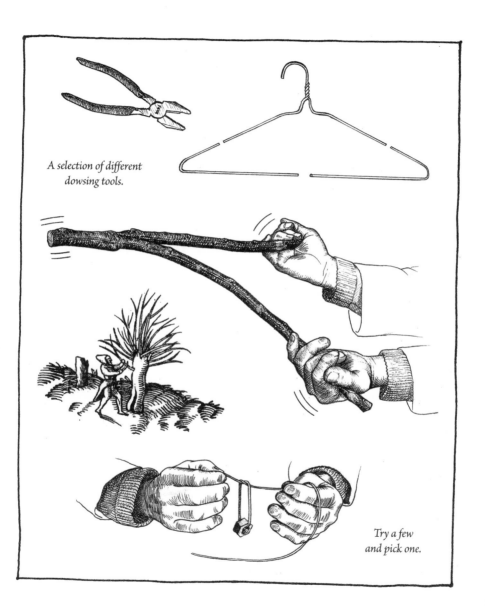

A selection of different dowsing tools.

Try a few and pick one.

Using the Tools
a simple start

The first essential is to establish a trustworthy *'yes'* or *'no'*.

Hold a pendulum in front of you with the cord between your thumb and forefinger, with the weight around six inches below your fingers. Swing it away from you and allow it to move freely. Concentrate and ask it firmly to show you a *'yes'*. In its own time it will change from a back and forward to a circular motion. Check to see if it is clockwise or counter-clockwise. Repeat the process for *'no'* and you'll find it revolves the other way. Practice this repeatedly until the pendulum becomes a natural extension of your hand. The tool sometimes changes its mind so check your *'yes'* every time before starting to dowse.

Using two rods, hold them in your hands about fifteen inches apart. They often cross for a *'yes'* and open out for *'no'*. Once they've decided, they don't usually mess about like pendulums.

A single rod gives a strong result. Hold it in front of you in your working hand, moving it slowly forward as you ask the question. If it turns the answer is *'yes'*, if nothing happens the answer is *'no'*.

Y-rods and bobbers do not respond for *'no'* and leap about for *'yes'*.

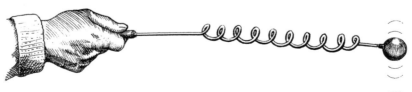

yes

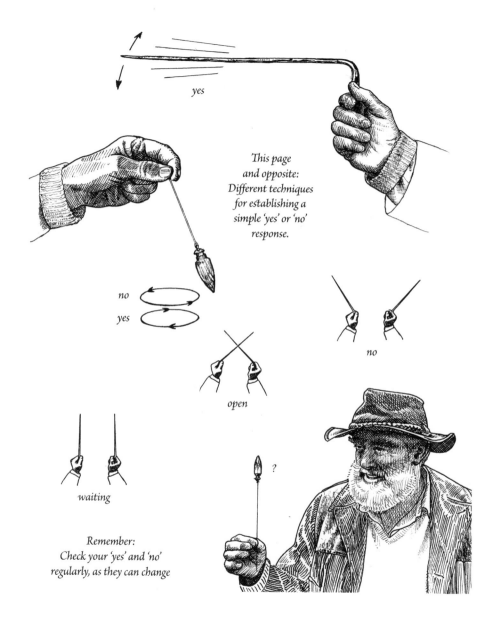

yes

This page
and opposite:
Different techniques
for establishing a
simple 'yes' or 'no'
response.

no
yes

no

open

waiting

Remember:
Check your 'yes' and 'no'
regularly, as they can change

?

PRACTICE
next steps forward

Working on the hugely important *'yes'* and *'no'* will have given you a chance to judge your responses to the different tools. When you've decided which one you prefer, practice with questions like *where is the kitchen sink?*. The tool will soon get the idea and point in the right direction.

Try dowsing separate glasses with bottled water, tap water and red wine, asking if they are okay to drink. Now try it with water from the drain. Check the red wine to see if a few more would do you any harm. Dowse to see if the cheese you've left in the fridge is alright for you and your family to eat. If not would it be good for the cat?

The answers will be *'yes'* or *'no'* but shouldn't be acted on until you have a lot of faith in your dowsing capability. Use your chosen weapon to find out if it's going to rain when you go shopping.

Will everyone be happier if you do go and visit your mother-in-law? Should you just drop everything and go to Ibiza?

Above all, practice your new talent.

Even though you do get wet between shops.

Above and below: Choose your divining instrument, select a target and try and find it. Just like the dowsers of centuries past, all you need to do is practice, practice, practice.

FIRST TRIALS
feeling the magic

Get used to handling your chosen tool. It's easier if you're not too ambitious or anxious at first. Work with it sitting, standing, walking, indoors, outside in the rain or under the bed until you are completely familiar with its movements.

Cheat a little to start with. Place a rope, cable or pipe on the grass or carpet and approach it with your eyes open, asking the tool to show you where it is. Now do it with eyes shut and preferably alone to avoid distractions. Get a friend to hide a bottle of your favourite wine in the garden, or a playing card under the carpet, and see if you can find it. Repeat, repeat, and repeat the exercise until your confidence grows.

It's all about tuning your mind. The aim is complete relaxation in body and thoughts but keeping one tiny part of your mind *totally* concentrated on the target. The dowsing tool provides a physical response to receptors in your consciousness which are capable of probing beyond normal sense horizons.

100% concentration makes you're right every time, very boring, and you can walk through walls, so a little humility helps. Above all don't despair if you can't do it first time. It *is* only a matter of practice and if you really need a drink you'll find the bottle.

WITNESSES & QUESTIONS
helping to focus

The sole purpose of a *witness* is to assist in concentration. Any help to improve visualisation of the target is valuable and witnesses can be pieces of pipe, wire, metal, wood, or phials of water which can be conveniently held in your hand or attached to your person. Professor Henri Mager's witness is a circular disc about four inches in diameter which is divided into eight equal sections of various colours which help to discern different qualities in water. Rod dowsers use one rod while the other hand indicates the different colours of the witness. Y-fork people sometimes need six fingers. There is no doubt that using a physical reminder of the target helps to keep the mind from wavering. It's difficult to lug a drainpipe about, but then they are easy to visualise.

An equally important discipline to learn is in phrasing the right questions. They have to be clearly defined, positive, and geared to receiving precise answers. Like working with a computer you get a reaction to your input, not a reasoned response. If the answer needs judgement of any kind the request isn't valid. Aim to narrow the field of search with each succeeding question until you nail the target.

It's disconcertingly easy to get answers to the question you *think* you've asked and be totally mislead. If your tank runs dry and you dowse for the distance to the nearest garage - make sure you ask for one that sells petrol.

WATERPIPES & STREAMS

easy to check

You probably have a rough idea where your watermain is, so try an experiment: Walk slowly across the area with dowsing tool at the ready, fix your supply pipe firmly in your mind, ignore the curious stares of your neighbour and ask it to show you the position. No bells will ring but rods will turn, pendulums swing, and Y-rods move up or down as your hands cross the pipe. Mark the position and try it again a couple of feet nearer the house until you have a positive line of points.

One way to find the depth is to stand on the line you've just found, walk slowly away from it at right angles and ask the tool to move at a distance equal to the depth of the pipe. This is known as the 'Bishop's Rule'. Another way is to use your simple *'yes'* and *'no'* by 'bracketing'. Stand over the pipe and ask if it is between one and five feet down; if *'yes'*, ask if it's between one and three feet, and so on. Go into inches if you want to be really fussy.

Deal with underground streams in the same way. With your *'yes'* and *'no'* you can also find the width, direction of flow, flow rate, purity and whether you should add it to your whisky.

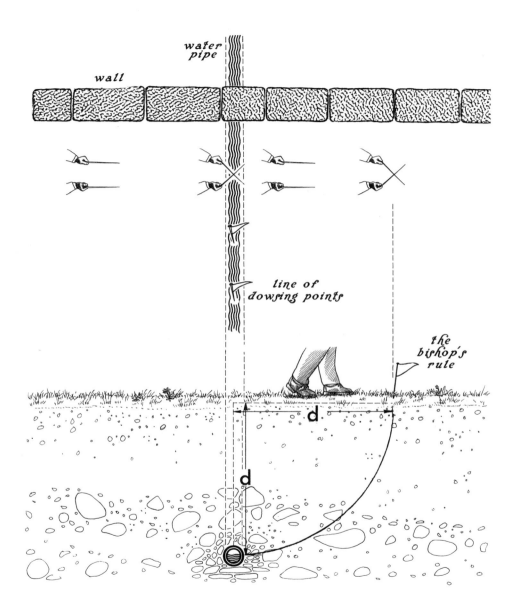

water
pipe

wall

line of
dowsing points

the
bishop's
rule

d

d

BUILDINGS & ARCHAEOLOGY
time savers

Huge amounts of time and money can be saved by the quick and accurate location of old foundations, sewage tanks, cables and drains. Archaeologists tend to have to take earth out by the thimbleful and a spot of dowsing can work wonders.

Directional dowsing is a useful start. Having decided exactly what you are looking for, find the direction of the target from where you stand by simply asking the tool to show you (just as you practiced with the kitchen sink). From a circular motion the pendulum will change to swinging in line with it. Rods will swivel to point at your objective from the site perimeter. Y-rods will dip or rise in the right direction as you turn around.

Move closer in the direction you've found and start defining your needs more clearly i.e "Show me a corner of the old wall, tank or Roman bath". With small objects ask the pendulum to whistle round, rods to cross, or bobbers bob directly over the medieval glass eye or priceless torque.

You can now use your '*yes*' or '*no*' bracketing technique to find out how old your treasure is and discover how deep you have to dig in the usual way.

Above: Dowsing can be a fantastic aid in discovering lost or buried features of an old garden. Ancient walls, waste heaps full of pottery, pipes, and even buried treasure can be revealed.

MAP & CHART
another reality

The concept of dowsing from a map or chart seems to trigger disbelief. It is, however, perfectly logical, since the essence of dowsing is to find things which are normally hidden. The map or chart in itself is not important, but acts as a representation of the area of search which enables you to create a dowseable reality.

Once you are in there you can work in the ordinary way. One method is to triangulate from three points of the map so that you can pin a position with three directional lines. Or with a bobber, single rod or pendulum you can use the square grid system by slowly moving a finger along two sides of the map, asking if your target is in the row your finger is on. After you've done it both ways you end up with one small square. Now, use a pencil to do the same operation in miniature. The larger the scale the more accurate you will be, so blow up the guilty square (on a photocopier, of course). Many a cell-phone and mudspattered rabbit-chasing terrier have been thankfully restored to their owners using these methods.

Specialist dowsers, who have to be very respectable, use maps to help the police find drugs, bodies and top secret laptops left in bars by MI5. American and British military dowsers have been involved, amongst other things, in underground tunnel, booby-trap, and mine detection.

It's just quantum mechanics, hooked up to the human body.

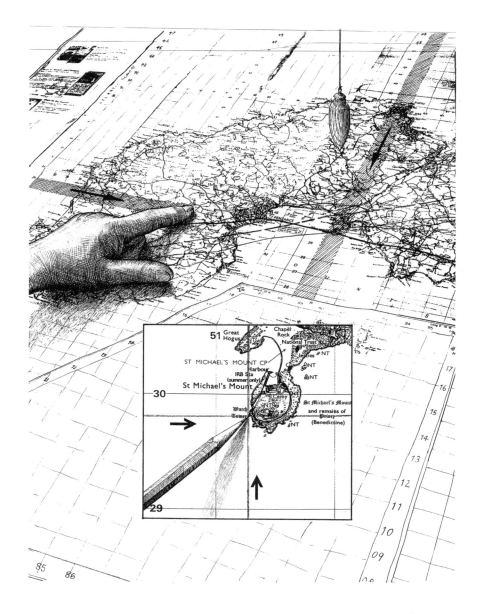

HEALTH AND ALLERGIES
a handy tool

There is a growing awareness that health risks may be associated with the proliferation of chemically-sanitised processed foods, and dowsing can provide an interesting new level of interpretation as to whether our intake is beneficial or otherwise. It can also be a useful tool in the medical field to access information on allergies.

Use a pendulum, single rod or bobber, leaving the other hand free to move. The standard 'yes' or 'no' technique works well if you run your finger down a list of chemicals, medicines, foods, drinks, dusts, pollens, stings and so on, asking the tool to indicate whether the subject is allergic to any of them. It's a quick way of eliminating the harmless ones in what can otherwise be a time-consuming business. Probably more importantly you can find out what is good for you. Fortunately Lagavulin comes very high on my positive list.

The rate of the swing of the pendulum, the speed and force with which the rods turn (I make flattened handles on my rods to give me a 'feel' of the movement), or the rapidity of the motion of the bobber can soon be recognised and assessed in a sort of personal Richter scale of one to ten. Some dowsers use calibrated scales to help analysis.

Using the same methods you can find out which potions have a healing effect, and whether it's okay to have another dram.

DOWSING **219**

BODY ENERGIES & CHAKRAS
an extra dimension

Our bodies don't end at the surface of the skin; we are surrounded by assorted energy fields which some people can sense but few of us discern with our five senses.

The *aura* is very basic and we have a number of other main biomagnetic fields called *chakras* which we share with every animal, insect, plant, stone and mini-piece of matter in the universe. Through them we are connected to everything on earth and finally to the cosmos.

Dowsing is a way of perceiving these fields as a reality. Use a pendulum, bobber or rod to show you where the aura starts. It will register at a point around twelve to thirty inches away from the body depending on the health of the volunteer and where he or she is standing, and as you follow the contour round it will show how the bio-field varies in depth in certain places.

If it's depleted at any point it could indicate that there is a potential problem in the area or that a physical defect is already there. Luckily you can help revitalise the aura and chakras by directing energy at them using your fingers like a pistol.

Some of the chakras are very subtle and it's easier to dowse them with your hands. You'll probably get a slight tingling or a feeling of resistance like a soft balloon.

CHURCHES
discretion is the better part

Many, if not most, ancient churches are built on sacred sites which were used as meeting places for social, ritual and spiritual events long before the Christian era. Succeeding religious authorities recognised the power of these places and, by superimposing their structures on them, sought to preserve the energy while establishing the new dogma. Earth energy is cosmopolitan and reacts to genuine prayer and ritual irrespective of which deity inspires it. An alignment of seven churches in Cambridge is shown opposite (*from Nigel Pennick*).

Unfortunately there is no simple structure to energy patterns in churches; through the ages eager clergy, anxious sinners and their builders have moved fonts and altars, and arranged for endless alterations of the present buildings with little understanding of the earth-energy balances which provide the ambience of sanctity, peace and purity. It often happens, with a good vicar and a congregation who attend for the right reasons, that the main power centre of the church stays firmly in position on the centre-line of the building, and about six inches in from the front of the altar. These are the churches which feel welcoming when you enter and it can be interesting to check the energy centre in the usual way, using discretion in the use of dowsing tools.

Many of the priesthood are very much aware of the energy fields and their effects. In fact quite a number are dowsers, but it's always better to have a quiet word first to avoid offence.

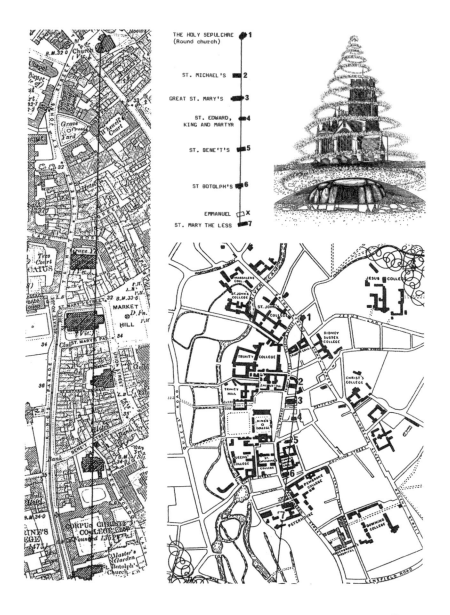

THE HOLY SEPULCHRE
(Round church) ─ 1

ST. MICHAEL'S ─ 2

GREAT ST. MARY'S ─ 3

ST. EDWARD,
KING AND MARTYR ─ 4

ST. BENE'T'S ─ 5

ST BOTOLPH'S ─ 6

EMMANUEL ─ X

ST. MARY THE LESS ─ 7

CATHEDRALS
sacred knowledge

A huge number of Gothic cathedrals were built in twelfth century Europe under the guidance and support of the Knights Templar. Their aim was to use their newly acquired knowledge of telluric currents (earth energies), resonance, sacred geometry, space, and colour to create stone monuments which would inspire mankind to reach ever higher levels of spiritual development.

They were acutely aware that the etheric human senses are profoundly affected by underground caves and dolmen, and often chose to place their new structures on these recognised and established power points.

The choice of site was delicate and deliberate, making the best use of the Earth's pure energy, one of its greatest but least understood gifts to us. The caves became crypts below buildings constructed by trained master craftsmen who used stressed stone and sound in geometric harmony to create the numinous balance of vibration and resonance.

For budding dowsers there is no more awesome place to practice earth energy work than around a cathedral. As the complexities begin to unravel it is possible to glimpse some of the sophistication of the knowledge behind the space, structure and its relationship with the Earth. Cuts us down to size a bit.

DOWSING THE EARTH'S FIELD
free connection

There is an inconceivably vast and complex network out there which makes our internet look primitive. Each one of us is already linked in, and while for a time we lost the delicate art of tuning in to the whispering energies of the universe, dowsing has re-opened a door for us to return to our evolutionary birthright.

Every field, garden and house has its own energy centres and you can locate the most powerful one in the same way as you found the kitchen sink. Work with it consciously and ask if you may communicate with it. It will respond to the right approach by manifesting energy lines like the spokes of a wheel in straight lines from the centre.

Walk slowly round the point asking the tool to show you where the lines are. Mark them on the carpet or grass. Usually they are bunched closer together in one or two directions and it's likely that other earth energy connections come in at these points. Walk in towards the centre on each radial (not necessarily in sequence) and ask to be shown where any other manifestation crosses the line. When you've located and marked them all you'll find a perfect Fibonacci spiral winding out from the centre. This is one of the basic building blocks of the universe and is so awesome that your hair will probably stand on end.

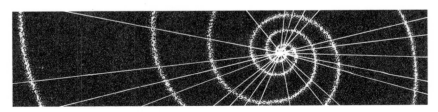

LEY & ENERGY LINES
the earth is listening

A ley line is essentially a straight alignment of at least four significant or sacred sites. They were named by Alfred Watkins (*see pages 12 and 251-56*) who was the first man to notice that there were lots of them all over the countryside (*see his drawing of leys around Stonehenge, opposite top*). While volumes have been written about the significance of these line-ups the main interest for dowsers is with the energy flows which weave around the lines and pulse in the sacred sites. It's almost as though the ley lines are there as pointers to places of power. The old people, who knew a thing or two about power points, went to enormous lengths moving great stones around the countryside to mark them with sophisticated geometrical structures.

Every energy line is made up from a marginally different set of frequencies giving each a 'signature' which can, with practice, be identified by a dowser as easily as a favourite label on a shelf. They are the Earths' equivalent of our nervous and meridian systems and throb to the rhythms of the universe. Undulating across the countryside in pairs, one polarity tends to hug the higher ranges and hilltops while the other seeks out valleys, plains and water. One example is 'Michael Line' of ancient sacred sites across the south of England, with its two 'Michael' and 'Mary' currents. The combined energies of their sporadic meetings create spiritually uplifting backwaters of balanced purity which have a profound effect on the bio-magnetic fields around our bodies.

Far Eastern cultures have been aware of the importance of these delicate energies for thousands of years, and have developed sophisticated expertise in their use in Feng Shui (*see Book III*).

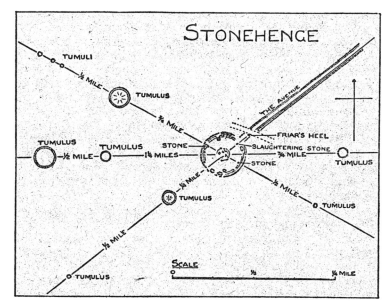

Left: *Leys around Stonehenge. An original drawing by Alfred Watkins.*

Below: *The famed Michael Line across Southern Britain has three components: The straight alignment; the female Mary current; and the male Michael current.*

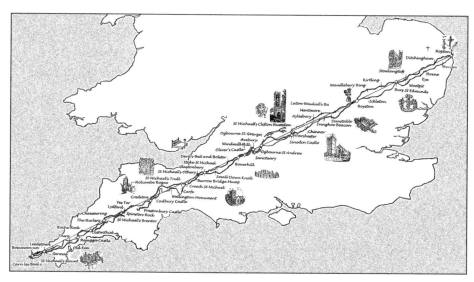

SACRED SITES
centres of power

Sacred sites and energy lines must have been of paramount importance to the ancients. It requires a disciplined society with unwavering convictions through generations to create monuments like Avebury and Stonehenge in Wiltshire, England. Even the lesser stone circles scattered around country required monumental effort to create.

Dowsing a stone circle to access its energy field is a rewarding exercise. There are often eight energy lines round the perimeter which seem to act as 'sensors', switching on the field for any consciousness willing to tune in. Find the power centre (not necessarily the geometric centre) in the usual way and from that point pick up the energy spiral. A number of lines radiate like irregular spokes of a wheel from the centre, each one passing through a stone. Each stone is connected to all the others, every one has its own spiral and radials, and the resulting field is a complex, vibrant energetic web (*lower right opposite*). Take time to dowse the separate magnetic fields of each stone and carefully phrase the questions you are prompted to ask.

One of the most powerful sites in Britain is on St Michael's Mount in Cornwall where two pairs of strong global earth energy lines meet in perfect harmony creating a vortex of peaceful stimulating space where cosmic energies connect with the Earth's field.

Above: St. Michael's Mount, Cornwall, where two pairs of global energy lines cross. The Michael and Mary lines run NE-SW, whereas the other pair, the Apollo and Athena lines, run NW-SE, crossing the Channel to St. Michael's Mount's twin, Mont St. Michel in Brittany (shown on the facing page). They then travel on to Bourges and Cluny in France, and on through Sacra di San Michele, Pisa, Siena, Assisi and Promontaro Gargano in Italy, then through Delphi and Athens in Greece (where they pass through temples to Apollo and Athena) and finally off to Mount Carmel and the Holy Land.

crossing energy lines, St. Michael's Mount, and the Merry Maidens Stone Circle, Cornwall

SACRED EARTH
global links

All over the world there are sacred sites which have long been connected with stories handed down through generations of indigenous people. These mythical folk-memories are an amalgum of occult knowledge and profound spiritual awareness, and they have so many factors in common world-wide that some form of prehistoric communication between sites must have existed.

Ethnic groups from Texas to Tashkent, from the Kalihari to Kabul and from the Chilean Andes to China each developed a special reverence for their local sites, and their legends show that while there are some differences in their interpretation of events and manifestations, there are positive connections between them which are contrary to accepted historical record.

Possible global earth-energy linkage structures have been suggested by Berenholtz of Los Angeles, Coon of Glastonbury and other international writers and thinkers. The energies of sites like Mt. Shasta (*opposite top*), Machu Picchu, and Uluhuru are as varied as the cultures which previously understood them, and as more and more people tune in to their frequencies, the old links between these sacred places are expanding and increasing in strength.

Dowsers are taking the opportunities now available to visit and assess similarities and variations of energy manifestations at these glorious, stimulating planetary acupuncture points, and are finding that exposure to the powerful energies is a richly rewarding experience.

It's a lot more exciting than lying on the beach.

Two examples of sacred sites. Above: Mount Shasta, California. Below: Angkor Wat, Cambodia.

EARTH'S ENERGY FIELD
cosmic internet

Druid legend has it that there are twelve main lines of energy round the world, not necessarily great circles, but joining and feeding the great power centres of the planet. These pathways are the equivalent of our spinal cord. The crossing places are very special and pulse with vortices of energy which connect with the universe. They are the gateways where peripatetic beings can come through into our density to learn and perhaps guide how we behave.

Joining these pathways are lesser energy lines which split, divide and subdivide endlessly, covering the globe on, under and above the surface until they are small enough to contact the energy centres of the minutest creatures and basic elements of the planet.

There is a growing interest amongst lateral thinking scientists and mathematicians in the perception and investigation of these natural fields and their effects on our biological development, particularly in the light of recent work on the measurable effects of sunspot activity on the Earth's magnetic field. The concept of being at one with the universe is easier to accept with this vision in our thoughts, and dowsing for its reality can make an important contribution to the expansion of our minds.

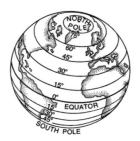

It's a lot of fun, too.

Left: An artists impression of one of the great energy lines of planet Earth, connecting ancient sites, important places in forests, animal lines, souls and galaxies.

Below: An early French map of the Earth's magnetic field lines. These move around, as do the positions of the north and south poles. The Earth's poles undergo a magnetic reversal on average every half a million years, the last one now being some 780,000 years ago, so we are well overdue a change right now. And in fact the poles they are a wandering.

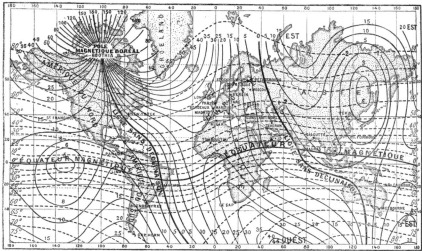

EARTH ENERGY RESPONSES
the common language

A direct response between the Earth and human consciousness seems impossible because of the language barrier between two such different beings. We have enough trouble communicating with dolphins who have to drop to their baby-talk to get down to our level. The Earth, however, seems to be looking for solutions by responding to stimuli and manifesting geometric symbols at power centres in her energy field.

This response alone is awesome, but dowsing has shown that the recently discovered spiral shape pulses with the rhythms of the Earth, the cyclic movements of Moon, planets, sun, the state of our minds and doubtless many other factors of which at the moment we are unaware.

Experiments have continued with ancient and modern artifacts placed on the energy centres and while by no means all of them stimulate a dowseable response, many of them activate a positive if sometimes asymmetric mathematical shape. We have found that natural energy forms can be profoundly affected by prayer and meditation and that the extent of any changes in the field pattern seems to be in direct proportion to the degree of mind concentration applied.

Not enough work has been done to come to any form of conclusion but this is an exciting new field for dowsers to work on, perhaps in conjunction with specialists in geology, resonance and magnetic fields.

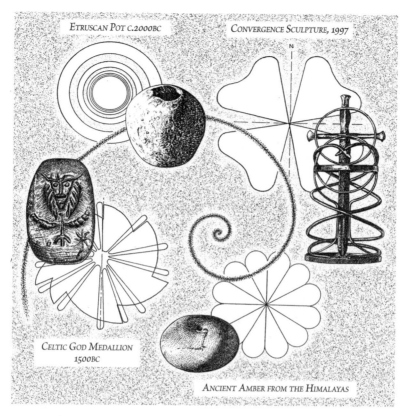

ETRUSCAN POT C.2000BC

CONVERGENCE SCULPTURE, 1997

CELTIC GOD MEDALLION
1500BC

ANCIENT AMBER FROM THE HIMALAYAS

Above: The fascinating shapes which can be dowsed when certain artifacts, ancient and modern, are placed on Earth energy centres.

Facing page: Neolithic carved tetrahedral ball from Towie, Aberdeenshire, Scotland, dated to c.3000BC. Left: Roman copper alloy dodecahedron, found in Tongeren, Belgium, dated to c.300AD.

Beyond Tools
our sensitive hands

There is a mystical excitement when first feeling dowsing tools move of their own accord, but none can touch, feel, manipulate and create as delicately as our own human hands. These can be programmed in the dowsing mode to a sense of awareness extending far beyond the skin. Learning to detect the body's ethereal boundaries with hands is a wonderful experience which profoundly changes our relationship with all of creation. However, it is of the greatest importance not to intrude on people, animals, plants or landscape when dowsing, and permission should always be obtained from whoever before starting.

Try pressing thumb and forefinger lightly together and becoming aware of changes of 'feel' as you work. Eventually you will find you are able to sense things without the response from your hands. Many people progress to a point where they see energy as coloured lines of light and some can apparently move into whatever environment they are researching. Dowse with rods or pendulums to identify shapes and images drawn by a friend, and you will gradually develop a form of telepathic communication which works without tools.

'Deviceless' dowsing can be used to mentally lock on to a water course and follow its meanderings, and is useful for work in sensitive areas where the obvious use of tools might cause offence. It can help discern sources of geopathic or social stress, or locate lost people, animals, car keys and dematerialised pairs of glasses.

TIME

a way to move through

There is no reason why our minds should be trapped in our earthly perception of time. The concept of dowsing out of present time is perfectly valid, but it needs a very special mental discipline to be sure of correct answers.

Start by bracket-dowsing to find the age of grandmother's antique cameo pendant. Check its age with an expert in the jewellery field, and use it to tune into the period. Once you've done that you can dowse normally holding the cameo in your hand as a witness, but of course you will have to train your mind to prevent an inadvertent return to 'now'.

Practice 'age' dowsing on an newly-felled tree trunk. Have it checked by a dendrochronologist. If you have difficulty in saying it or finding one, count the annular growth rings yourself.

There are many talented experts in psychometry. This is an ability to access facts about objects, events and people by handling artifacts and tuning in to their past. It's a form of dowsing and works remarkably well when you have learned to prevent your rational mind from interfering.

Future events open a different can of worms. This is divination rather than dowsing and the confusion of the two terms triggered quite some opposition from the Church based on their interpretation of Deuteronomy 18;10. In my opinion it can't work because I believe that the future holds an infinite number of possibilities.

Not many dowsers win the lottery.

Left: Dowsing the years using tree rings can be a great way to hone your skills. Get an old log and see if you can identify the year of a particular ring. Make a guess and ask the pendulum or dowsing rod if your guess is too high, or too low.

Below left: A 1930s American lottery ticket. Dowsing future events is not a good idea and mostly doesn't work. Leave the future for another day.

Below: See if you can guess what time it is using dowsing alone.

ORIGINAL
Lucky Dime
FIVE DAY

FIVE DAYS FIVE
10 Cent SPECIAL
Week of
JULY 28, 1930

Remote Viewing
through the curtain

Dowsing deals with perceptions of events and objects which are normally hidden. *Remote viewing* is a highly specialised version of the art where the viewer develops an ability to tune, with a high degree of concentration, to specific targets anywhere in the world and beyond. Restrictions of time and travel no longer apply and experts can 'see' locations, situations and actions as they are happening. Accurate viewing requires a considerable mental discipline but this can gradually be acquired with practice by honing standard dowsing techniques. The trick is to transfer the complex energies which normally cause the rod or pendulum to move in a simple 'yes' or 'no', into the creation of a mental picture of the event.

Unfortunately some of the more advanced talents in this exciting field have been persuaded by military and political 'experts' to spend a lot of time in embassies trying to find out what the chaps next door are doing, and this tends to restrict the natural development of the skill. When we get beyond this archaic, sometimes paranoid, application of this wonderful human talent and more of us become proficient viewers, we may all have to think about becoming more honest. Difficult to cheat in business or run a war if the other side knows what you're up to.

This amazing major dowsing breakthrough could one day help man's evolutionary progress simply by forcing us to be more open with each other.

Beyond the Veil
quo vadis

While working on Earth's energies with her myriads of frequencies, you may occasionally come across a few which are not in resonance with the place or person. All natural earth energy is benign but sometimes it has been influenced by a less than pleasant human consciousness, and as a result of this can generate feelings of discomfort or even fear. Practiced dowsers can ask for these to be changed to healing frequencies in a way that does not affect any other being. There are many ritualistic ways of doing this with crystals, stones, metal pipes and even burning effigies, but if you are coming from the right place, all you have to do is ask. The effect can be extraordinarily beneficial and the process is very simple.

In dowsing we have a tool which stimulates senses beyond the usual five. It is one way of letting us recognise the limitations of our present perceptions. With the realisation that the social, spiritual, and moral restrictions which have historically controlled our thought patterns can be questioned, modified or lifted comes the freedom to make our own decisions about the life-style we would like to follow. Each of us needs the courage to accept the responsibility for the results of our decisions.

We can *all* do it if we work together with love, care and concern for the Earth in all its manifestations.

BOOK V

Above: The 1000-year old Serpent Mound of Ohio in the Mississippi Valley
of the USA suggests a sinuous flow of more mysterious energies.
Facing page: Alfred Watkins' 1921 map of eight leys through
Capel-y-Tair-Ywen, near Hay-on-Wye.

LEYS

SECRET SPIRIT PATHS

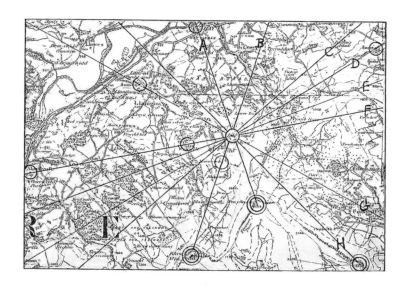

Danny Sullivan

INTRODUCTION

On June 30 1921, Herefordshire businessman Alfred Watkins was driving along a road in Blackwardine, near Leominster. Attracted by the nearby archeological investigation of a Roman camp, he stopped his car to compare the landscape on either side of the road with the marked features on his map.

Whilst contemplating the landscape around him, he saw, in the words of his son, "like a chain of fairy lights", a series of straight alignments of various ancient features, such as standing stones, wayside crosses, hill forts and ancient churches. The discovery, he later wrote, came to him "like a flash".

Enthusiastic commentators since have interpreted it as a mystic vision (*see illustration opposite*), which the methodical and practical Watkins would have certainly indignantly denied. Watkins was not the first person to notice alignments at ancient sites, but he was the first to propose that alignments existed all over the land and, crucially, to give them an appropriate name, *leys*, because of the frequency with which this Saxon place name, meaning a cleared strip of land, occurred along them.

Since the day Alfred Watkins made his discovery public, ley lines have become associated with prehistoric trackways, ancient astronomy, UFOs, mysterious earth energies, dream lines, song lines, black dogs, ghosts, flying shamen and spirits of the dead.

What a long, strange trip it's been.

THE MYSTERY OF LEY LINES
UFOs and strange energies

It's a dull imagination that isn't fired on first hearing of the concept of ley lines. From Alfred Watkins' simple discovery of lost ancient trackways in 1921, ley lines have evolved to encompass a wide field of theory and speculation.

In the early part of the 20th century research began to appear which speculated that ley lines should be identified with astronomical alignments, or spirit or fairy lines (*e.g. see illustration opposite by L. Dalliance, Paris, 1887*). These and other ideas will be covered later in this book. However, the modern revival in ley hunting was in fact largely triggered by the post war flying saucer craze.

In the 1950s French ufologist Aimé Michell had claimed that sightings of UFOs, when plotted on a map, fell into straight lines which he called 'orthotenies'. One of the earliest alien abductees, Buck Nelson, had written that flying saucer pilots tapped into lines of magnetic force in the earth to power their craft. Then, in the early 1960s, ex-RAF pilot Tony Wedd, an enthusiastic believer in UFOs, put these two fantastic concepts together with Alfred Watkins' leys and thus the ley as a line of magnetic force was born.

The sixties counterculture embraced ley lines as part of the cultural revolution and the mystical energy lines quickly became the accepted explanation for leys. Before long dowsers claimed to be able to locate hidden energies at ancient sacred sites such as stone circles and standing stones and eventually claimed to be able to dowse the leys that run between them.

THE FIRST LEY HUNTERS
the Straight Track Club

Alfred Watkins quickly got to work verifying his initial discovery. He travelled extensively in his home county of Herefordshire photographing sites and accumulating an impressive collection of data, which was published in 1925 as *The Old Straight Track*.

He had concluded that the alignment of prominent hills and the ranks of minor mark points between them represented the routes of prehistoric traders carrying salt, pottery and flint. Ignored by the archaeologists of the day it quickly became a best seller and ley hunting soon became a popular pastime.

Within two years the *Straight Track Postal Portfolio Club* was established by ley enthusiasts to investigate leys for themselves. They circulated their researches in a series of portfolios, which were posted in turn to each member. Many leys were proposed, some of which clearly could never have been traders' tracks, and soon members started to question Watkins' key discoveries.

Though many strange theories were proposed for leys, no-one seemed to be any closer to finding a satisfactory explanation. With the outbreak of war in 1939 the Club eventually broke up and Watkins' theory was largely forgotten until the 1960s.

Opposite top left: Alfred Watkins announces the first ever excursion of the Straight Track Club in Hereford in 1933. A splendid time is guaranteed for all. Opposite, top right: Cover illustration from 1920s edition of the Ordnance Survey maps. Opposite: Alfred Watkins' map of two putative Herefordshire ley lines. Notice how he has cut up his maps into thin horizontal strips, and pasted them vertically above one another. From his 1922 book Early British Trackways, Moats, Mounds, Camps and Sites.

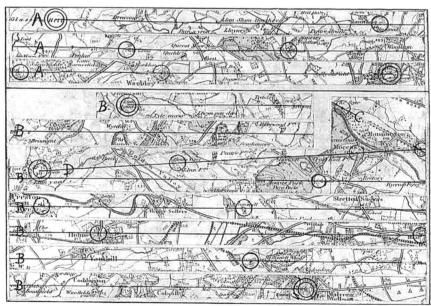

Astronomical Alignments
Watkins, Lockyer, Thom and Stonehenge

Sir Norman Lockyer's research in 1901 on the astronomical orientation of ancient temples showed that certain alignments of stones through the centre of Stonehenge had been arranged to point to the moment of sunrise or sunset on particular days of the year (*opposite*).

Alfred Watkins lost no time in revisiting Stonehenge to follow up what Lockyer had not fully developed—the evidence of other mark points for those astronomical alignments. He found good evidence for four such alignments. More corroboration was to come from Admiral Boyle Sommerville, a Straight Track Club member who noted that several stone rows, circles and dolmens in the Hebrides and in Ireland were precisely aligned to sunrise and sunset on significant days in the year. Such alignments then continued in straight lines to marks, notches, cairns or earthworks on or near hilltops several miles away.

A similar alignment can be seen at Newgrange, in Ireland where the passage to the central chambers of the tomb is oriented towards the point of midwinter sunrise. On the same line lie two decorated kerbstones, a burial mound and one of the stones of the surrounding stone circle (*see pages 302-303*).

Above: The midsummer solstice alignment from the centre of Stonehenge. On June 21st every year the Sun rises over the Heel Stone (from helios, Greek for sun), which aligns with the Avenue.

THE HOLY LINES OF GERMANY
the work of Teudt and Heinsch

Alignments of ancient sacred sites are not confined to Britain. In 1939 the German historian Josef Heinsch published a paper, *Principles of Prehistoric Sacred Geography*, in which he spoke of a lost magic principle by which holy sites had been located in the remote past. The sites, he claimed, were points on the lines of great geometrical figures that had been constructed to certain fixed angles and units of measurement based on simple fractions of the Earth's dimensions. This ancient pattern, he said, was still recognisable in the present landscape because of the adoption of pagan sites by the Christian Church.

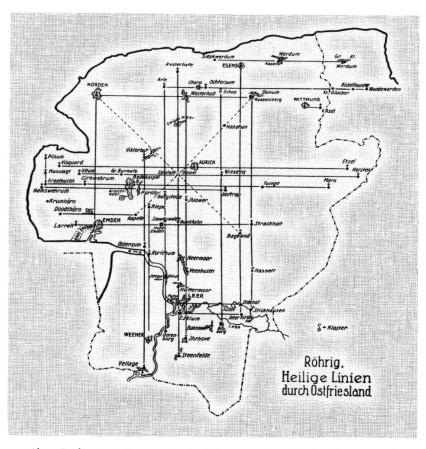

Röhrig,
Heilige Linien
durch Ostfriesland

Above: Ley hunting in Germany. Cardinal alignments of a multitude of German sacred sites by one of Wilheim Teudt's contemporaries. *Left:* Watkins had a second German contemporary, Wilhelm Teudt, an evangelical parson who claimed that a rock-cut chapel in the Externsteine, one of several natural twisted stacks of rock in West Saxony, was a solar observatory and that 'astronomical lines' linking numerous sacred sites radiated outwards throughout northern Germany. He called these lines *heilige Linien* or holy lines, but the adoption of Teudt's questionable theories by Himmler during the rise of the Nazis led to his ideas being consigned to obscurity.

PATHWAYS TO THE GODS
Nazca lines, Inca ceques and Bolivian tracks

At Nazca in Peru dozens of straight lines are laid out across the desert. Elsewhere in the Peruvian desert other straight lines made from small heaps of stones link low mounds with prominent hills. Near Lima straight lines radiate from a central space like the spokes of a wheel. They are not roads, but link together ancient sacred places called *wak'as*.

Seventeenth century Jesuit texts record the one-time existence of invisible lines radiating out from the centre of the ancient Inca city of Cuzco. These lines are known as *ceques* and were believed to be sacred pathways. Today they are only visible as alignments of shrines and churches exactly in the manner of English leys.

In Bolivia similar long straight tracks can be found running dead straight for miles across the undulating Andean altiplano from hills and piles of stones to white painted chapels on the summits of low hills.

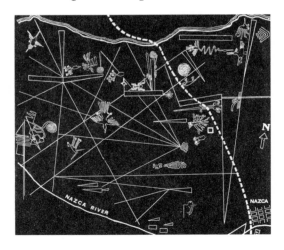

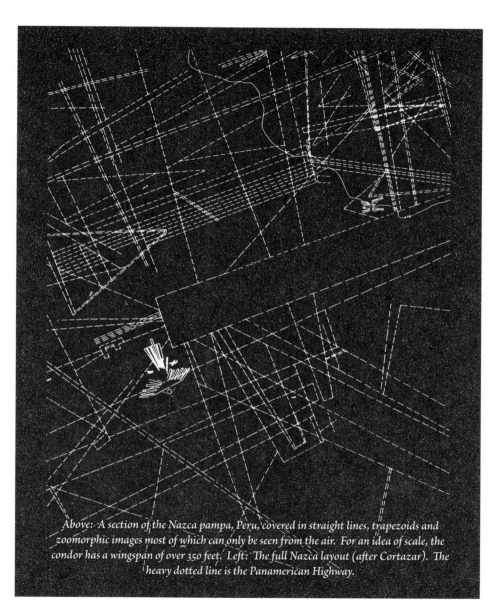

Above: A section of the Nazca pampa, Peru, covered in straight lines, trapezoids and zoomorphic images most of which can only be seen from the air. For an idea of scale, the condor has a wingspan of over 350 feet. Left: The full Nazca layout (after Cortazar). The heavy dotted line is the Panamerican Highway.

Road, Mound And Meridian
alignments of the ancient Americans

Elsewhere in the Americas fragments of ancient straight road systems can still be traced. They invariably link holy or sacred places.

In Yucatan, in Mexico, the Maya constructed dead straight ceremonial roads through the jungle called *sacbeob*. In New Mexico infrared satellite photography has revealed a system of dead straight roads centred on Chaco Canyon (*below*), the site of many ancient ruined ceremonial and religious buildings known as *kivas*. The road system is a mystery as the Anasazi people who built them had neither the wheel nor the horse. Rather than linking communities the roads connect specific places in the landscape which suggests a symbolic purpose. Archaeologists have identified an alignment of ancient Anasazi cities along a north south meridian over several hundred miles long, part of which is marked by the Chacoan Great North Road.

Prehistoric linear earthworks in Wisconsin (*main picture*) have astronomical orientations and in Mississippi various ancient Indian circular and effigy mounds were laid out in linear ranges (*side pictures*).

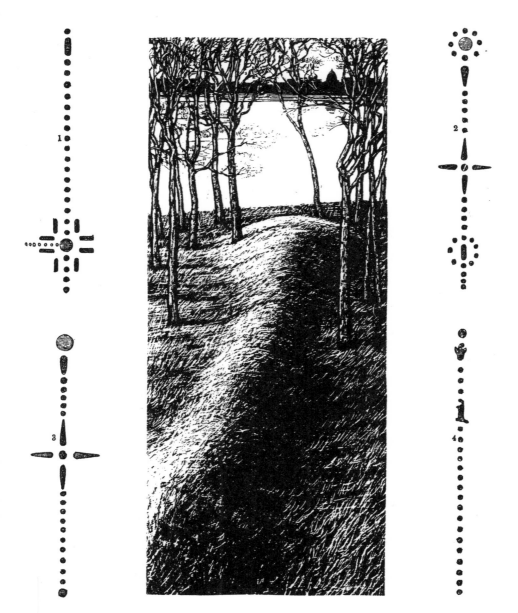

ASTRONOMICAL ALIGMENTS
pointing to heaven from earth

Watching the sun rise and set over a year, a pattern appears. At the beginning of the year it rises in the southeast and draws a small low arc in the sky before setting in the southwest. As the days lengthen both the sunrise and the sunset move north, more and more quickly every day, until at the equinox on March 21st the sun rises due east and sets due west. As the days continue to lengthen the sunrises and sunsets move ever northward, but more slowly now, until at midsummer on June 21st, the sun stops for the summer solstice, before repeating the pattern, with sunrises and sunsets moving south, past the east-west line of the autumn equinox on Sept 21st, until the Dec 21st winter solstice.

Halfway between the solstices and equinoxes are the cross-quarter days, still celebrated in many cultures, the most famous being May Day.

The moon follows the rough rising and setting pattern of the sun, but does the whole swing every month, with full moons rising opposite setting suns. In addition the moon breathes in and out, either side of the sun, over 18.6 years, producing lunar standstills (*as shown opposite*).

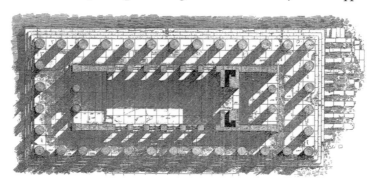

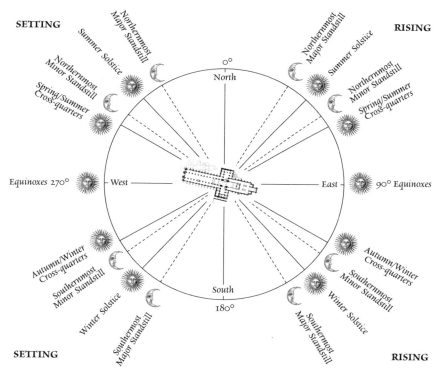

SETTING   Northernmost Major Standstill   RISING

Summer Solstice

Northernmost Minor Standstill

Spring/Summer Cross-quarters

North   0°

Northernmost Major Standstill

Summer Solstice

Northernmost Minor Standstill

Spring/Summer Cross-quarters

Equinoxes 270°   — West —   East —   90° Equinoxes

Autumn/Winter Cross-quarters

Southernmost Minor Standstill

Winter Solstice

Southernmost Major Standstill

South   180°

Autumn/Winter Cross-quarters

Southernmost Minor Standstill

Winter Solstice

Southernmost Major Standstill

SETTING   RISING

Above: The key solar and lunar points on the horizon to which archaeological sites may be aligned. A distant hilltop or other landscape feature may agree with one of these astronomical alignments or denote a day of the year, and thus the birthday of a dedicatory saint. The rising and setting positions of bright stars, such as Sirius, are also often used.

Left: Like most Christian churches, the majority of Sicilian Greek temples (e.g. the 500 BC Temple of Concordia at Agrigento, shown opposite), are aligned precisely to the east, to the equinox sunrise, on or close to March 21st and September 21st, the two special days of the year when day and night are equal all over the world.

THE SOLAR YEAR IN EIGHT PARTS

IMBOLC: ~ FEB 4TH
SPRING EQUINOX: ~ MARCH 21ST
BELTANE: ~ MAY. 5TH
MIDSUMMER SOLSTICE: ~ JUNE 21ST
LAMMAS: ~ AUG. 7TH
AUTUMN EQUINOX: ~ SEPT. 23RD
SAMHAIN: ~ NOV. 6TH
MIDWINTER SOLSTICE: ~ DEC 21ST

Equinoxes and Solstices

the most basic astroarchaeological alignments

Throughout the ancient world, important sites and long alignments were aimed at the rising and setting of the sun on the four keys days of the year, the summer and winter solstices (the longest and shortest days of the year), and the spring and autumn equinoxes.

In England, Stonehenge is aligned to the summer solstice sunrise and also to the winter solstice sunset (which always oppose one another on a level horizon). In Ireland Newgrange (built 3200 BC) is aligned to the midwinter sunrise. The oldest stone circle yet discovered is at Nabta Playa in the Egyptian desert. It is dated to 4800 BC and is an egg-shaped circle whose axis, like Stonehenge's, points to the northeasterly midsummer sunrise and the southwesterly midwinter sunset. More examples are shown on the page opposite.

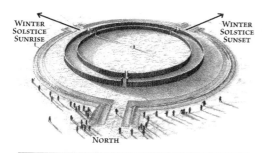

Left: Artist's impression of Goseck Circle, Saxony-Anhalt, Germany (4900 BC), an early example of one of hundreds of palisaded ring-ditches. Two of the three entrances are precisely aligned to the winter solstice sun, one to the sunrise (SE) and one to the sunset (SW).

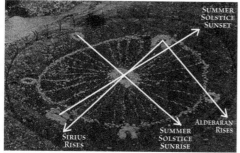

Left: Majorville Sun Cairn Ring, Alberta, 3000 BC) marks key dates of the solar year plus lunar cycles.

Below and opposite: The Treasury of Atreus, Mycenae, Greece. 1250 BC). The equinox sun rises in the east, over Mount Zara, before shining through the triangular window over the doorway onto the far wall of the wonderful interior beehive chamber.

LUNAR EXTREMES
important examples from the ancient world

The Newark Earthworks in Newark, Ohio were built by the Hopewell culture around 350 AD and consist of a three sections of huge earthworks (*see opposite, and also pages 298-301*). To give a sense of scale, the great circle is 1,054 feet across (321 m), so large that in 1875 the county fair was held inside it (*below*). A huge irregular octogon at the northeast end of the complex demonstrates advanced lunar surveying. The moon's risings and setting swing monthly from the north to the south, but the amount of the swing varies slightly over 18.6 years. It is this variation which is marked by the clever shape of the octagon.

In Wiltshire, England, the impressive stones of Stonehenge also track the 18.6-year variation in the extent of the monthly swing of the lunar rising and settings. But, in addition, at the latitude and setting of Stonehenge the lunar extremes also synchronise with the key solar positions. These essential risings and settings fall on the arms of a perfect octagram as shown (*opposite*).

Drawing the octagram as shown, from the circle defined by the midsummer Hele Stone, its arms cross to give the size of the 56-hole Aubrey circle, which was used to predict eclipses.

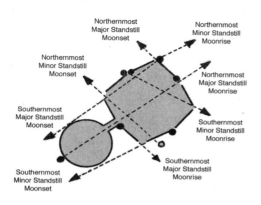

Above, right, & facing page: The 300 AD Newark earthworks, Ohio, showing lunar extreme risings and settings.

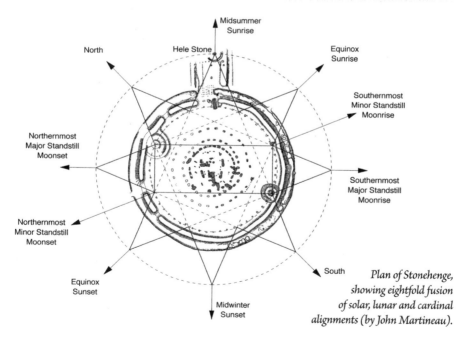

Plan of Stonehenge, showing eightfold fusion of solar, lunar and cardinal alignments (by John Martineau).

MEGALITHOMANIA

what were the ancients up to?

Off the northwestern tip of the British Isles, beyond the Isle of Skye, lie a small group of islands called the Outer Hebrides. On the largest of these, the Isle of Lewis, may still be found one of the most undisturbed set of megalithic long distance alignments yet unearthed.

In an area five miles wide a collection of small stone circles offer a fascinating glimpse into the neolithic mind. It was only in the 1960s that Oxford professor Alexander Thom realised that stone circles, although sometimes circular, are also often precisely flattened circles, egg-shapes and ellipses, a little like eyeballs, and so possess two axes. On the Isle of Lewis (*e.g. at Callanish, below*) we can observe how circles separated by some miles nevertheless seem to precisely 'look' at each other. Study the six examples opposite, which are spread out in the area, and notice how various stone circles point to one another.

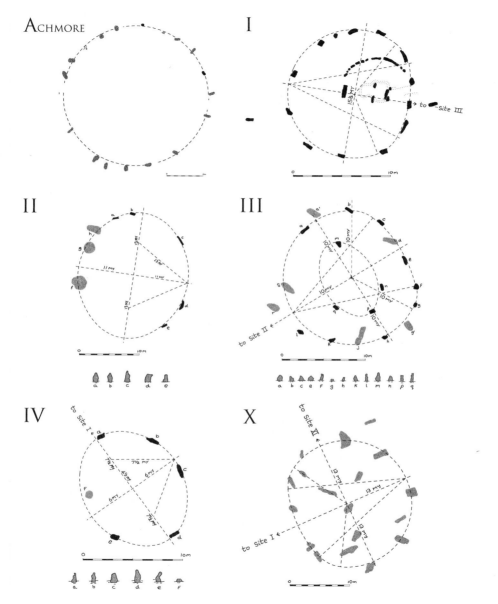

ACHMORE

I

II

III

IV

X

DRAGON LINES
enhancing good luck in ancient China

Invisible straight lines can also be found in other parts of the world. The Chinese science of geomancy, known as *feng shui (see Book II)*, was originally developed for determining the best location for a tomb.

Feng shui tradition believes that harmony in landscape and life can be achieved through the manipulation of natural forces that course through 'veins' in the Earth. These forces, in certain circumstances, manifest themselves as lung mei, or dragon lines, which run in straight lines. Lung mei are also spirit paths, as the Chinese, like so many ancient cultures, believed that spirits preferred to travel by the straightest route. Thus it was, in most instances, considered unlucky to build a house at the end of a straight road or path.

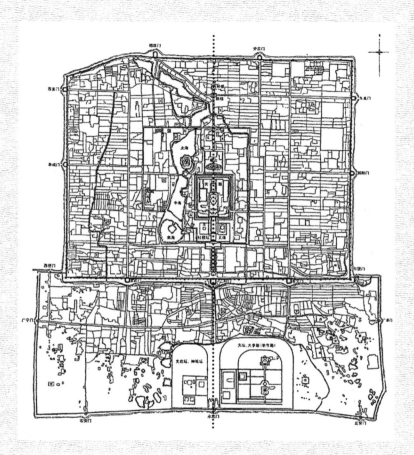

*Above: The Forbidden City, centre of old Beijing, China, lies on an ancient noth-south
dragon line that passes through the city gate, the Emperor's palace and a sacred mound.
Left: Antique print of the old western gate of the Forbidden City. The laying out of cities
on a North-South-East-West grid, with four gates in the four sides, was common in the
ancient world. The Romans built their cities in this way, with the Forum at the centre.*

FAIRY PASSES

keeping the lines clear in Ireland

In a similar tradition to the Chinese, the fairies or 'little people' of Irish folklore had their favoured routes which ran straight between fairy forts, or raths, circular earthworks of known antiquity. These fairy roads are known as 'passes' and are sometimes, but not always, marked by physical roads.

It was considered unlucky and even dangerous to build on or to block a fairy pass. Calamity would befall anyone who did so. To this day, some Irish houses have special doors on each side of a house which need to be opened on particular days of the year to allow the safe passage of the fairy host. Illustrations by Richard Doyle (*below*) and Arthur Rackham (*opposite*).

GEOLOGICAL FAULT LINES
following telluric currents

Ley lines and their accompanying phenomena may have something to do with underground geological fault lines. Studying UFOs and other strange balls of light in the 1950s, French reseacher Aimé Michell noticed that they often followed the paths of underground fault lines, and that these fault lines also tracked certain important French leys.

Recent work by Howard Crowhurst has revealed that the extensive alignments of standing stones at Carnac in Brittany, France, also follow geological fracture lines, whilst at the same time also indicating important sun and moon alignments. Did the ancient builders somehow sense the underground faulting, or is this just a coincidence?

Could geological piezoelectrical effects also explain the altered states of consciousness that some people experience at these places?

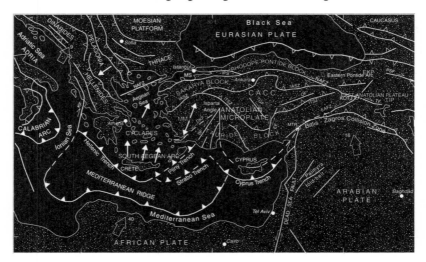

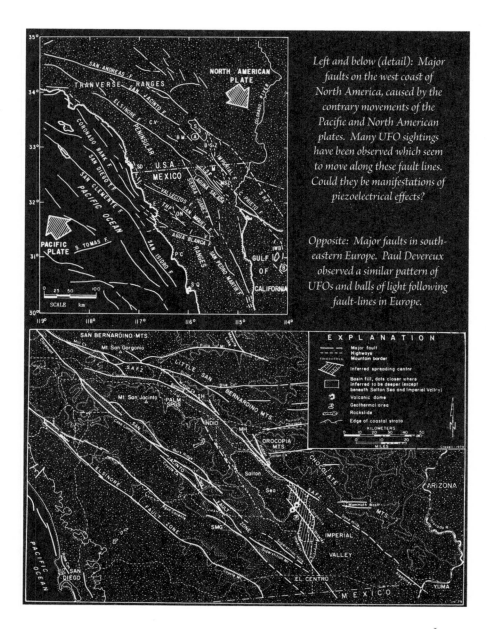

Left and below (detail): Major faults on the west coast of North America, caused by the contrary movements of the Pacific and North American plates. Many UFO sightings have been observed which seem to move along these fault lines. Could they be manifestations of piezoelectrical effects?

Opposite: Major faults in south-eastern Europe. Paul Devereux observed a similar pattern of UFOs and balls of light following fault-lines in Europe.

DREAM ROADS
and death roads

Evidence for invisible sacred pathways can be found in the religious beliefs of aboriginal peoples across the world. In Australia the beliefs and knowledge of such alignments can be found in the traditional stories of the Dreaming, a mythical period in aboriginal history set at the dawn of time when mythological creators or gods emerged from the featureless earth and began to wander aimlessly across it. Every place where they camped, made fires, dug for water or performed ceremonies they marked with a natural feature, such as a rock, hill or watercourse. Those wanderings across country are preserved in the songs and stories of present day aborigine tribes.

Each tribe has possession of one part of the whole creation myth and the finishing place of a 'line of songs' is where the myths and songs change hands to another tribe and thus form a mythical tribal boundary.

The invisible lines linking the various songs and stories are the lines of communication between the tribes which when drawn together represent a mythical map of Australia (*shown right, after David Mowaljartai*).

Song lines also appear as alignments of choirs across Europe (*see opposite*).

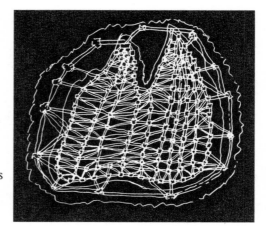

The singing of hymns and psalms in churches and cathedrals supposedly enchanted the surrounding landscape. Many of Alfred Watkins' leys linked medieval churches and churchyards. In the Netherlands it was decreed by law that the dead had to be carried for burial along a specially designated road called a *dodweg* or 'death road'. These were invariably dead straight. In Germany in the 10th and 11th centuries it was the deliberate practice to lay out towns to a sacred geometric scheme. A cathedral was built at the centre of the town and four churches were erected in the cardinal directions, forming a cross. Often the churches were linked to the cathedral by straight roads, and sometimes existing pagan sites were incorporated into these. Left: A church line and pilgrimage route in Zurich, Switzerland. Fraumunster, the bridge, Wasserkirche and the Grossmunster align with a blue stone (black dot, centre of picture), the geomantic centre of the city. (J Murer, 1576). Below: Speyer, where the axis of the cathedral continues as the main street or ceremonial way to the city gate and points towards the prominent Kalmit mountain.

THE JOURNEY OF THE SOUL
funeral paths and corpse ways

The tradition of carrying a corpse for burial along a special road is prevalent throughout Western Europe and may be linked to the fear of ghosts and wandering spirits.

Dutch death roads may have been straight, but contemporary German death roads are seldom straight and neither are the medieval funeral paths and corpse ways of the British Isles. In the Middle Ages some villages and hamlets were required by Church law to bury their dead at the nearest church that held the burial right. Funeral parties would use a designated route, known as a 'burial path', 'coffin path' or 'church road' to convey the coffin.

There are many traditions and beliefs bound up in the rites of death and burial, and many protective measures were undertaken before, during and after the funeral to protect the living from the spirits of the deceased. It is possible that the straight funeral route was deliberately avoided so as to confuse the spirit of the dead person if it tried to return home, as spirits were believed to prefer travel in straight lines. The belief in straight spirit travel occurs throughout the world.

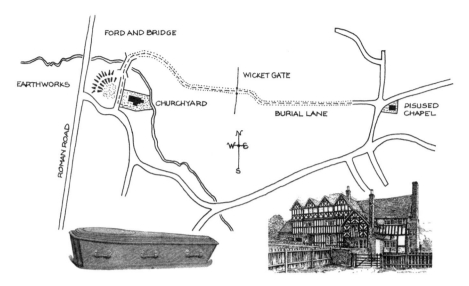

Above: The last journey. Burial Lane at Feckenham, Worcestershire.
One of thousands of abandoned dedicated funeral paths across Europe.

SPIRIT PATHS & GHOST ROADS
the universal concept of straight spirit flight

The belief in straight spirit travel is global. German death roads may not have been straight, but *Geisterwege* 'ghost roads' most certainly are.

German folklore records that ghost roads always run straight over mountains and valleys and through marshes and start and end at cemeteries. Elsewhere in Germany tradition recalls other straight spirit paths such as the *Leichenflugbahn* or 'Flightpath of the Corpses' in East Prussia, where on certain nights the dead from the cemeteries situated at each end of the line travel to visit one other. Houses built on the line regularly suffer damage on the nights when the spirits fly.

Halfway across the world in Columbia the Kogi Indians, descendants of the extinct Tairona culture, tend the ruins of great cities in the jungle reaches of Santa Marta. Straight stone causeways link the cities as do other invisible spirit roads (*below*). The Kogi shamans when in trance regularly travel along these invisible routes. Their courses are preserved in the linear markings on a standing stone in one of their villages.

Upper: *The paths of Chuckchee shamen during fly-agaric hallucinations (from Wasson 1971). Lower: A Chuckchee map of the journey of a human soul to the spirit world.*

SUPERNATURAL HIGHWAYS
linear hauntings and apparitions

An explanation for some leys might be the spirit path, as ghostly linear journeys are common in folklore. Examples include the wandering ghostly monk who makes regular journeys between a church and a haunted house, phantom coaches that speed along sections of old road at night, or spectral funeral processions taking the same route to a churchyard year after year. Sometimes these spirit paths have a physical counterpart, by way of an old paved track, or can be successfully plotted on the map to show their straightness.

In many parts of Britain ghostly Black Dogs haunt stretches of old highways, often immortalised in pub names. Before the war Theo Brown plotted Black Dogs sightings in Devon and Cornwall on the map and found that straight lines could be drawn through many of them.

Today mysterious Black Cats are more often seen.

Opposite: A spectral Black Dog that takes the straight path (from a 1577 pamphlet);
A classic phantom coach (note the absence of the horses' heads); Mystery Black Cat.
Above: Headless Horseman, from Washington Irving's Legend of Sleepy Hollow, *1820.*

WHAT IS A LEY LINE?
an introduction to examples which follow

The following pages describe and list alignments of the types discussed in this section. Included are some of Alfred Watkins' own discovered leys, some of a similar nature that have been found by modern ley hunters inspired by Watkins' vision, astronomical alignments, acknowledged prehistoric alignments of sites and stones, sacred pathways, funeral routes, death roads and spirit paths.

All of the alignments given here have at one time or another come under the heading of 'ley lines'. From these lists it is clear that there is no one single type of landscape line that can definitively be called a ley, but these examples demonstrate mankind's continual obsession with the straight line or path in the landscape.

Examples have been selected that take in some of the more famous prehistoric sites. Others have been picked for those who enjoy combining their interest in megalithic sites with walking in the country, including examples from Ireland, France, Belgium and Holland.

What is a ley line? Is it the paths of disembodied spirits, travelling dead straight between places they lived and died and loved and maybe even further afield?

What is a ley line? Is it maybe an geological electromagnetic effect or a telluric current of mysterious Earth energies running between between sacred sites.

What is a ley line? Is it an alignment to the Sun on a special day of the year, or an alignment to the Moon, at its extreme rising or setting, extended across the landscape?

What is a ley line? Is it just an alignment between a handful of interesting sites, maybe recording an old track road, animal path or trade route? Pictures by Ulrich Magin.

A Holy Hill Alignment
Wilmington Ley, Sussex, England

Looking for illustrations of ancient surveyors Alfred Watkins seized upon the antique chalk hill figure of the Long Man of Wilmington. It is fitting therefore that the Long Man should lie on a ley.

The first ley marker is the 12th century St. Mary's and St. Peter's church in the village of Wilmington, Sussex. Legend says it is connected by a tunnel to the crypt of the next ley point, the Norman Wilmington Priory (*shown below*). Legends of tunnels often occur on leys. The third marker is the "Long Man" (*see below and opposite*). The top of the hill on which the Long Man lies is marked by the fourth point, Windover Hill round barrow, 135ft in diameter. The line can be extended further north where it crosses a hard-to-find Bronze Age bowl barrow. Many leys start or end at a prominent hill.

Above: Watkins adopted the chalk hill figure of the Long Man of Wilmington as his Stone Age ley surveyor, or Dodman (picture by Eric Ravilious). The figure is a 237ft long, featureless outline of a human figure holding a long staff in each hand (Watkins' surveyor's staffs); the date of the figure is uncertain, but it is possibly pre-Roman. Left: Figure from the Torslunda Plaque, Sweden, c.700 AD, showing a figure carrying two spears, possibly another early surveyor named Dod.

Church Leys in Oxford
the axes of the town defined

In *The Old Straight Track* Alfred Watkins draws attention to the alignments of churches in some of Britain's old cities, notably Hereford, Bristol, Oxford and London.

In Oxford two church leys cross at St Martin's Carfax at the centre of the city and in fact define the two main axes of Oxford, Queen Street - Carfax - High Street and Magdalen Street - Cornmarket Street - St. Aldate Street, running approximately north-south and east-west.

The north-south line includes St. Giles (*a*), St. Mary Magdalen (*b*), St. Michael's (*c*), St. Martin's Carfax (*d*), St. Aldate (*e*) and crosses the Thames at 'Oskna Ford', now Folly Bridge (*4*).

The east-west line links St. Peter's in the Castle (h) (now demolished), St. Martin's Carfax (d), All Saints (g) and St. Mary the Virgin (f). St. Martin's Carfax lies on the highest part of the old city and was once the assembly point for council, justice and commerce.

The streets that follow these two lines deviate to avoid the churches in a manner noticed by Watkins in many other leys.

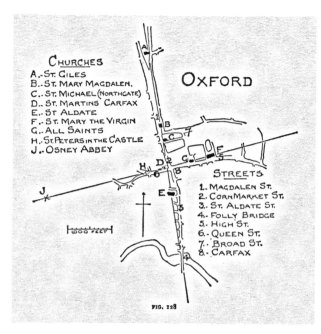

CHURCHES
A.- ST. GILES
B.- ST. MARY MAGDALEN.
C.- ST. MICHAEL (NORTHGATE)
D.- ST. MARTINS CARFAX
E.- ST ALDATE
F.- ST. MARY THE VIRGIN
G.- ALL SAINTS
H.- ST. PETERS IN THE CASTLE
J.- OSNEY ABBEY

OXFORD

STREETS
1. MAGDALEN ST.
2. CORNMARKET ST.
3. ST. ALDATE ST.
4. FOLLY BRIDGE
5. HIGH ST.
6. QUEEN ST.
7. BROAD ST.
8. CARFAX

1000 FEET

FIG. 128

Left: Alfred Watkins' own map of the medieval church alignments in the city of Oxford. Two ancient ley lines may have informed the positions of no less than seventen churches. Did these leys even define the street pattern of Oxford?

Facing page: The ruins of Osney Abbey, the westernmost point along the East-West ley line.

Below: 18th century view of the city of Oxford.

A SCOTTISH ROYAL LEY
a line of kings, Argyllshire, Scotland

The Kilmartin valley, in Argyllshire, Scotland, is home to an extraordinary concentration of prehistoric monuments dating from 4000 to 1200 BC. The dominant feature of Kilmartin is a straight line of burial cairns that follows the contour of the valley. The sites include an unnamed cairn north of Crinian Moss, the small and denuded Rowanfield cist (whose axis points along the ley), Ri Cruin or the King's Circle, a well preserved prehistoric tomb dating from 4000 BC containing three chambers and carved stones, a standing stone incised with cup and ring marks, Nether Largie South chambered cairn, 130ft in diameter and dating from 3500 BC and the tomb of a king or queen, the site of a chambered cairn destroyed at the turn of the century, and two more royal tombs, Nether Largie mid-Cairn, 100ft across, and Nether Largie North, dating from 3000 BC. The final tomb on the line is Glebe Cairn, once the tallest on the line. If projected further north the ley passes through the hill fort of Dun na Nighinn and terminates at the hill fort and natural pyramidal peak of Dun Chonnalaich.

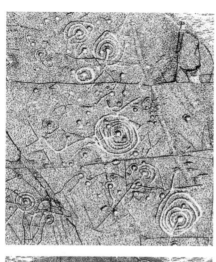

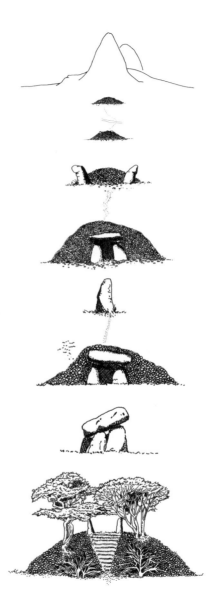

Above: The Kilmartin Valley has one of the highest concentrations of ancient rock art in the world. Right: The royal burial mounds of the Kilmartin valley trace a straight line of eleven sites that lead to a sacred mountain peak. Left: Temple Wood stone circle, also in the Kilmartin Valley.

A SUNRISE LINE
Stonehenge, Wiltshire, England

Perhaps the most famous of all ancient astronomical alignments is the summer solstice alignment at Stonehenge, Wiltshire (*see too page 266*).

On the longest day of the year, when viewed from the centre of the monument, the sun can be seen rising over the outlying Heel Stone between the massive uprights that form the central ring. The earth-banked Avenue that leads away from Stonehenge is aligned in the same direction for several hundred yards.

The antiquary William Stukeley first noted this strange phenomenon in 1740 when he wrote that the axis of Stonehenge and the Avenue is directed to the north-east 'whereabouts the sun rises when the days are longest'.

Alfred Watkins noted in *The Old Straight Track* that the alignment also passes through two Bronze Age barrows to the southwest of Stonehenge. Stukeley noted another barrow once visible on the skyline on Haradon Hill and lining up with the Avenue marking the point on the horizon where the summer solstice sun would rise.

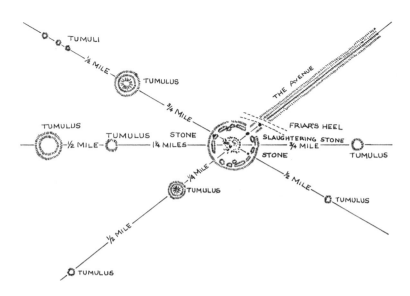

TUMULI

½ MILE

TUMULUS

¾ MILE

THE AVENUE

TUMULUS   TUMULUS   STONE   FRIAR'S HEEL
½ MILE   ¼ MILES   SLAUGHTERING STONE   ¾ MILE
                                         STONE   TUMULUS

¼ MILE   ½ MILE
                                           TUMULUS
TUMULUS

½ MILE

TUMULUS

Above: Alignments around Stonehenge (after Alfred Watkins). Below: The Avenue pointing away from Stonehenge to a barrow on the distant Haradon Hill that marks the summer solstice sunrise.

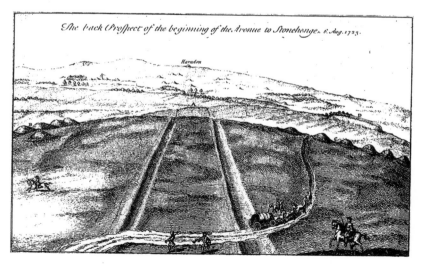

The back Prospect of the beginning of the Avenue to Stonehenge. 8. Aug. 1723.

Haradon

ORCADIAN LEYS
Orkney, Scotland

Orkney is famous for its fine collection of megalithic monuments: the Ring of Brodgar henge and circle of stones, the Stones of Stennes (*below*), the remains of another henge and stone circle, and the vast chambered mound of Maes Howe.

The latter has its passage oriented directly to the point on the horizon where the midwinter sun sets. To reinforce this alignment a standing stone was erected over 900 yards away at Barnhouse as a foresight. Magnus Spence, an Orcadian school-master, first noted this and other solar alignments in 1894.

A line linking the Watchstone, an 18ft high monolith and Maes Howe points to the equinox sunrise. These alignments can be clearly seen both on the map and on the ground.

Alignments upon the Ring of Brodgar point to hills where fires were once lit to mark the Celtic festivals of Beltane (1st May) and Samhain (1st Nov). Alexander Thom, who surveyed the sites in the 1970s, found alignments to the moon from the Ring of Brodgar.

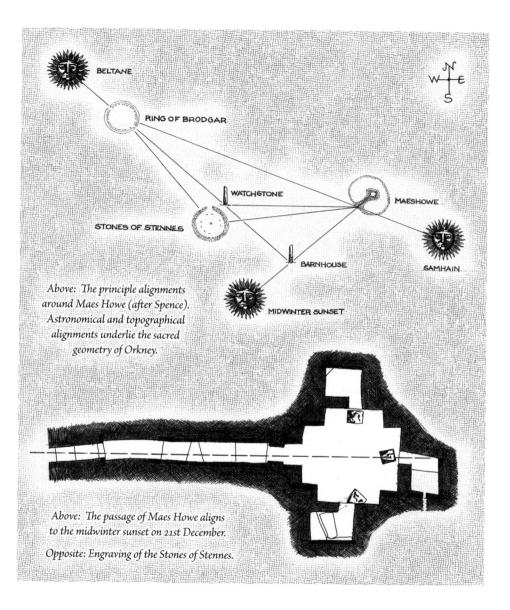

BELTANE

N

W E

S

RING OF BRODGAR

WATCHSTONE

MAESHOWE

STONES OF STENNES

BARNHOUSE

SAMHAIN

Above: The principle alignments around Maes Howe (after Spence). Astronomical and topographical alignments underlie the sacred geometry of Orkney.

MIDWINTER SUNSET

Above: The passage of Maes Howe aligns to the midwinter sunset on 21st December.

Opposite: Engraving of the Stones of Stennes.

THE KENNET AVENUE
Avebury, Wiltshire, England

When the antiquary William Stukeley wrote about the Avebury megaliths in the 18th century he interpreted the complex of huge standing stones as a gigantic serpent temple; the now lost Beckhampton avenue being the tail, the henge and the stone circles its coiled body, and the Kennet Avenue and the Sanctuary on Overton Hill, the neck and head. Since these fanciful interpretations, writers and archaeologists have referred to the remaining Kennet Avenue as 'sinuous'. It is not. Close inspection reveals that the two parallel lines of megaliths were built in discrete and straight sections over a long period of time. Furthermore, votive offerings and human burials were placed at the points where the avenue changes direction and alongside the outer edges, thus confirming a connection between the lines and death rituals.

The avenue today is largely a restoration and consists of two lines of evocatively shaped megaliths that define a sacred pathway between the Sanctuary and the Avebury henge. Archaeological investigations have revealed that people walked along the outsides of the avenue and not between the rows of stones. Was that route perhaps preserved for the spirits of the dead?

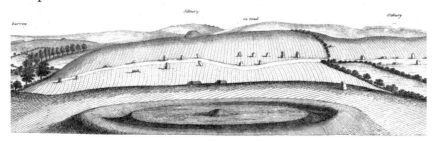

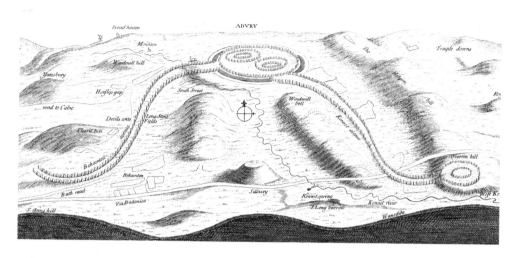

Three of William Stukeley's engravings of Avebury from 1743. Facing page: A side view of the eastern Kennet Avenue. Above: The full Avebury temple as envisaged by Stukeley. Below: The great stones where the Kennet Avenue meets the outer circle.

PATHWAY TO THE SUN
Warwickshire and Worcestershire, England

A Warwickshire legend tells of a burial path that once existed over Brailes Hill. The path was said to run for 23 miles to Bredon Hill in neighbouring Worcestershire - a long way for a funeral!

An alignment of sites runs from Brailes to Bredon Hill that might be the origin of the burial path legend. It runs due west from Castle Hill in Brailes, a reshaped natural hill that may have been a Norman castle, over Dover's Hill, the possible site of a turf maze, through Saintbury cross, a crossroads at Hinton Cross, an earthwork at Elmley Castle, and onto the Banbury Stone, an elephantine shaped mass of rock at the edge of an Iron Age hill fort on Bredon Hill.

Projected westwards the line bisects the grand Iron Age British Camp on the Malvern ridge (*shown opposite*) where it marks the position of the equinoctial sunset on March 21st and Sept 21st.

The burial path referred to in the legend may be the ancient pilgrim's trackway, now marked by roads and public footpaths, that snakes around the course of the alignment passing burial places along its route and skirting the lower slopes of Brailes Hill on its way to Bredon.

A second interesting ley crosses this first one at Bredon Hill. It runs from 7th century Pershore Abbey, through the corpse route of 11th century Elmley Castle's church of St Mary, across Bredon Hill's Iron Age hill fort, through Beckford's Saxon church of St John, through Little Washbourne's ancient manor house and 12th century church, before ending at Winchcombe Abbey (founded in the 8th century).

Facing page: The Iron Age terraces of British Camp, at the centre of the line of the Malvern Hills

EHNEW

BOYNE VALLEY LEYS
County Meath, Ireland

Three enormous Neolithic chambered mounds, Newgrange, Knowth and Dowth, dominate the Boyne valley in Co Meath, Ireland. Newgrange contains a passage and central chamber which is illuminated by the midwinter rising sun, Knowth has two passages aligned directly east and west and Dowth has two passages, one of which is aligned directly on Newgrange. The Dowth alignment is augmented by two of the standing stones in the circle surrounding the Newgrange mound, which lie exactly on the alignment. In a similar fashion, two more of the stones in the circle fall on a line drawn through an outlying burial mound, Newgrange and Knowth.

Both leys cross at a stone in the central chamber of Newgrange that archaeologists have designated R21, and from this stone lines run to each of the surrounding stones in the circle pointing to astronomical and topographical features. R21 also aligns with the engraved kerb stone at the entrance to Newgrange and a kerb stone at the rear. Both are marked with straight vertical grooves which align with the passage and the midwinter sunrise.

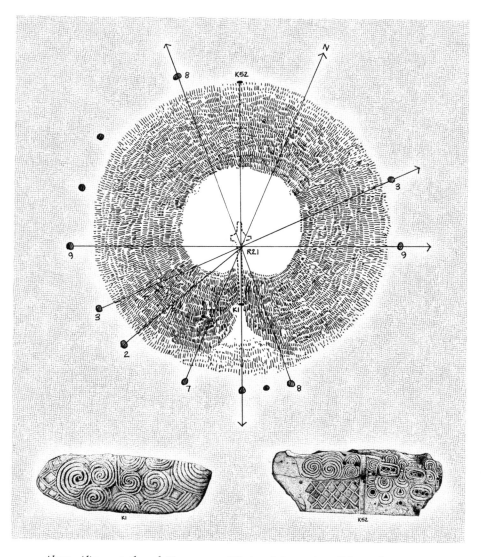

*Above: Alignments through Newgrange. 1. Winter solstice sunrise. 2. Winter solstice sunset.
3. Summer solstice sunrise. 7. North-south meridian. 8. To Knowth. 9. To Dowth.*

YORK MINSTER LEY
York, England

Situated within the city walls of York is a medieval church ley. This alignment is spectacularly visible from the tower of York Minster.

The best way to walk the ley is from its starting point, a spit of land between the Foss and Ouse rivers, which was once Templar land. The ley passes through the site of St. George's chapel, a Templar building, the Norman castle, Clifford's Tower, with its 11th century chapel, the spired church of St. Mary's, dating from the 11th century (now York Heritage Centre), and on to the 15th century All Saints Pavement, a church built on the site of earlier 11th and 7th century churches. All Saints is the oldest church on the line and sits at the crossroads at the centre of the city.

The next sites along the line are the 14th century St. Samson's church, now a Senior Citizen's Centre and the Minster itself, St. Peter's cathedral. The ley passes directly below the 11th century tower at the crossing of the nave and transepts.

The line terminates at the 13th century Archbishop's Palace chapel, but is inaccessible to the public.

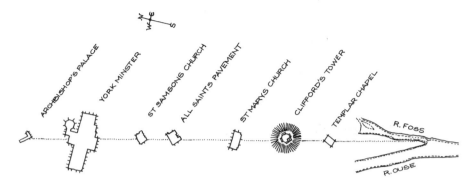

Above: An alignment of seven key medieval ecclesiastical buildings in York terminates at its south end on an important spit of land between the rivers Foss and Ouse, a geomantic arrangement reminiscent of ancient Chinese Feng Shui practices.

Above: York Minster rises above the roofs of moonlit medieval York. Although the E-W axis of the Minster does not conform to the ley, various features inside demonstrate awareness of it.

THE FAIRY STEPS
Cumbria, England

Supernatural encounters are often reported on the corpse road from Arndale to Beetham church in Cumbria. The path, which consists of a series of straight sections, follows a dead straight course from Hazelslack Tower Farm, named after the ruined stone fortress that still stands on the farm, to the Fairy Steps. At Whin Scar the straight corpse road is forced to make a series of dog-leg turns as it ascends the scar in two flights of stone steps. The second flight is known locally as the Fairy Steps and is an impossibly steep rock-cut stairway at the bottom of a very narrow gully. The idea that pall-bearers could manoeuvre a coffin up this cleft is hard to credit. It is at the Fairy Steps where tradition has it that your wish will be granted by the fairies if you can skip up the stairway without touching the sides. The author has attempted this feat without success. In places the cleft is as narrow as a foot at shoulder height. Those with the second sight are believed to be able to witness the fairy folk skipping up the steps.

Above: Corpse cross at Lamplugh, beside a Cumbrian corpse road. Left: The Fairy Steps in Cumbria. Below: The Lodore Falls, site of more Cumbrian fairies. Opposite: Fairies in the wind, by Arthur Rackham.

The Menhirs of Carnac
Brittany, France

The best known of the Breton megalithic sites are the multiple lines of huge standing stones near the village of Carnac in southern Brittany, some dated to 4000BC. The largest group of stone rows is at Kermario.

The cromlechs that stood at both ends of the long rows are now gone but a restored passage mound still stands in line with the southernmost stone row. Cromlechs are spacious rings of close-set standing stones that were probably used for open air rituals connected with death and burial.

The next largest group, at Le Menec, has twelve roughly parallel stone rows running between two egg-shaped cromlechs (*see opposite*).

The Kerlescan rows (*shown below*), north of Carnac, also run to a cromlech. At the western end, alongside the cromlech there is a *tertre tumulaire*, a rectangular burial mound. Kermario means 'place of the dead' and Kerlescan means 'place of burning', an indication of activities that once may have taken place at the ends.

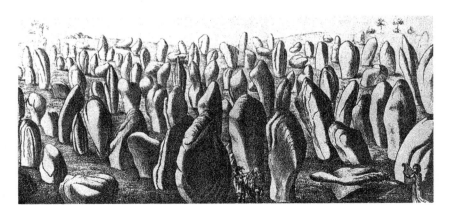

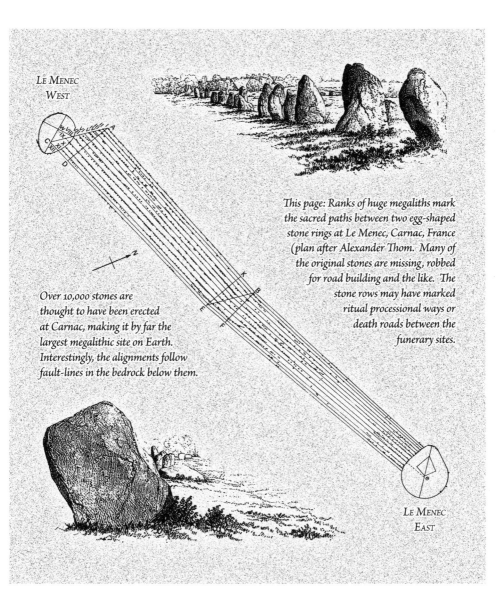

LE MENEC
WEST

Over 10,000 stones are
thought to have been erected
at Carnac, making it by far the
largest megalithic site on Earth.
Interestingly, the alignments follow
fault-lines in the bedrock below them.

This page: Ranks of huge megaliths mark
the sacred paths between two egg-shaped
stone rings at Le Menec, Carnac, France
(plan after Alexander Thom. Many of
the original stones are missing, robbed
for road building and the like. The
stone rows may have marked
ritual processional ways or
death roads between the
funerary sites.

LE MENEC
EAST

THE STONEHENGE CURSUS LEY
a prehistoric funeral route

The Stonehenge Cursus is a two-mile long rectangular earthen ditched enclosure that lies about half a mile north of Stonehenge itself. The antiquary William Stukeley first noticed it in 1723 when he interpreted it as a Roman racecourse, hence 'cursus'. The Stonehenge Cursus links a group of round barrows at its western end to a long barrow at its eastern extremity. Alfred Watkins first noted that a line drawn along the straight northern ditch passes through the Cuckoo Stone to the east, a standing stone not marked on the 1:50 000 map (*see below*).

Excavations by Mrs Cunnington, in the 1930s, revealed the circular henge monument now called Woodhenge, through which to his delight Watkins was able to extend his ley. This alignment was later given archaeological credence in 1947. The links between straightness and the dead at the Stonehenge Cursus are very persuasive and indeed the Woodhenge excavations revealed the body of a child who had apparently been sacrificed and buried at the centre of the henge. The line can be extended further east to where it strikes the horizon at Beacon Hill, thus finding its Watkinsian terminal point.

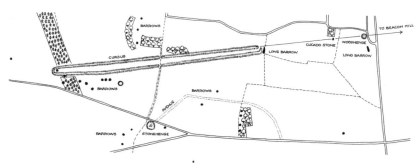

Above: The enigmatic Stonehenge cursus points to the Cuckoo Stone and the centre of Woodhenge.

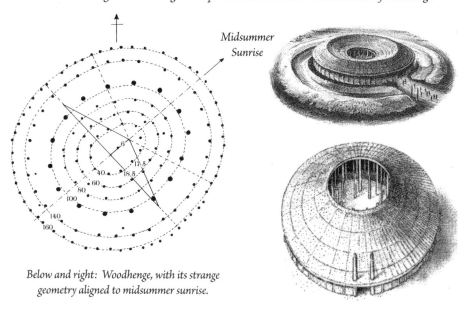

Midsummer
Sunrise

*Below and right: Woodhenge, with its strange
geometry aligned to midsummer sunrise.*

A BELGIAN ALIGNMENT
Wéris, Belgium

This is an alignment of contemporary megalithic monuments that is acknowledged by Belgian archaeologists as deliberate and planned.

Two miles outside the town of Erezée at Bohaimont at Oppagne stands a group of three menhirs, which were re-erected in 1906. The tallest stone is 8ft tall. The line is at right angles to the alignment, which leads northwards to a half-buried allée-couverte (or passage grave) near Wénin. The next site on the line is a 12ft tall menhir built into a wall at the side of the road. Over half a mile further on the line passes over the Dolmen de Wéris (*opposite*), a major dolmen over 36ft long with a huge capstone. Both dolmens are orientated upon the alignment. Further along the line to the north are the remains of fallen menhirs, broken up at the end of the 19th century. These may have formed another line like the Oppagne group marking the end of the alignment.

3. MENHIRS, OPPAGNE

*Above: Megaliths on the Wéris alignment. Upper: The ruined dolmen at Wéris. Lower:
Three menhirs at Oppagne. Etchings by John Palmer. Opposite: Stones at Weris.*

THREE DUTCH DEATH ROADS
Hilversum, Netherlands

Straight medieval *doodwegen*, or death roads, are still visible in parts of the Netherlands. They were built for the specific purpose of carrying the dead to burial, and their specification and upkeep were the subject of decrees and periodic inspections. Medieval laws forbade the transportation of corpses on other types of road.

This splendid example comes from Westerheide, a heath between Laren and Hilversum, in north Holland, an area dotted with Bronze Age barrows. Three dead straight doodwegen converge on the isolated St. Janskerhof (St. John's cemetery). The three roads are equally spaced forming a triangle pointing at the chapel of St. John. The present day chapel is only a century old, but it replaced an earlier building said to date from the 1600's or earlier.

The death road from the village of ës-Graveland is believed to have been laid out in 1643. The other two, from the villages of Bussum and Ankerveen, are of uncertain date but are believed to be older. They are not Roman roads as they lie outside the boundaries of the Roman occupation of the Low Countries.

Leys are a complex and many-faceted subject. I hope by now you've at least started to get a sense of the beast that they are, by following the examples covered in the pages. I heartily suggest you get out and walk some, or get your map out and find some more. Happy ley hunting!

Opposite: Three dead straight doodwgen on the barrow-studded heath of Westerheide.
all aim in on the isolated churchyard of St. Janskerhof, St. John's chapel and cemetary.

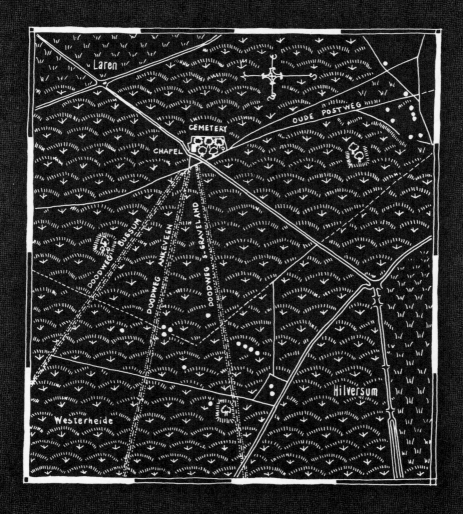

Laren

Oude Postweg

CEMETERY

CHAPEL

DOODWEG—O-BUSSUM

DOODWEG ANKEVEEN

DOODWEG S-GRAVELAND

Hilversum

Westerheide

BOOK VI

To save a Mayd St. George the dragon slew,
A pretty tale if all is told be true.
Most say there are no dragons, and tis sayd
There was no George; pray God there was a mayd.

A LITTLE HISTORY OF
DRAGONS

Joyce Hargreaves

"His horns resemble those of a stag, his head that of a camel, his eyes those of a demon, his neck that of a snake, his belly that of a clam, his scales those of a carp, his claws those of an eagle, his soles those of a tiger and his ears those of a cow."
Wang Fu, Han dynasty, describing the nine features of the Lung Dragon

INTRODUCTION

The Dragon is the most nebulous, complex and ambivalent of all the animals that inhabit the jungle of the imagination. This fabulous creature, the symbol of the geomancer's art, has been the subject of myth and traveller's tales for the last 4000 years. Although it has never been seen apart from its snake incarnations, its image has been used in religion, alchemy, heraldry and medicine (to name but a few of its aspects), throughout all cultures and histories of the world, primitive, classical, medieval and oriental.

A dragon can primarily be considered to be a symbol of the many different aspects of the powers of the Earth, both good and bad. When associated with water, it may represent the fertility of the soil, or herald floods and drought. It can also be seen as a sign of the heat within the Earth—appearing in mythology as Typhon, the son of mother Earth, the fire-breathing dragon representing the volcano.

Sites of ancient dragon legends, hills, caves, mounds and lakes are often taken over by later religions and depictions of the dragon still linger in places where they are least expected, like Christian churches.

A pagan dragon can be found in a number of churches with foliage sprouting from its mouth, denoting fertility. Perhaps too the dragon-slayer is equally pagan in concept, and descends from the Green Man and other fertility deities, pressuring the dragon via the spear into releasing its generative forces of nature.

This little book will probably not answer all your questions about dragons, but will, I hope, introduce you to some of the more amazing ideas that surround them.

WHAT IS A DRAGON?

a wingless flying serpent

Early naturalists believed that the dragon was a real animal—often maps of foreign countries were inscribed with the words "here be dragons", usually on areas of unexplored wilderness, and books like the 17th century *Historie of foure-footed Beastes* by Edward Topsell showed depictions of dragons next to reptiles such as lizards and snakes. Today, with our ability to visit nearly every part of the world, we can be almost certain that the dragon, in the general form that we visualise it, does not physically exist anywhere on Earth.

A modern description of a dragon might be that it has four legs, a long snakelike body with a barbed tail, a fierce wyvern's head, bat's wings, sharp claws and teeth, and emits fire from its mouth. However, in earlier times the dragon and serpent shapes were completely interchangeable.

The words *Drakon* and *Draco* were used throughout the Greek and Roman Empires to describe a large snake, and the word 'Dragon' is derived from both of these names. Drakon not only referred to a large snake but also to a flying creature (although, like most Chinese dragons, it mysteriously did not need wings to achieve flight). Classical and earlier texts make little distinction between legless serpents and dragons.

Above: *The dragon's legendary strength and bravery were possibly the reason why Alexander the Great was said to have been fathered by one.*

Opposite: *A winged dragon and serpent from Edward Topsell's 17th century classic treatise* A Historie of Foure-Footed Beastes.

TIAMAT
in the beginning

The account of the creation epic *Enuma Elish* (the Babylonian genesis) was discovered in the form of a long poem on seven tablets excavated at Ninevah in Iraq. The inscriptions date from the 2nd millennium BC, and, when translated, revealed the story of the dragoness Tiamat.

The tablets tell how in the beginning there was nothing but two elements: *Apsu*, the spirit of fresh water, and *Tiamat*, the spirit of salt water and chaos, portrayed as a dragoness with a serpentine body, horns, and a long tail. In the myth Tiamat gives birth to many children, the Gods, who kill their father to prevent him from destroying them. Their mother's rage at this act leads her to make war against her brood and she spawns eleven monsters; the viper, shark, scorpion man, storm demon, great lion, dragon, mad dog and four nameless ones.

The God Marduk then agrees to fight Tiamat. Armed with a bow and arrows, lightning and a net of four winds, he advances upon his enemy, and after an epic struggle manages to catch Tiamat in his net and drive an evil wind into her mouth, rendering her powerless and destroying her life. He divides Tiamat's body into two parts which become the upper and lower firmaments (the earth and sky)—the Babylonian world order.

Tiamat thus symbolises primeval chaos, water and darkness.

Opposite: Marduk and Dragon. Above, top: The imperfect fusion of the traditions of Babylonian and Egyptian mythology created Tiamat, seen here fighting Marduk (drawing based on a design from the second millennium BC). Lower, above: Head of Tiamat, and scorpion man from a Babylonian boundary stone.

Yggdrasil's Dragons

at the root of the world tree

In Old Norse tradition, the ash tree Yggdrasil, Cosmic Tree of Life, stands at 'the still point of the turning world' supporting the universe. Its branches overhang all the worlds and reach far into the heavens. The three great roots at the base of the tree descend into a tripartite underworld—one twisting towards the frost giants, another reaching the judgement seats of the Aesir, and the third standing over Niflheim where Hel reigns. Underneath Hel's domain dwells the dragon Nidhogg 'The Dread Biter', gnawing at the root from below, attempting to destroy the universe. While Nidhogg is the evil threatening the universe, the Midgard (or Jornungand) Worm is the bane afflicting the Earth, lying in the seas encircling the land with its tail in its mouth, creating and regurgitating the oceans of the world. The legend tells that if its tail is ever wrenched out of its mouth, then calamity will befall the Earth.

In the legend the hot-tempered, red-headed, weather-God Thor decides to smite Midgard's worm with his fearsome hammer. He persuades the giant Hymir to take him fishing and, by baiting his strong fishing line with a succulent ox head, succeeds in hooking his prey.

> *"I can tell you this for certain: nobody ever saw a more blood-freezing sight than Thor did, as his eyes goggled down at the serpent and the great worm from below blew a cloud of poison. At that, they say the giant Hymir blenched, then turned yellow in his terror what with the sea swishing into the boat and out of the boat! But Thor grabbed his hammer and flung it above his head just as Hymir fumbled for the knife he used for chopping bait and hacked Thor's fishing rod overboard! The serpent sank down into the depths of the sea".* Snorri Sturluson [1178–1241].

Thor, mortified at his failure, thumps Hymir, who falls into the sea.

The Tree of Life with the Midgard worm circling the Earth. Frontispiece from Northern Antiques, *1847. After Thor's first failed attempt to slay Midguard Worm, the two of them eventually kill each other at Ragnarok, the 'Doom of the Gods'.*

THE SIGN OF THE GODDESS
coils and cunning curves

From the earliest times, dragons in the West have been connected with the feminine. In early Mediterranean art, the Mother Goddess is often shown in the company of a serpentine dragon. A cylinder seal from the Tigris Euphrates valley, inhabited in 4000 BC by the Sumerians, shows the great Goddess Bau on the left of the tree of life, while behind her rears a great serpent dragon representing her lifegiving powers.

In the Pelasgian myth of creation, the universal Goddess Eurynome creates the great serpent Ophion as her mate. Eurynome soon becomes pregnant and gives birth to the 'Universal Egg'. Ophion coils around the egg until it hatches and out falls everything in the Universe from the sun to the smallest ant. But Ophion grows vainglorious and boasts that it is he who is the author of the whole of creation. This enrages Eurynome who hits him over the head with the heel of her shoe, kicks out his teeth and throws him into the dark caves beneath the earth.

In Egyptian hieroglyphics the term 'goddess' is expressed by the image of a cobra, and the Egyptian Goddess Neith is portrayed as a great golden cobra. Later statuettes of Cretian Goddesses found in the temple of Minos show them holding sacred adders in their hands. Like the Great Goddess these can cause both terror and swift death.

Opposite page: Ophion coiled around the egg.
Left: Babylonian Boundary Stone 1120BC.
Above: Sumerian figure holding two snakes.
Below: Cretian Goddess holding two adders.

THE NAGA
watery serpent spirits

Nagas are the semi-divine, semi-human serpent spirits of Indian origin who are known throughout South East Asia. The Naga King Mucalinda is reputed to have sheltered the meditating Buddha from chilling winds and rain for seven days, protecting him with his hoods and coils. Another legend holds that the king of Ancient Cambodia married a reptilian Naga princess from a huge Pacific kingdom, from whom we are all descended. Nagas and the female Naginis are depicted in three different ways: completely serpentine; human with serpents emerging from the back of the neck; and half human-half serpent.

Their natures are also threefold: animal, human and divine. Dwelling in springs, lakes and rivers, Nagas control all waters, from clouds, rain and fertility to floods and droughts.

Mahayanists divide Nagas into four groups: *Divine Nagas* who produce clouds and rain; *Earthly Nagas* whose duty it is to make sure that all outlets are open and that rivers are running freely; *Hidden Nagas* who guard the treasures of the world; and *Heavenly Guardian Nagas* who, as 'Guardians of the Threshold' protect the heavenly palace and the temples of many major and minor deities. Guardian Nagas are often portrayed as coiled serpents with human heads, protecting the mysterious sacred pearl of divine wisdom at the centre of their coils.

Opposite left & above left: Garuda, Vishnu's mount, eloping with enemy Naga Kanya; a happy Naga couple with entwined tails; both from Halebidu, India, c 1100 AD. Above right: Fu-Hsi, the ruler of the mythical third age of China [2852-2738 BC], and his consort Nu Kua were reputedly both Nagas. They are portrayed with their tails entwined in a fourfold pattern. Fu-Hsi holds a compass and Nu Kua a plumb line and a set square - measuring implements to create order out of chaos. Right: A Nagini stone relief from Gondwana, India.

CHINESE & JAPANESE DRAGONS
important invisible families

Ancient Chinese writers describe four types of dragon: the *Tian-Lung* (Celestial Dragon), who guards the dwellings of the gods; the *Fucang-Lung* (Dragon of Hidden Treasures), who guards the hidden wealth of the Earth; the popular *Shen-Lung* (Spiritual Dragon) who controls the rain and winds and whose five-toed Imperial image the Emperor alone was permitted to wear; and the celebrated *Ti-Lung* (Earth Dragon) who holds the rivers and streams in its power.

There are nine major types of Chinese dragon, including the *Ying-Lung* (Winged Dragon), *Jiao-Lung* (Horned Dragon), *Pan-Lung* (Coiling Dragon), *Huang-Lung* (Yellow Dragon) and various others (*see appendix, page 399*). In addition there are nine *Dragon Children* which adorn many Chinese structures (*see page 332-3*). The number nine is considered especially lucky in China. Dragons have nine attributes and 117 scales, 81 of them male ($3^2 \times 3^2$) and 36 female ($3^2 \times 2^2$). Chinese dragons are all associated with the masculine Yang force (the phoenix symbolises Yin).

Chinese and Korean Imperial dragons have five toes on each foot, all other dragons have four toes, but Indonesian and Japanese dragons have three, possibly after the earlier Chinese three-clawed Han style.

Japanese dragons include the *Ryu* which is a large dragon with no wings, and the *Tatsu* native Japanese dragon which is smaller but has large wings. In Japanese art the dragon is never wholly visible, instead appearing partially hidden in the swirling winds or waves it represents.

i.

ii.

Opposite page: Jade dragon ornament;
a dragon carp; the only winged Chinese
dragon is the Proper Conduct Dragon;
and a dragon pot decoration.
This page: i. Tatsu; ii. Hai Ryio,
Japanese bird dragon; iii. Shen Lung;
iv. The dragon king, Lung Wang.

iii.

vi.

FENG SHUI & THE AZURE DRAGON
dragons in the landscape

The 2,500 year-old Chinese art of *Feng Shui*, or 'wind and water', is used to select an auspicious site and design for a building, where the Earth's 'vital spirit' or 'cosmic breath' (*ch'i* in Chinese) is balanced.

The topography of the landscape, its mountains, waterways and valleys, have all been formed by wind and water; it, in turn, affects the local flow of these powerful forces. Four symbolic animals are used:

A hill resembling a huge *Black Turtle* should lie to the north, to the south the *Red Phoenix* suggests open vistas, sunshine and water. In the east the *Azure Dragon* (*shown with the Phoenix below*) rules jagged rocks like a huge spine, while the *White Tiger* in the west prefers low, round smooth rocks. As the Azure Dragon is Yang and male, so too are mountains, large rocks, steep waterfalls and ancient pines. The White Tiger represents Yin, the female principle, ruling low-lying places, valleys and damp spots.

Above: Feng Shui Dragon by Chow Hon Lam. A diviner of Feng Shui will study the raised portions of the land, the veins of the dragon, in relation to the valleys, and note auspicious places where there is a harmonious balance of Yin and Yang. The ideal site, or Dragon's Head, is best found beside a hill which rises to the east, northeast or southeast, with one precipitous face and the other sloping gently down to a valley to the south. In general the most favourable position for a structure exists when, looking out over a sparkling stream or slowly meandering river, the hills of the Azure Dragon are positioned to the left and a mountain supports your back.

DRAGONS OF THE AMERICAS
jewelled watery lightning serpents

The dragons of the North American Indians are more serpentine in shape than many of their European counterparts. They have a snake-like body and are nearly always portrayed with a horn or two, or a jewel, growing out of the tops of their heads. Large and immensely powerful, these serpents are again regarded as water deities and, like Chinese dragons, live mainly in lakes and rivers, creating storms and lightning.

In many North American myths, from Mexico to Alaska, the path of lightning marks the swift darting of lightning snakes, and, also during storms, feathered reptiles (*sisiutl*, *haietlik* or sea wolves) rise out of rivers. These are depicted on masks worn by the Indians for ceremonial dances, symbolising the fertility associated with rain and lightning.

The feathered serpent also appears widely throughout ancient South America—as the central Aztec deity Quetzalcoatl (literally 'quetzal-bird snake'), known to the Maya as Kukulkan, and in 3,000 year-old Olmec representations. As the magical morning star, Venus, Quetzalcoatl emerges from the mouth of the earthbound feathered serpent. The inventor of the calendar, he is also, like the Chinese Yellow Dragon, credited with bringing the art of writing to mankind.

Note the wind and water combination of feathers and serpent.

Above: Wall relief, Pyramid of the Feathered Serpent, Xochicalco, Mexico, c 800AD. Below: Quetzalcoatl as the Feathered Serpent, Tenochtitlan, Mexico; Opposite: Quetzalcoatl from a manuscript; Haietlik Serpent; Canadian 442 Squadron Haietlik Lightning Snake motif.

THE HYDRA
many-headed water dragon

The mythological Hydra embodies the fertilising powers of water. Living things that are hard to destroy are still sometimes called 'hydra-headed'. One of the earliest representations of the Hydra appears on a 1400 BC cylinder seal from Syria (*shown below*), and portrays part of a myth where the fertility god Baal conquers the seven-headed dragon Latan, a creature identified with the watery forces of chaos and disorder.

In Greek mythology, the description of Heracles' fight with the Lernaean Hydra shows her powers of renewal (*see two illustrations, opposite*). The Hydra was an awe-inspiring sight—she had a prodigious dog-like body and eight or nine reptilian heads (one of which was immortal). For every head that Heracles cut off, the beast reproduced two. Eventually he set the neighbouring woodland alight and seared the neck stumps with red-hot brands, and buried the immortal head beneath a rock. This battle may record the suppression of the Lernaean fertility rites, as new priestesses, like the regenerated heads of the Hydra, constantly appeared in the temple on the banks of the river Anymone until it was burned down.

The Bible has its own famous Hydra in *Revelations* 12:3: *"and behold a great red dragon, having seven heads and ten horns, and seven crowns upon his heads."*

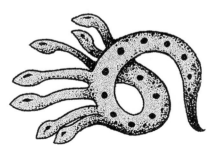

The Constellation Draco
winding around the pole

The Greek word *Drakon* comes from a verb meaning 'to see' or 'to watch' and dragons have great reputations as guardians of wisdom and treasure. In Greek mythology the dragon Ladon guarded the apples on the Tree of the Hesperides for the Goddess Hera. Ladon, who was the parthenogenous (virgin-born) son of Mother Earth, had 100 heads and, with 200 eyes, was the obvious choice for a guardian. However, even with these advantages, he was no match for the hero Heracles who shot him with an arrow and stole the apples. To commemorate this feat Heracles bore the likeness of a dragon on his shield, described by Homer as: *"A scaly horror of a dragon, coiled full in the central field, unspeakable, with eyes oblique, retorted, that askant shot gleaming fire."* The Goddess Hera wept bitterly at the death of Ladon and set his image among the stars as the constellation of the serpent Draco. Draco, also known as the Red Dragon, is a large constellation of stars which winds around the celestial and the ecliptic north poles and can be seen in the northern sky positioned close to Heracles.

Another Greek myth tells a different story—of the time that Zeus and his followers battled with the gods of an earlier mythological order high on Mount Olympus. In the struggle that ensued the new gods drove out the old ones and Draco, who as a Lord of Chaos was counted among the elder gods, was cast into the sky by the Goddess Athene. She sent his body spinning into a knotted circle where he remains to this day, inextricably tangled with the north pole, and daily turning with it on the slowly drifting axis of the northern sky. In fact, the star Thuban (Draconis), third from the tip of Draco's tail, was the pole star, centre of the heavens, in 2700 BC, the age of Stonehenge and ancient Egypt.

Draco, from a 12th century Sufi book of constellations, and a circular representation of some of the circumpolar stars showing Heracles brandishing his club while standing on the head of Draco.

THE FIREDRAKE
shooting across the sky

Heavenly comets, shooting stars (meteors), lightning and the Aurorae Borealis (northern lights) have long caused wonderment on earth, and historically they have all been documented somewhere as dragons. This includes the extraordinary phenomenon called the *draco volans*—the Firedrake—the glittering celestial event noted by early medieval meteorologists. The Anglo-Saxon Chronicle records that *"... excessive whirlwinds, lightning, storms and fiery dragons were seen flying in the sky."*

A brilliant head attached to a long luminous tail gives a comet a very draconian appearance, though some thought that it consisted merely of a conglomeration of vapour in the lower air. In 1571 William Fulke wrote said of it:-

"I suppose it was a flying dragon, wherof we speake, very fearfull to loke upon as though he had life, because he moueth, where as he is nothing els but cloudes and smoke ..."

The term 'Firedrake' can apply to meteors, and in Scotland strange lights in the sky were often called Fiery Drakes. In northern mythology, Firedrakes were cave-dwelling dragons who guarded hoards of gold in gravemounds and because of this were believed to be the spirits of the departed. In time they became the symbols of triumph over death.

In the Norse *Volsunga* saga, the giant Fafnir transforms himself into one of these fire dragons (*see illustration opposite*).

Above: In many cultures, comets were said said to be dragons. Below: Arthur Rackham's drawing of the dragon Fafnir from 'The Ring of the Nibelung'. In the Norse saga, the giant Fafnir transforms himself into a fire dragon and hides his gold in a remote cave. Fafnir's brother Regin persuades a young student, Sigurd, to kill him. The youth is able to do this, and afterwards cooks the dragon's heart but accidentally sucks his finger. As the dragon's blood touches his lips he understands the language of birds, and these, like the dying Fafnir, inform him that Regin will try to kill him. So he finally draws his sword and cuts off Regin's head.

TYPHON
the fire dragon

It is not just air and water which flow. Fire too undulates, and the ancestor of all fire-breathing dragons is surely the monstrous Greek god Typhon. The final son of Gaia, the Earth Mother, and fathered by Tartarus, the void, he represents one of her most destructive aspects. His body from the thighs down was composed of coiling, poisonous serpents, his wings blacked out the light of the sun and his heads touched the stars. A most terrifying sight, Hesiod describes him thus:

"...and from his shoulders grew a hundred serpent's heads, heads of a dread dragon that licked with dusky tongues, and from the eyes of his wonderous heads fires flashed beneath his brows and from all his heads fire burned as he glared."

Zeus waged a bitter battle with the monster, eventually driving Typhon to Sicily where he was crushed under the volcano Mount Etna. Today his fires still belch forth from its core and his mouth spews flaming rocks and larva, the fiery molten earth which shapes the world.

Typhon also rules the fourth element, air, in its dangerously hot form. Hot winds coil and spiral to produce the cyclonic storms we still call 'typhoons', the word having been borrowed by the Persians and Arabs.

IMAGO TYPHONIS
IVXTA APOLLODORVM.

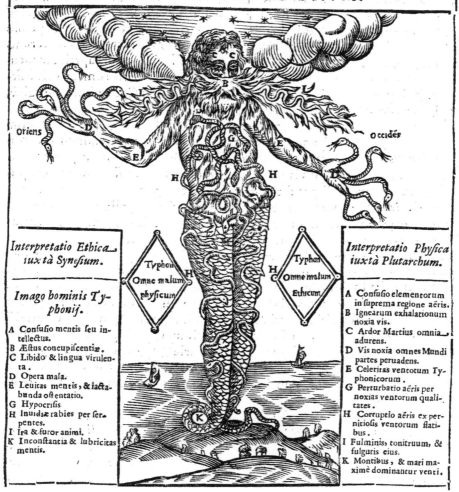

Oriens · Occidés

Typhon Omne malum physicum · *Typhon Omne malum Ethicum*

Interpretatio Ethica iuxtà Synesium.

Imago hominis Typhonij.

A Confusio mentis seu intellectus.
B Æstus concupiscentiæ.
C Libido & lingua virulenta.
D Opera mala.
E Leuitas mentis, & iactabunda ostentatio.
G Hypocrisis.
H Inuidiæ rabies per serpentes.
I Ira & furor animi.
K Inconstantia & lubricitas mentis.

Interpretatio Physica iuxtà Plutarchum.

A Confusio elementorum in suprema regione aëris.
B Ignearum exhalationum noxia vis.
C Ardor Martius omnia adurens.
D Vis noxia omnes Mundi partes peruadens.
E Celeritas ventorum Typhonicorum.
G Perturbatio aëris per noxias ventorum qualitates.
H Corruptio aëris ex pernitiosis ventorum flatibus.
I Fulminis, tonitruum, & fulguris eius.
K Montibus, & mari maximè dominantur venti.

Imago Typhonis, from Oedipus Aegyptiacus by Athanasius Kircher, 1652.

THE DRACONIOPIDES
taste the fruit of the tree

When a new religion conquers an earlier one, old customs and gods are either incorporated into the new order or they become demonised. In the Judeo-Christian era the dragon was in for a shock. While Christianity personified the Egyptian Osiris and Greek Dionysus in the figure of Jesus, ancient horned and fertility deities were combined into the sinister horned and hooved Satan, and dragons of wisdom, flow and fertility became envoys of negative, destructive power.

Thus a serpentine dragon, Lilith, appears at the very beginning of the Bible in the Garden of Eden persuading Eve to eat forbidden fruit—a Hebrew text reminds us "... for before Eve was Lilith". She is described elsewhere as the first wife of Adam who refused to lie beneath him (and obey his commands), so when Adam spurned Lilith and married Eve in the garden of Eden, she revenged herself on Adam's wife. She further appears as a night phantom and enemy of newborn babies—the very opposite of a good and loving mother. Lilith is thus probably a distortion of a venerable ancient deity worshipped long before Judaism.

Interestingly, the later Roman depiction of the ancient Egyptian goddess Isis, who ruled fertility and motherhood, was as a snake with a human head. In medieval times Lilith was depicted the same way (*opposite*).

Left: The Draconiopides in the Garden of Eden, stained glass window, Ulm Cathedral, Germany, 1420. Below: Lilith tempting Eve, German woodcut, 1470. Bottom: Temptation and Expulsion, after Michaelangelo, Sistine Chapel, Rome. In medieval times Lilith was shown coiled around the Tree of Knowledge, with the head of a beautiful woman and the body of a serpent, tempting Eve with the apple. This composite and mermaid-like creature is known as a Draconiopides. Facing page: Draconiopedes peering round the Tree of Life at Eve, who offers Adam the forbidden apple.

THE WORM
coiled around a hill

A Northern European dragon who has a serpentine shape but lacks wings or legs is termed a 'Worm' or 'Lindworm', from the Norse *ormr* meaning 'dragon'. The embodiment of stuck or stagnant energies, the Worm has very few redeeming features. Described as a serpent with a horned, reptilian or horse-like head, its traditional natural habitat is in wet or damp places, like lakes, wells, the sea, or bogs, where it may also sometimes be found coiled around a small conical hill.

There are many references to the Worm in Great Britain; the Gurt Vurm of Shervage Wood lived in Somerset, and near Pitempton, in Scotland, is the broken base of a Pictish cross called Martin's Stone. Carved at its base is a fat serpent lying across a zig-zag line. It is here, in legend, that a wormlike dragon was slain by a man named Martin.

The legend of the Northumbrian Lambton Worm tells of the Lambton heir catching an unpleasant-looking worm while fishing, which he throws into a well. There it grows and grows until it is a danger to everything. The heir rectifies his mistake by standing on a stone in the middle of a river wearing a knife-studded suit of armour.

When the worm tries to crush him, its body is cut to pieces which are swept away in the river's fast flowing current, thus preventing it from regenerating.

Childe Wynd thrice kisses the Laidly Worm & rescues his Sister the Princess Margaret.

Top left: The Laidly Worm, of Spindlestone Heugh, is a tale of a Northumberland princess, turned into a dragon by a jealous stepmother. Other pictures on this page show the Lambton Worm, and the hero with the spikey armour.

THE LAMBTON WORM

THE WYVERN
beware the eyes

Early depictions of the dragon show it in the form of a serpent, and the Wyvern is halfway between the shape of a Worm and a fully-fledged four-legged dragon. There are Chinese, Toltec and Pictish equivalents of the beast, and possibly these were the models that were used to change the shape of the visually-not-very-dynamic serpentine version.

When illustrating a fight between a courageous hero or saint and a dragon, a serpent can look a little undramatic or not particularly vicious; it needs—so to speak—a makeover, to appear more aggressive and formidable while doing battle with the valorous hero.

Over a period between the 11th and 12th centuries AD changes were seen in the Worm's serpentine shape in sculpture and manuscript art. It was transformed into a ferocious beast with bat-like wings, a fierce looking head and two legs, and was named a Wyvern, from the French *wivere* meaning 'viper' and 'life', its new name invoking the vital flowing energies of the dragon. But it was also inverted in some European countries and depicted as a vicious and fierce predator, taking instead of giving life. In some cases the Wyvern does not even have to catch its victims for it possesses a strange power over other living things—if a creature looks into a Wyvern's glittering emerald eyes, it will be hypnotised and lured into its greedy mouth.

Draco Æthiopicus.

Above, top: Multiple sightings of a Wyvern, 1150.
Lower: Various examples of wyverns from manuscripts.

La Wouivre

a natural mystic flowing through the air

Portrayed with the head and upper body of a voluptuous woman the beneficent French Wyvern known as the Wouivre has a ruby set into her head between her eyes, or in place of them, by which she can guide herself through the underworld. In some traditions this precious eye is a luminous ball that hangs in the air in front of her. The only chance to steal her jewel is when she is bathing and leaves the stone unguarded on the ground. If that should happen she would be as blind as a bat.

In his 1387 Le Noble Hystoire de Luzignan, Jean d'Arras tells the ancient story of Melusine or Melusina, the Countess of Lusignan, who was reputed to have been transformed into an immortal Wouivre. Over the ages which followed she watched over her descendants, warning them of impending disasters by screeching three times.

The term Wouivre is also given to snakes that glide and to rivers that snake, including the subtle telluric currents of geomancy. As such the Wouivre is also related to the *genius loci*, the 'spirit of the place', as she hovers protectively over the highlands and the countryside. She dwells in mountainous regions, ruins, abandoned chateaux and frequents the area around Nevers, where her name is transformed into 'Wivre'.

A Medieval woodcut of Melusine of Avalon, Countess of Lusignan, a Wouivre with a blue and white tail. On Saturdays she would hide from her husband and turn into a Dragon. When he found out she retreated to a town in the French Alps, and lived on the Apollo-Athena line (p. 57).

THE BASILISK
king of serpents

The Basilisk is the king of serpents, and monarch of smaller reptiles. In early images it appears as a serpent with a narrow pointed head topped by three crest-like excrescences, but it was later portrayed with a thicker and heavier body, two bird-like legs and a crown instead of a crest.

The Basilisk lives in the desert, which it creates through its venomous withering breath. One searing glance from its glowing eyes is enough to kill a man instantly. This murderous stare can also be the Basilisk's downfall for the sight of its reflected stare in a mirror will strike it dead. Two creatures can kill a Basilisk: the weasel (by biting it to death) and the cockerel (whose crowing sends it into a terminal fit).

During the first century AD the deserts of North Africa were said to be infested with these creatures and desert travellers often used to take a number of cockerels as protection against them. But reports soon began describing a different type of Basilisk which had the head of a cock. This creature was at first called a Basilcock and later a Cockatrice.

The Cockatrice was born from a toughened, spherical, unshelled egg laid by a seven year old cock under Sirius the dog star and hatched by a toad or snake on a dung heap.

HE BECAME AWARE THAT THE BASILISK WAS CLOSE BY HIM

Basiliscus. Βασιλίσκοσ. Basilisck.

Of the COCKATRICE.

Basiliscus ein gifftig thier.

Gallus οφιομορφος, Serpentina
cauda conspicuus. Florentiæ in horto
Magni Ducis Hetruriæ Francisci: ea-
forma quâ hic exprimitur omnium
admiratione visus.

Various images showing Cockatrices (opposite left, above right), and Basilisks (opposite right, above, and right, as portrayed by Athanasius Kircher in the 1600s). To medieval Christians, the cockatrice represented sin and sudden death and was one of the four aspects of the devil.

THE AMPHISBAENA
the double-headed dragon

The Amphisbaena is a double-headed dragon or serpent, usually portrayed with bird's claws, pointed bats wings and the extra head at the end of its tail. It is said to be capable of giving a venomous bite with both sets of fangs. Amphisbaenas are hard to kill: when cut in half, the two parts can join back together, and it can also cover ground very fast, both backwards and forwards (its name in Greek means "goes both ways"). In 1893 John Greenleaf Whittier wrote about it in a poem *The Double-headed Snake of Newbury.*

> *'For he carried a head where his tail should be,*
> *And the two of course could never agree,*
> *But wriggled about with main and might,*
> *Now to the left and now to the right;*
> *Pulling and twisting this way and that,*
> *Neither knew what the other was at.'*

According to Pliny the Elder, the amphisbaena is reputed to give protection in pregnancy when alive and cure rheumatism when dead—a typically ambivalent state of affairs.

The dual nature of this two-headed beast also describes the solar (positive, active, masculine) and lunar (negative, passive, feminine) forces of the Earth as symbolised by the caduceus. In Christian symbolism, unsurprisingly, it is the negative side of the amphisbaena which receives emphasis, appearing as the 'Adversary'—a concept later attached to the devil—which must be fought and mastered by heroes and saints. Modern psychology in fact defines a dragon as 'something terrible to overcome', for only he who conquers a dragon becomes a hero.

Top left: St. Michael
fighting an Amphisbaena,
detail of a piece of
embroidery.

Above: Two examples
of Amphisbaenas from
medival and modern
artworks.

Left: Amphisbaena on gold,
from an early illuminated
manuscript.

Opposite: Amphisbaena
from an early book.

HOLY DRAGON-SLAYERS
fixing the serpent

Pictures of dragon-slayers often show the saint's spear forcing the dragon's head to the earth, or poised in front of its open mouth. This echoes the traditional method of recharging serpentine, telluric currents by piercing the ground with a rod to fix the energy flow.

Earthly St George, patron saint of England, is often identified with earlier pagan gods like the fertility figure of the Green Man or Jack-in-the-Green and especially with the Celtic God Belinus, who also fought with a dragon. Historically, however, he poses a problem as none of his British contenders have any reputed connection with a dragon.

Heavenly St Michael is the chief archangel, and represents the sun. Often invoked for his healing energies, he rules high places and mediates health-giving solar powers, taking over the roles of the Graeco-Roman Aesculapius and the Hellenic Seraphis both of whom have a healing serpent as their symbol.

The Bible describes St Michael's battle with the dragon:- *"Michael and his angels fought against the dragon, and the dragon fought and his angels and prevailed not ... he was cast out into the earth."*

Above left: After Raphael, an early 1900's engraving by J. L. Petit.   Above right: Dürer's etching of St. Michael casting out the dragon.   Below: A drawing by F Anstey of the slaying of a family of dragons. Opposite, left to right: The three most important Christian dragon-killing saints: St Michael; St Margaret (who, though eaten by a dragon, burst it asunder with her cross); and St George.

HERALDIC & WAR DRAGONS
red, white and green

The heraldic dragon is one of the most artistic of all heraldic creations and the one with which we are most familiar today. Its four legs, neck and back are covered with scales, while the under part of its body is scaled in rolls of a much larger size. Its tongue and tail are barbed and its wings are those of a bat. Although heraldry is essentially medieval in origin, the use of the dragon as a personal device was in use from much earlier times—Marduk, slayer of Tiamat (*see page 324*), had a dragon as his emblem and Heracles bore a dragon effigy on his shield.

The legend of the Welsh flag describes how King Vortigern designed a fortress at Dinas Emrys which proved impossible to build for as soon as a wall was raised, it collapsed. A lad named Merlin said that beneath the foundations two dragons were battling in an underground lake, shaking the walls and causing them to fall. This proved to be true, for a red dragon and a white dragon were seen there fighting, and the red dragon eventually obtained suzerainty. The legend is based on history, and probably describes an actual battle, as when armies rode out it was the custom for each side to group beneath a dragon standard of an identifying colour. In this particular instance the red dragon, the British (or Welsh), overcame the white dragon, the Saxons (or English). A red dragon on a green and white ground, known as the Red Dragon of Cadwallader, later became the national flag of Wales.

Merlin became adviser to King Arthur, son of Uther Pendragon who had a vision of a flaming dragon which was interpreted as a sign that he would become king. Uther took the name 'Pendragon' ('Head Dragon'), and both he and Arthur used the dragon as their heraldic symbols on their arms and helmets.

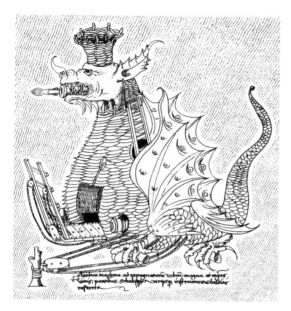

Left: A dragon war machine from Roberto Valtrio's 'De Re Militari'. Dragons on banners, standards and shields are signs of valour and courage and represent the power of a ruler. The draco windsock banner was widely used in the Roman Empire, and the Persians and Scythians also bore dragons on their standards. A windsock consisted of a pole, held by a soldier called a Dragonarius, which had a carved wooden Dragon's head mounted on top of it. A tube of cloth was attached to the head and, when the banner was held aloft, it filled with wind, writhing and billowing like a living creature. This scared the enemy and assisted the archers by showing them the strength and direction of the wind. Even today there is a regiment of English guards called 'Dragoons'.

Below: Left: The dragon in this heraldic drawing is not devouring its prey - the image instead represents enlightenment coming out of wisdom. Centre: From A.C. Fox-Davies's "A Complete Guide to Heraldry", a German dragon which is known as the Lindwurm, of the same kind as the Red Dragon of Wales. Right: Another heraldic dragon.

DRAGONS IN ALCHEMY
the mysteries of the earth

The literature surrounding the secretive and magical art of Alchemy is rich with dragons, where they assist in the physical and psychological chemistry lessons and appear in different ways for various hidden purposes— "The dragon slays itself, weds itself, impregnates itself."

The most famous of all alchemical dragons is the Ouroboros, the great serpent devouring itself, as depicted romantically on the front of this book, and reminding the student that "All is One" and that the universe undergoes periodic cycles of destruction and creation.

Winged dragons in alchemy generally represent the mercurial volatile elements, i.e. substances in the vessel which can evaporate, while wingless dragons signify fixed ones, although many alchemists regard all dragons as representing Mercury, the spirit, or life force. Dragons sometimes fight, where they illustrate psychic disorder or the conflict between unrefined Sulphur (soul) and Mercury (spirit).

The two-headed amphisbaena (*page 42*) becomes, in alchemy, the caduceus (*below, left and right*), the winged rod with two serpents twined about it carried by youthful Hermes and symbolising the harmonious intertwining marriage of opposites which is the alchemist's objective.

In alchemical symbolism, it is only by the killing of the dragon that the transmutation of the Prima Materia can take place and so produce Luna, the White Queen or unicorn, the virgin divinity in nature.

Left: Sol and Luna hunting and subduing the dragon. Their fear of the uncontrolled dragon power makes the dragon cower. Later they will no longer fear the dragon but embrace it and learn from it. Emblem 50 from Michael Maier Atlanta Fugiens: De Secretis Naturae Chymica, 1617.

Left: A man sleeps in his grave encoiled and embraced by the Universal Soul of the Earth spirit. The soul recognises the labyrinthine ways of dragon and is awakened by it to the connected life. Emblem from Michael Maier Atlanta Fugiens: De Secretis Naturae Chymica, 1617.

The Serpent Power
the kundalini of the earth

The image of the caduceus, with its pair of serpents climbing up a central staff, is very ancient indeed, and finds its most widespread application in the yogic and tantric traditions of ancient India. Here it appears as the essential blueprint for the human body—a pair of serpent heads springing from the base of the spine, volatising (i.e., gaining wings) by spiralling upwards toward the heavens and framing the seven spinning energy centres known as the chakras.

This amphisbaena embodies a power known as *kundalini*, similar to the Chinese *ch'i* and Japanese *qi*, and, like the Chinese *yin* and *yang*, thought of as consisting of a balance of female and male energies. In India these are Shakti, the mother of the universe, and Shiva, the purifier (*shown together below left*). A central purpose of yogic physical and mental exercises is to awaken the kundalini and allow it to rise and transform the individual.

Left: An alchemical emblem showing the divine hermaphrodite fusing with the serpent energies of the awakening kundalini which rises and spirals from a mastered amphisbaena on which the figure stands.

Above: The seven chakras or psychic centres of the ancient Indian system, corresponding to the seven endocrine glands of modern biology. These are only truly awakened when the serpent power is liberated.

Left: According to the tantric yogic tradition Kundalini is curled up in the rear part of the root base chakra in three and a half turns around the sacrum. When awakened the serpent energies rise up the spine as a transformative caduceus of balanced male (Shiva) and female (Shakti) principles allowing the individual to truly fuse with the universe.

Dragon Lines

the blood runs deep

The term 'ley' or 'ley line' denotes a series of straight alignments of ancient sites such as standing stones, hill forts, sacred springs and ancient churches, many of which have connections with dragon mythology.

The longest of the English leys is the St Michael's line of dragon sites that stretches along the May Day sunrise line from the westerly tip of Cornwall through St Michael's Mount (*below*), Glastonbury, Avebury and Bury St Edmunds. Recently, two huge serpentine energy currents have also been discovered by dowsers following the alignment: one is male and follows the high places, often churches dedicated to St Michael; the other female current stays low and passes through wells, springs and churches dedicated to St Mary and Margaret.

Another long straight alignment traces an alignment of sacred sites across Europe. This too appears to consist of two dowseable currents, one male (Apollo) and one female (Athena) forming a huge landscape caduceus across Europe, marking the passageway of the Earth Spirit.

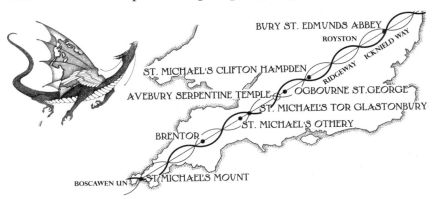

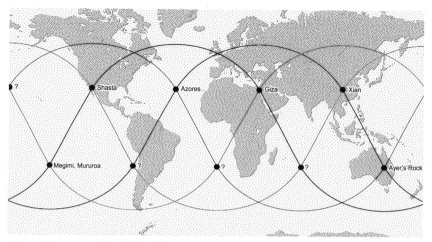

Above: A suggestive plait of three global dragons lines, with ten crossing places. Two further points at the poles give twelve in all, the number of vertices of an icosahedron. Facing page: England's 'Michael Line' joins the easternmost and westernmost tips of England and is supported by a pair of serpentine energy lines which pass through a vast number of ancient sites. Below: The Apollo-Athena line, with its similar pair of male and female energy currents (see pages 57 & 231). These start out in Ireland passing through sites dedicated to Michael and Mary respectively, but by the time they reach Greece are passing through temples dedicated to Apollo and Athena.

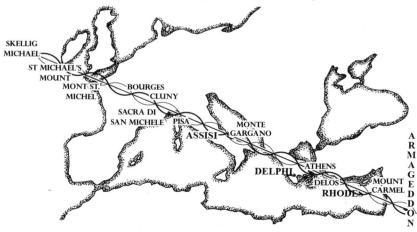

THE RAINBOW SERPENT
always half invisible

The idea of dragon or serpent lines in the landscape finds its earliest expression in the art and myths of the native peoples of Africa and Australia. In western and central Africa a pair of snakes, Danbhalah (the male divine serpent) and Aida Hwedo (the female rainbow serpent) represent wisdom incarnate, and in Australia, as in so many ancient cultures, the earliest legend of all concerns a very similar reptile.

The Aboriginal story begins in the distant Dreamtime when there were no animals, birds, trees, bushes, hills or mountains. The Great Rainbow Serpent stirred and set off to look for his own tribe. In the course of his wanderings he left huge impressions on the landscape, gorges, mountains, creeks, rivers and hills, both destroying and creating the environment. When he tired of shaping the Earth he dragged his massive body into a water hole and sank into its depths. Today he is long gone, but his spirit still shines after rains fall—as the rainbow.

The 'songlines' or 'dreamings' left by the Rainbow Serpent and other creation beings are still marked by alignments of natural features, some visible and some invisible. They criss-cross the entire continent of Australia, each possessing its own storyline and song structure.

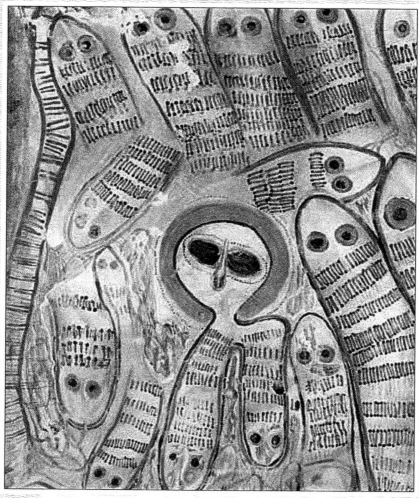

Above: A 50,000 year-old Australian aboriginal rock painting of a human face surrounded by nearly 20 serpent spirit beings.

THE EARTH DRAGON
and her fire-breathing core

What has scales, breathes fire and flies? The Earth does. Throughout this book we have seen the figure of the dragon associated with elusive currents and energies, from the Chinese art of Feng Shui to the enigmatic French Wouivre, whether looking for the dragon's backbone in a line of hills in the aboriginal bush or following a medieval dragon-line of ancient churches across Europe. It was only in the last half of the twentieth century, years after mankind had split the atom, rediscovered the dinosaurs and photographed distant galaxies, that scientists finally realised that the whole earth was very like a scaly fire-breathing dragon.

A huge continuous backbone of mountains runs down the centre of every ocean on Earth, spewing fire and new rock underwater to form the ocean floor, which spreads out on both sides, pushing the continental plates apart. Elsewhere, plates collide, and ocean floor is subducted back into the molten mantle beneath the ancient floating continents. The story of the Earth is locked into its stones, as pressure gradients, magnetic reversals, crystal and mineral seams, and wind and water patterns. Perhaps this is the dragon the ancients were referring to. Perhaps we have been living on a dragon all along.

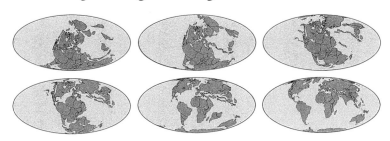

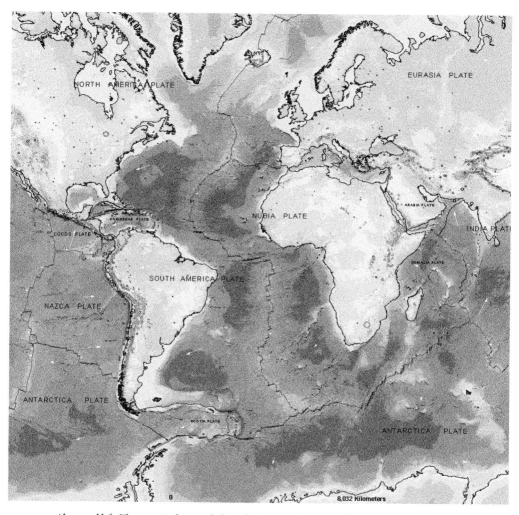

Above and left: The tectonic plates underlying the Americas, Europe and Eastern Asia (1970s graphic from the Smithsonian Institution). The Earth is a thinly covered ball of molten rock, the temperature at its centre being hotter than the surface of the sun. The plates shift and jostle, carrying the continents around. Fire-breathing volcanoes bring valuable minerals to the surface. The dragon guards her treasure.

APPENDICES & INDEX

Coordinates of Selected Sites

Alexandria - 31°11'53"N, 29°59'09" E
Angkor Wat - 13°24' 45"N, 103°52' 01"E
Arbor Low - 53°10'08"N, 1°45'42"W
Avebury - 51°25'43"N, 1°51'09"W
Baalbek - 34°0'25"N, 36°12' 11"E
Babylon - 32°32'32"N, 44°25'15"E,
Bimini (north) - 25°46'0"N, 79°16'43"W
Bosnian Pyramids - 43°58'37"N, 18°10'41"E
Bryn Celli Ddu - 53°12'28"N, 4°14'05"W
Canterbury - 51°16'45"N, 1°05'03"E
Caral - 10°53'28"N, 77°31'24"E
Callanish - 58°11'51"N, 6°44'42"W
Carnac, Brittany - 47°34'17"N, 2°57'01"W
Chavin - 9°36'47"N, 77°13'58"W
Chichen Itza - 20°40'59"N, 88°34'07"W
Copan - 14°51'30"N, 2°57'05"W
Coral Castle - 25°30'02"N, 80°26'40"W
Cuzco - 13°31'06"S, 78°51'48"W
Delphi - 38°28'53"N, 22°29'46"E
Easter Island - 27°07'20"N, 109°21'05"W
Giza - 29°58'45"N, 31°08'03"E
Glastonbury Tor - 53°08'39"N, 2°41'50"W
Gobekli Tepe - 37°13'26"N, 38°55'21"E
Jericho - 31°51'01"N, 35°26'10"E
Jerusalem - 31°46'15"N, 35°13'20"E
Kilauea - 19°25'12"N, 155°17'24"W
Knossos - 35°17'52"N, 25°09'48"E
Knowth - 53°42'04"N, 6°29'28"W
Lhasa - 29°40'02"N, 91°10'10"E
Long Meg - 54°43'41"N, 2°40'02"W

Luxor - 25°42'00"N, 32°38'22"E
Machu Picchu - 13°09'50"S, 72°32'46"W
Mecca - 21°25'38"N, 39°48'53"E
Mohenjo-Daro - 27°19'31"N, 68°08'00"E
Nabta - 22°30'29"N, 30°43'32"E
Nan Madol - 6°50'41"N, 158°20'06"E
Nazca - 14°41'31"S, 75°09'00"W
Newark Octagon - 40°03'17"N, 82°26'39"W
Newgrange - 53°41'41"N, 6°28'30"W
Ohio Serpent Mound - 39°01'30"N, 83°25'41"W
Ollantaytambo - 13°15'26"S, 72°16'02"W
Paracas - 13°51'10"S, 76°17'50"W
Quito - 13°46'47"S, 78°31'27"W
Rennes le Chateaux - 28°52'11"N, 42°53'57"E
Rollright Stones - 51°58'33"N, 1°34'15"W
Rosslyn - 55°52'21"N, 3°07'12"W
Saqqara - 29°52'17"N, 31°12'49"E
Silbury Hill - 51°24'56"N, 1°51'24"W
St.Michael's Mount - 50°06'26"N, 5°29'12"W
Stonehenge - 51°10'43"N, 1°49'30"W
Tara - 53°34'46"N, 6°36'42"W
Teotihuacan - 19°41'33"N, 98°50'38"W
Tiahuanaco - 16°33'24"S, 68°40'22"W
Tikal - 17°13'23"N, 89°37'24"W
Tonga - 21°08'12"S, 175°02'53"W
Troy - 39°57'28"N, 26°14'18"E
Ur - 30°57'46"N, 46°06'11"E
Wandlebury - 52°9'29" N, 0°10'58"E
Xian Pyramid - 34°16'13"N, 108°49'02"E
Yonaguni - 24°17'47"N, 123°50'37"E

Uvg Grid Points

1) **31.72°N 31.20°E**
On the Egyptian continental shelf, at approximately the midpoint between the two outlets of the Nile at Masabb Rashid and Masabb Dumyat. Very close to Behdet.

2) **52.62°N 31.20°E**
On the Sozh River east of Gomel, at the boundary junction of Ukraine, Belarus, and Russia. Numerous megalithic sites and Venus figurines from Paleolithic era found.

3) **58.28°N 67.20°E**
In marshy lowlands just west of Tobolsk

4) **52.62°N 103.20°E**
In the lowlands north of the southern tip of Lake Baykal, at the edge of highlands

5) **58.28°N 139.20°E**
In the highlands along the coast of the Sea of Okhotsk

6) **52.62°N 175.20°E**
Slightly east of Attu at the western tip of the Aleutian Islands

7) **58.28°N 148.80°W**
Edge of continental shelf in the Gulf of Alaska

8) **52.62°N 112.80°W**
Buffalo Lake, Alberta, at the edge of highlands in lowlands

9) **58.28°N 76.80°W**
Just east of Port Harrison on Hudson's Bay

10) **52.62°N 40.80°W**
Gibbs Fracture Zone

11) **58.28°N 4.80°W**
Loch More on the north-west coast of Scotland

12) **26.57°N 67.20°E**
On the edge of the Kirthar Range bordering the Indus River Valley, directly north of Karachi

13) **31.72°N 103.20°E**
At the east edge of the Himalayas in Szechuan Province, just west of the Jiuding Shan summit

14) **26.57°N 139.20°E**
At the intersection of Kyushu Palau Ridge, the West Mariana Ridge, and the Two Jima Ridge

15) **31.72°N 175.20°E**
At the intersection of Hess Plateau, the Hawaiian Ridge, and the Emperor Seamounts

16) **26.57°N 148.80°W**
Northeast of Hawaii, midway between the Murray Fracture Zone and the Molokai Fracture Zone

17) **31.72°N 112.80°W**
Cerro Cubabi, a highpoint just south of the U.S. Mexico border near Sonoita and lava fields

18) **26.57°N 76.80°W**
Edge of continental shelf near Great Abaco Island in the Bahamas

19) **31.72°N 40.80°W**
Atlantis Fracture Zone

20) **26.57°N 4.80°W**
In El Eglab, a highland peninsula at the edge of the Sahara Desert sand dunes

21) **10.81°N 31.20°E**
Sudan Highlands, edge of White Nile marshfields

22) **0° 49.20°E**
Somali Abyssal Plain

23) **10.81°S 67.20°E**
Vema Trench (Indian Ocean) at the intersection of the Mascarene Ridge, the Carlsberg Ridge, and Maldive Ridge into the Midindian Ridge

24) **0° 85.20°E**
Ceylon Abyssal Plain

25) **10.81°N 103.20°E**
Kompong Som. a natural bay on the southern coast of Cambodia southwest of Phnom Penh

26) **0° 121.20°E**
At the midpoint of Teluk, Tomini, a bay in the northern area of Sulawesi

27) **10.81°S 139.20°E**
Midpoint of the mouth of the Gulf of Carpentaria

28) **0° 157.20°E**
Centre of the Solomon Plateau

29) **10.81°N 175.20°E**
Midpoint of the vast abyssal plain between Marshall Islands, Mid-Pacific Mountains, and the Magellan Plateau

30) **0° 166 80°W**
Nova Canton Trough

31) **10.81°S 148.80°W**
Society Islands

32) **0° 130.80°W**
Galapagos Fracture Zone

33) **10.81°N 112.80°W**
East end of the Clipperton Fracture Zone

34) **0° 94.80°W**
Junction of the Cocos Ridge & the Carnegie Ridge, just west of Galapagos Islands.

35) **10.81°S 76.80°W**
Lake Punrrun in Peruvian coastal highlands

36) **0° 58.80°W**
State of Amazonas. at tip of minor watershed highlands

37) **10.81°N 40.80°W**
Vema Fracture Zone

38) **0° 22.80°W**
Romanche Fracture Zone

39) **10.81°S 4.80°W**
Edge of Mid-Atlantic Ridge in Angola Basin, just southeast of Ascension Fracture Zone

40) 0° 13.20°W
   Gabon highlands, at intersection of three borders
41) 26.57°S 31.20°E
   Luyengo on the Usutu River in Swaziland
42) 31.72°S 67.20°E
   Intersection of the Mid-Indian Ridge with the Southwest Indian Ridge
43) 26.57°S 103.20°E
   Tip of the Wallabi Plateau
44) 31.72°S 139.20°E
   Lowland area east of St. Mary Peak (highest point in the area) & north east of Spencer Gulf
45) 26.57°S 175.20°E
   At the edge of the Hebrides Trench, just southwest of the Fiji Islands

46) 36.72°S 148.80°W
   Undifferentiated S Pacific Ocean(?)
47) 26.57°S 112.80°W
   Easter Island Fracture Zone
48) 31.72°S 76.80°W
   Nazca Plate
49) 26.57°S 40.80°W
   In deep ocean, at edge of continental shelf, southeast of Rio de Janeiro
50) 31.72°S 4.80°W
   Walvis Ridge
51) 58.28°S 31.20°E
   Enderby Abyssal Plain
52) 52.62°S 67.20°E
   Kerguelen Plateau
53) 58.28°S 103.20°E
   Ocean floor, midway between Kerguelen Abyssal Plain and Wilkes Abyssal Plain

54) 52.62°S 139.20°E
   Kangaroo Fracture Zone
55) 58.28°S 175.20°E
   Edge of Scott Fracture Zone
56) 52.62°S 148.80°W
   Udintsev Fracture Zone
57) 58.28°S 112.80°W
   Eltanin Fracture Zone
58) 52.62°S 76.80°W
   South American tip, at the edge of the Haeckel Deep
59) 58.28°S 40.80°W
   South Sandwich Fracture Zone
60) 52.62°S 4.80°W
   Bouvet Fracture Zone
61) NORTH POLE
62) SOUTH POLE

Grid Points from William Becker & Bethe Hagens, as based upon their UVG Planetary Grid model.

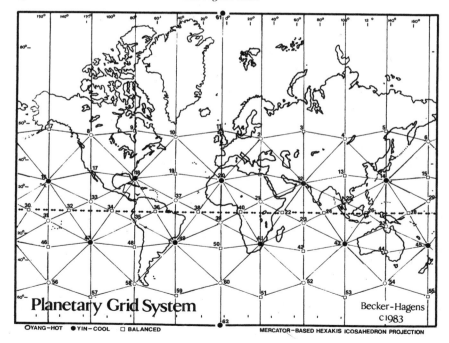

Planetary Grid System

Becker-Hagens
c 1983

○ YANG–HOT   ● YIN–COOL   □ BALANCED

MERCATOR–BASED HEXAKIS ICOSAHEDRON PROJECTION

TYPES OF DIVINATION

A - ABACOMANCY: *Divn. by dust.* ACULTOMANCY: *Divn. by needles.* AEROMANCY: *Divn. by atmospheric conditions such as clouds, wind, thunder, lightning and other meteorological phenomena.* AGALMATOMANCY: *Divn. from statues.* AICHMOMANCY: *Divn. from sharp objects.* AILUROMANCY: *Divn. from cats.* ALECTRYOMANCY: *Augury involving the eating patterns of sacred chickens.* ALEUROMANCY: *Divn. using flour.* ALOMANCY: *Divn. using salt.* ALPHITOMANCY: *Special cakes made of barley flour.* ALVEROMANCY: *Divination by sound.* AMATHOMANCY: *Divination using sand:* AMBULOMANCY: *Divn. by walking.* AMNIOMANCY: *Divn. from placenta.* ANEMOSCOPY: *Divn. from the wind.* ANTHOMANCY: *Divn. from flowers:* ANTHRACOMANCY: *By reading burning coals.* ANTHROPOMANCY: *Divn. from a human sacrifice.* ANTHROPOSCOPY: *By reading physical attributes in humans.* APANTOMANCY: *Omens from things that present themselves by chance, especially animals, such as a black cat crossing your path.* ARACHNOMANCY: *The appearance and behaviour of spiders.* ARCHEOMANCY: *Reading sacred antiquities:* ARIOLATION: *Divn. from altars.* ARITHOMANCY: *Numerology of words and phrases.* ARUSPICINA: *By examining entrails.* ASPIDOMANCY: *Channelling while sitting on a shield or in a circle.* ASTRAGALOMANCY: *Divn. by casting the knuckle bones of sheep (see too reading with dice, cleromancy & astragyromancy).* ASTRAPOMANCY: *Reading lightning flashes.* ASTROLOGY: *Divn. using stars and planets, their patterns and cycles.* AUGURY: *Divn. from the appearance of bird formations.* AUROMANCY: *By reading auras.* AUSPICY: *By observing birds. Also avimancy.* AUSTROMANCY: *Divn. from the wind.* AXIOMANCY: *Divn. from axes:* **B** - BAZI: *Chinese Astrology also known as Four Pillars.* BELOMANCY: *Divn. by arrows.* BIBILOMANCY: *Divination from books, including rhapsodomancy, also called stichomancy.* BLETONOMANCY: *By observing water currents.* BOTANOMANCY: *Pyromancy by burning leaves and branches.* BRIZOMANCY: *Dream Divn.* BRONTOMANCY: *Divn. from thunder.* BUMPOLOGY: *By reading bumps.* **C** - CANOMANCY: *Divn. from dogs.*

CAPNOMANCY: *Pyromancy by smoke.* CARTOMANCY: *Divn. using modern playing cards related to tarot.* CATOPTROMANCY: *Scrying using a mirror.* CAUSINOMANCY: *Pyromancy by objects cast into the fire.* CEPHALOMANCY: *Augury from the skull or head of a donkey or goat.* CERAUNOSCOPY: *Aeromancy using thunder and lightning.* CEROMANCY: *Divn. from melted wax.* CHALOMANCY: *Divn. by the sounding of gongs and bowls.* CHAOMANCY: *Aeromancy using aerial visions.* CHINESE ASTROLOGY: *Divn. based on a 12-year cycle and involving 12 animals of Shengxiao, which, unlike the zodiac signs of Western astrology, are not based on the configuration or movement of the planets or stars.* CHIROMANCY: *Divn. using the palm of the hand including an analysis of hand shape, fingers, and fingernails. Also called chirgnomy, chirology, or palmistry.* CHORIOMANCY: *By reading pig's bladders.* CHRESMOMANCY: *Divn. by the ravings of a lunatic.* CLAIRAUDIENCE: *A form of clairvoyance by hearing.* CLAIRVOYANCE: *Divn. by seeing the future ahead of time. Different forms are clairaudience, metagnomy, precognition.* CLAMANCY: *A reading from the random shouts of a crowd.* CLEDONOMANCY: *Divn. by chance happenings or rumours.* CLEIDOMANCY: *A form of radiesthesia or dowsing using a suspended key.* CLEROMANCY: *By casting lots, also Divn. with dice Also astrgalomancy.* COMETOMANCY: *Divn. from the tails of comets.* CONCHOMANCY: *A reading from shells.* COSCINOMANCY: *Dowsing using a suspended device.* COSQUINOMANCY: *Divn. from hanging sieves.* COTTABOMANCY: *Divn. by wine in a bowl.* CRITHOMANCY: *Reading the markings on freshly baked bread.* CROMNIOMANCY: *A reading from onion sprouts:* CRYPTOMANCY: *Divining omens from hidden messages.* CRYOMANCY: *A reading from ice.* CRYSTALLOMANCY: *Scrying with a crystal ball.* CYATHOMANCY: *Divn. using cups.* CYBERMANCY: *Divination using computer technology.* CYCLICOMANCY: *Divination from swirling water in a cup.* CYCLOMANCY: *A divinatory reading using wheels, and noticing their rotation.* **D** - DACTYLIOMANCY: *Dowsing with a suspended ring.* DACTYLOMANCY: *Reading finger* movements. **DAPHNOMANCY**: A form of pyromancy, the burning of laurel leaves. **DENDROMANCY**: A reading from trees particularly oaks, yews or mistletoes. **DOBUTSU URANAI**: Modern Japanese Divn. based on date of birth assigning an animal type and personality. **DOWSING**: Divn. using a pendulum, L rods or traditionally a forked hazel twig. Different forms include cleidomancy, coscinomancy, and dactylomancy. Also called radiesthesia. **DOMINOMANCY**: Divn. using dominoes. **DRIMIMANCY**: Divn. using bodily fluids. **E** - **ELEOMANCY**: Divn. using oil. **ENTOMOMANCY**: Augury from the appearance and behaviour of insects. **FAVOMANCY**: Divn. from beans. **FEI XING GONG FA**: Divn. using the principles of Chinese metaphysics. **GEOMANCY**: Divn. by the patterns in the earth, also the practice of reading and enhancing the built and natural environment. **F** - **FENG SHUI**: Chinese art of reading and harmonising the environment. **FLORAMANCY**: A reading from a flower or plant freshly picked by the seeker. **G** - **GELOSCOPY**: A reading from laughter. **GRAPHOLOGY**: Assessment of a person's character from handwriting. **H** - **HAKATA**: African method of casting carved bones. **HALOMANCY**: Pyromancy by casting salt into a fire. **HARUSPICY**: Augury from the entrails and body part of animals. **HEPATOSCOPY**: Haruspicy using the liver. **HIEROMANCY**: Divn. from the entrails of a sacrifice. **HIPPOMANCY**: Divn. from horses. **HORARY**: Divn. from an astrological chart drawn at the moment of the question. **HYDROMANCY**: Scrying by water. **HYOMANCY**: Divn. from wild hogs. **I** - I **CHING**: Chinese method of Divn., Mandarin is Yi Jing, also known as the Book of Changes. **ICHNOMANCY**:

Reading footprints. **ICHTHYOMANCY**: Augury from the shape and entrails of fish. **IFA**: An African method of geomancy. **IRIDOLOGY**: A reading from the iris of the eye. **J** - **JIAOBEI**: A Chinese Divn. tool. Wooden moon blocks tossed in pairs to give a yes/no answer. Also known as poe. **JYOTISH**: Vedic astrology, claimed to the oldest form of astrology. **K** - **KAU CIM**: Chinese fortune sticks where a box is shaken until one stick falls out to give a reading. Also Chien Tung or qiantong. **KIPPER CARDS**: A German card deck with very literal meanings rather than the symbolic and intuitive forms of tarot cards. **KNISSOMANCY**: Divination from the vapours of incense. Also libanomancy. **L** - **LAMPADOMANCY**: Divn. using an oil lamp or a torch flame. **LECANOMANCY**: Divn. from a basin of water. **LENORMAND**: A popular card deck in France and Germany invented in the 1850 named after the fortune teller Marie Anne Adelaide Lenormand. **LITHOMANCY**: Divn. using gem stones. **LYCHNOMANCY**: Divination from the flames of candles. **M** - **MACHAROMANCY**: Divination using knives. **MARGARITOMANCY**: Divn. from pearls. **MAHJONG**: A reading using mah-jong tiles. **METAGNOMY**: Hypnotic trance originally evolved for predicting malady and cure. **METEORMANCY**: Aeromancy using meteors and shooting stars. **METOPOSCOPY**: Divn. from lines on the forehead. **MI KAYU URA**: Japanese Shinto Divn. ritual using rice or bean gruel to predict the weather and harvests for the year. **MOLEOSCOPY**: Assessing character from moles on the body. Also meilomancy. **MOLYBDOMANCY**: Divn. using molten metals. **MYOMANCY**: Divn. from the colour and movement of mice. **MYRMOMANCY**: Interpreting the behaviour of ants. **N** - **NECROMANCY**: Communing with the dead using automatic writing, a ouija board, or through a psychic. **NECYOMANCY**: Summoning the dead. A type of necromancy associated with the dark arts. **NEPHOMANCY**: Divn. from clouds. **NGGAM**: Divn. from Cameroon and Nigeria using the actions of spiders and crabs. **NUMEROLOGY**: Numbers are analysed to understand lives and personality. This practice is also called numeromancy or arithomancy. **NUMISMATOMANCY**: Divination using coins. **O** - **OCULOMANCY**: Divn. from the eyes. Also iridology. **OENOMANCY**: Divn. from the patterns made by wine. **OGHAM**: Celtic inspired Divn. using "staves", wood from sacred trees carved with the Ogham alphabet. **OLOLYGMANCY**: Divn.

from the howling of dogs. **OMIKUJI**: Japanese fortune paper strips, literally meaning "sacred lot", drawn at a temple. Similar to Chinese Kau cim: **ONEIROMANCY**: Divn. using dreams. **OOMANCY**: Divn. from eggs. **OPHIOMANCY**: Augury from the colour and movement of snakes. **ORNITHOMANCY**: Divn. using the sound, appearance and flight of birds. **OSTEOMANCY**: Bone reading. **OUIJA**: A spirit board with marks, such as the alphabet, which is used to communicate with the dead. **P** - **PALLOMANCY**: Dowsing with a pendulum. **PALMISTRY**: Divn. using the palm of the hand, including an analysis of hand shape, fingers, and fingernails. It is also called chirognomy, chirology, or chiromancy. **PEGOMANCY**: Hydromancy using a sacred pool or spring. **PESSOMANCY**: Divn. by drawing or casting of specially marked pebbles, also called psephomancy. **PHYLLOMANCY**: Divination from the leaves of plants or trees. **PHYLLORHODOMANCY**: Divination using rose petals. **PHRENOLOGY**: Assessing character from the presence of bumps on the head. **PHYSIOGNOMY**: Character analysis using physical features. **PLASTROMANCY**: A reading from the cracks formed by heating a turtle's plastron. **PODOMANCY**: Reading the soles of feet. **PRECOGNITION**: A form of clairvoyance giving knowledge of the future. **PSYCHOMETRY**: A form of clairvoyance where holding an object gives you information about the people and history connected to the object. **PSYCHOGRAPHY**: Channelling spirit using automatic writing. **PTARMOSCOPY**: Divn. by interpreting sneezes. **PYROMANCY**: Divn. by fire. Different forms include botanomancy, capnomancy, causinomancy, daphnomancy, halomancy, pyroscopy, and sideromancy. **PYROSCOPY**: Pyromancy by burning a sheet of paper on a white surface and examining the resulting stains. **R** - **RADIESTHESIA**: French for Dowsing. **RHABDOMANCY**: Divining or dowsing for water or minerals using rods or wands. **RHAPSODOMANCY**: A form of bibliomancy from poetry. **ROADOMANCY**: Reading star constellations. **RUNES**: The symbols of an ancient alphabet that are used for Divn. **S** - **SCAPULOMANCY**: Augury from the patterns or cracks and fissures on the burned shoulder blade of an animal. **SCRYING**: Divn. by gazing into a reflective surface. Different forms include crystallomancy, catoptromancy, and hydromancy. **SEANCE**: A meeting of people typically led by a medium who communicate with the dead or astral spirits. **SELENOMANCY**: Divn. from the

moon. **SHUFFLEMANCY**: Divn. using the shuffle function on a digital media player. **SIDEROMANCY**: Pyromancy by burning straws on red hot iron and reading the patterns, movements, flames and smoke. **SKATHAROMANCY**: Interpreting beetle tracks. **SORTES VERGILIANAE**: A form of bibliomancy from works of the Roman poet Virgil. **SORTILEGE**: Divn. by the casting or drawing of lots. Different types include astragalomancy, belomancy, bibliomancy, pessomancy (also known as psephomancy), rhapsodomancy, and stichomancy. It is also called cleromancy. **STERCOMANCY**: Divn. using the seeds in bird droppings. **STICHOMANCY**: Divn. using books. Also called bibliomancy. **STOICHEOMANCY**: From the Iliad and the Odyssey. **T** - **TAROMANCY**: A reading using tarot cards. **TASSEOGRAPHY**: Divn. from a cup using tea leaves or coffee grounds. **TELAESTHESIA**: Interpreting of physical disturbances of the body, such as throbbing, twitching, itching or whistling in the ears. **TEPHROMANCY**: Divn. from the ashes of ritual and sacrifice fires. **THEOMANCY**: The consulting of an oracle that is inspired by the gods, such as the Oracle of Delphi. **THERIOMANCY**: Divn. from the behaviour of animals. **TURIFUMY**: By interpreting the shapes in smoke. **TYROMANCY**: Divn. from cheese. **U** - **UMBROMANCY**: Divn. using shade. **UROMANCY**: Divn. using urine. **URTICARIAOMANCY**: Divn. from itches (see telaesthesia). **W** - **WATER DIVINING**: Dowsing for underground water (also called water witching). **X** - **XYLOMANCY**: Divn. using wood, such as twigs, branches or logs. **Z** - **ZOOMANCY**: Augury from the appearance and behaviour of any animal. ✐

Feng Shui - The 10 Stems

The ten Heavenly Stems "contain water" and "reflect the Milky Way". Their (24 Mountain) directions are "opened" by the careful siting of gateways, doors, windows, views, watercourse entry and exits, roads and paths.

Stems 3, 4, 7 & 8 are "lucky" and linked with Gen and Xun Gua which have mixed Yin and Yang and so are fertile.

Stems 1, 2, 9 & 10 are "Unlucky" and linked with Qian and Kun Gua which are overwhelmingly Yang or Yin respectively.

Stems 5 & 6 are central, the "Tortoise Shell" or middle of the universe; they are used to control the dispersal of Sha.

1. **Jia** 甲 depicts a shell or bud, hard and enclosing, a fingernail or guard's helmet, protecting what is precious.

2. **Yi** 乙 is a sprout appearing out of the mother plant, the expression of creativity.

3. **Bing** 丙 represents the fire in the hearth of the house.

4. **Ding** 丁 is a hammered-in nail, the penetrating power of Heaven, virile, potent, able to stand on its own.

5. **Wu** 戊 is a scythe, cutting and reaping.

6. **Ji** 己 is sorting, the warp and weft of weaving.

7. **Geng** 庚 is winnowing, the hard work of getting the precious grain out of the husk.

8. **Xin** 辛 is accurate and bitter, offending superiors, punishment and fear, the bite of the tiger.

9. **Ren** 壬 is a servant shouldering a pole with two water buckets, bearing the burden, supporting life, child bearing.

10. **Gui** 癸 is a bow bent with arrows ready to fly, a secret movement of waters, the fertility of life in sperm and ovum.

The 12 Branches

The 12 Earthly Branches mark the 12 terrestrial compass directions and the location of Earthly Dragon Qi. They also indicate the 12 double hour divisions of a day, months in a year, and years of Jupiter's solar orbit. The year begins at Winter Solstice, midway through Branch 1 (due north), and the rest of the branches relate compass directions to moments in time. The branches also indicate best directions relative to a person's birth year, and the best times of the year for initiating projects connected with building or burying.

The **Xia Li** (Thousand Year) calendar describes time (years, months, days and double-hours) in recurring cycles of sixty Stem and Branch combinations, also found in the 60, 72, 120 and 240 direction Dragon rings on some Luopans.

1. **Zi** 子 is a baby wrapped in swaddling clothes, Winter Solstice, gate of death and life, hidden power of Yang in Yin.

2. **Chou** 丑 is a young plant supported by a stick with binding to help growth at the beginning.

3. **Yin** 寅 is hands joining in greeting and reverence.

4. **Mao** 寅 is a pair of doors opening, the rising sun, Spring Equinox, the power of Wood and the Qing Dragon.

5. **Chen** 辰 is a woman with hands hiding her belly, pregnant and timid, and movement in a Spring egg.

6. **Si** 巳 is a fully-grown fetus, and fruits forming.

7. **Wu** 午 is opposition, the strong vertical power from Heaven, Summer Solstice, the heat of fire at its zenith.

8. **Wei** 未 is the roots and stem of a tree heavily laden with fruit, the power of Heaven coming to the Earth.

9. **Shen** 申 represents two hands holding a rope between them, expanding power, connection to the Spirits.

10. **You** 酉 is a liquor fermenting in a jug, distillation, harvest, Autumn Equinox, Heaven coming into Earth.

11. **Xu** 戌 is a scythe, weapon, injuring or killing, cutting what is unnecessary, clearing the ground before sowing.

12. **Hai** 亥 is a man and woman making love, Yin and Yang combining under a roof to conceive.

DESIGN OF BEIJING

Like the importance of the head to a Dragon, the Feng Shui of the capital (and within that the design of the Imperial Palace or President's residence) affects the fortunes of the entire country—the capital is also the metaphorical centre of the universe. Beijing is located at the head of the northern Mountain Dragon Range, the Qi flowing from the northern and western hills to the city, a microcosmic metaphor for the topography of China. The site was chosen because of its resemblance to the "Regal Throne" located near the celestial North Pole, the surrounding mountain ranges providing a reflection of the stars of the Zi Wei constellation. The Heavenly Emperor resides at the Zi Wei star, while the surrounding stars form the Imperial Court of Heaven, representing the Empress, Concubines, Princes, Lords and Mandarins. Ancient Chinese cosmology regards all earthly forms such as countries, cities and even individual beings as reflections of the celestial stars in heaven.

Tai Wo Palace, the seat of the Imperial Throne and the most important building in Beijing, is oriented on the four cardinal points determined by the four altars of the Sun, Moon, Earth and Heaven. These are laid out following the Former Heaven Ba Gua—the altar of Heaven to the south, Earth to the north, Sun to the east, and Moon to the west. Other altars to the gods of land and grain, agriculture, hills and rivers, and silkworms, are located along the main axes. The Eight Altars bring peace and harmony to the capital and the entire country by providing timely offerings to spirits. They form the principal metaphysical design elements in the planning of Beijing.

In order to increase the good Heavenly Yang Qi flowing from the Mountain Dragon range in the north-west into the city, pagodas and towers were built to the north-west and west of Beijing to direct the Qi to the Imperial Palace, starting from the sacred spring on Uchun Shan from which the Emperor obtained his drinking water. The only structures that are higher than the Tai Wo Palace are the Coal Hill Pavilion at the back of the palace to the north, and the Buddhist stupa and temple of Yamataka. Yamataka is the spiritual protector of Beijing and the White Pagoda stupa gives blessing and protection to the Emperor from the northwestern and northern heights.

Ming and Qing Dynasty Beijing was laid out according to the Early and Later Heaven Ba Gua and the interaction of the Five Elements, and provides an excellent example of Chinese metaphysics in application.

SOUTH represents the Fire element, the metaphor for technology, civilization and progress. The main city gate by which the Emperor rules and brings prosperity and progress to the country lies to the south.

NORTH represents Water, money and wealth: a Drum Tower and Bell Tower are located to the north of the Imperial Palace. The bell was rung in the morning to herald the opening of the city gates and the drum was

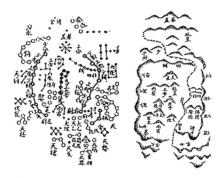

struck in the evening to herald their closing. The bell belongs to the Metal element, which gives rise to the Water of the North and ensures the healthy development of the state treasury; the drum belongs to the Earth element, controlling and sealing the prosperity.

EAST represents the Wood element, growth and prosperity, and in the original design a forest was planted just outside the East Gate to enrich the Wood of the East.

WEST represents the Metal element, war, disputes, and other bad omens: there are three lakes to the West of the Imperial Palace, which reduce the harmful effects of the Metal element, as Metal feeds Water. The two main Stars representing the Emperor also reside in the West: a twin pagoda temple is built to the West of Tien An Men to denote them. An early hill form, now Bu Bu Shan Cemetery, is also located in the West. Earth gives rise to Metal: weakening and rebuilding it by Feng Shui allows the Metal element to be used as a tool by humanity.

NORTHEAST denotes the trigram *Gen*, symbolizing young men: the temple of Confucius and the State University are located in this corner.

SOUTHEAST denotes the trigram *Xun* and symbolizes intellectual fame and literature, which is increased by the Wen Chang Pagoda. An area of lakes and marshes, now public gardens, nourishes the Wood element of the Southeast.

SOUTHWEST denotes the trigram *Kun*, the people, flat land–this corner of the city was mainly residential cottages and flat land. The Emperor travelled out of Beijing to visit the country via the Southwestern Gate of Humans.

NORTHWEST represents the trigram *Qian*, Gods, Buddha and the ancestors: the high pagodas and temples are mainly located in this direction, while the North Lake here reduces the harmful effect of the Metal element of the Northwest.

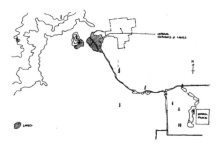

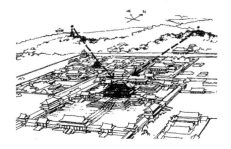

THE 60 JIA ZI

THE 10 HEAVENLY STEMS

No.	Ch.	Nam.	Yn/g	Nature	Elmnt	Season
1	甲	Jia	○	Adaptable	Wood	Spring
2	乙	Yi	●	Flexible	Wood	Spring
3	丙	Bing	○	Generous	Fire	Summer
4	丁	Ding	●	Leader	Fire	Summer
5	戊	Wu	○	Loyal	Earth	Centre
6	己	Ji	●	Nurturing	Earth	Centre
7	庚	Geng	○	Stamina	Metal	Autumn
8	辛	Xin	●	Attention	Metal	Autumn
9	壬	Ren	○	Moving	Water	Winter
10	癸	Gui	●	Still	Water	Winter

THE 12 EARTHLY BRANCHES

No.	Ch.	Month	Yn/g	Anim.	Nature	Elmnt
I	子	Zi	○	Rat	Quick-witted	Water
II	丑	Chou	●	Ox	Steadfast	Earth
III	寅	Yin	○	Tiger	Authoritative	Wood
IV	卯	Mao	●	Rabbit/Hare	Homely	Wood
V	辰	Chen	○	Dragon	Charismatic	Earth
VI	巳	Si	●	Snake	Seductive	Fire
VII	午	Wu	○	Horse	Free	Fire
VIII	未	Wei	●	Sheep/Goat	Creative	Earth
IX	申	Shen	○	Monkey	Fun-loving	Metal
X	酉	You	●	Rooster	Practical	Metal
XI	戌	Xu	○	Dog	Faithful	Earth
XII	亥	Hai	●	Pig/Boar	Perfectionist	Water

THE 60 JIA ZI – STEMS AND BRANCHES

Stem	1	2	3	4	5	6	7	8	9	10
Branch	Jia	Yi	Bing	Ding	Wu	Ji	Geng	Xin	Ren	Gui
I Zi	1924 1984		1936 1996		1948 2008		1960 2020		1972 2032	
II Chou		1925 1985		1937 1997		1949 2009		1961 1921		1973 2033
III Yin	1974 2034		1926 1986		1938 1998		1950 2010		1962 1922	
IV Mao		1975 2035		1927 1987		1939 1999		1951 2011		1963 1923
V Chen	1964 2024		1976 2036		1928 1988		1940 2000		1952 2012	
VI Si		1965 2025		1977 2037		1929 1989		1941 2001		1953 2013
VII Wu	1954 2014		1966 2026		1978 2038		1930 1990		1942 2002	
VIII Wei		1955 2015		1967 2027		1979 2039		1931 1991		1943 2003
IX Shen	1944 2004		1956 2016		1968 2028		1980 2040		1932 1992	
X You		1945 2005		1957 2017		1969 2029		1981 2041		1933 1993
XI Xu	1934 1994		1946 2006		1958 2018		1970 2030		1982 2042	
XII Hai		1935 1995		1947 2007		1959 2019		1971 2031		1983 2043

Left: The 60 JIA ZI are composed of same-polarity combinations of the 10 Stems and 12 Branches. Years, months, days and double-hours are represented as recurring cycles of alternating Yang and Yin, always following the same diagonal sequence as shown. Use the table to find the Stem and Branch for your year of birth and then refer to the tables above..

Below: Earthly Branches appear as four Element triangles, each composed of Three Stages: Sheng (birth), Wang (growth) and Mu (death), the San He or Triple Harmony, shown (below left) with the Liu He Harmonic Combination. The best branches in which to locate a front door, stove, bedroom and altar are those which harmonize with your birth year. Avoid the Zhong Sha or Direct Kill and its two related branches, and the Liu Sha Antipathy (below right).

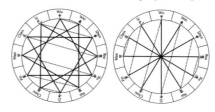

24 MOUNTAINS

THE TWENTY-FOUR MOUNTAIN directions of the Luopan were created during the Tang Dynasty using the magnetic north-south axis as the frame of reference, called the *Correct Needle of the Earth Plate*, or *Di Pan*. The twelve Branches alternate every 30° around the compass with eight of the ten Stems (omitting the earth pair) and the four intercardinal (corner) *Ba Heaven Gua* trigrams from the *Later Heaven Ba Gua*. Study the example on the facing page.

The four *Gua* in their intercardinal Mountain positions represent spirit doorways, all potentially inauspicious with reference to watercourse directions and gateway placement. For Stems and Branches refer to the appendices on the previous page. Here are the four *Gua* Mountains:

GEN 艮, Mountain, NE, is *Yin* power, the womb conceiving and giving birth, dawn, the Chinese New Year *Li Chun*, Celtic *Imbolc*, the Feast of Brigid, Goddess of the Hearth.

XUN 巽, Wind, the SE Mountain, is the invisible power of Heaven which stirs everything into motion, *Beltane*, the weaving of colours around the Maypole.

KUN 坤, Earth, the SW Mountain, is the abundant mother, bountiful and fruitful, giving on all three *Yao*, Celtic *Lughnasad*, the Festival of the Goddess of Grain.

QIAN 乾, Heaven, the NW Mountain, is the *Yang* power going deep into *Yin* in order to be protected, corresponding to *Samhain*, the release of Spirit from form.

The *San He* Luopan contains three identical yet rotated 24 Mountain rings, each with several supporting rings.

The inner *Earth Plate* has *Wu* aligned to magnetic south and reveals whether a particular directional influence is effective principally on the spiritual, mental and emotional plane (Stems), material and social plane (Branches), or mediating and stabilizing plane (*Gua*). It is used to establish direction and orientation, to determine where a tomb or house "sits" and "faces," and to judge the quality of Earth *Qi* in the Mountain Dragon veins influencing the site. The *Sitting Direction* is the direction from the centre to the back of the site and the

Facing Direction that from the centre to the front of the site. The Sitting and Facing Mountains are ideally both *Yin* or *Yang*, with the axis of orientation not too close to the unstable *Qi* of a border. The ring is also useful for the placement of features in a design as it can be used to activate a particular quality of *Qi*.

The intermediate *Central Needle of the Human Plate* ring, the *Ren Pan*, is rotated 7.5° counterclockwise from the Earth Plate and was added in the Tang Dynasty. It is used to judge the quality of the small hills (called "Sand" or "Sha") in front of the Xue, as well as local hills and large rocks, trees and outbuildings, using the Five Elements.. The outer *Seam Needle of the Heaven Plate* ring, the *Tian Pan*, was added during the Southern Song Dynasty. It is rotated 7.5° clockwise from the Earth Plate, and is used to assess water flows, including wells, driveways and roads, and grasp good water and wealth. Water is auspicious if flowing from a vigorous direction, or to an unfavorable direction, but inauspicious towards a vigorous direction.

Above: Tang Dynasty [618–907AD] bronze astrological mirror showing the 4 Spirits, 8 trigrams, 12 Animals representing the Branches, 24 Mountains and 28 Lunar Mansions.

AN EXAMPLE LUOPAN

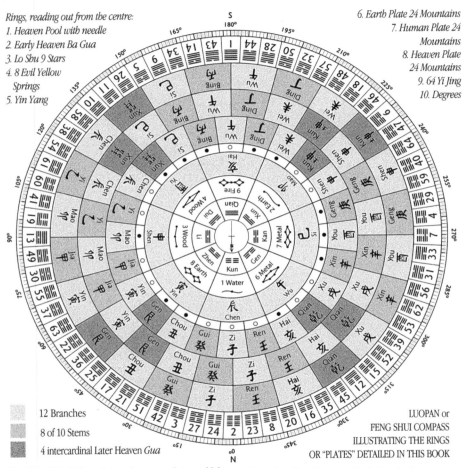

Rings, reading out from the centre:
1. Heaven Pool with needle
2. Early Heaven Ba Gua
3. Lo Shu 9 Stars
4. 8 Evil Yellow Springs
5. Yin Yang

6. Earth Plate 24 Mountains
7. Human Plate 24 Mountains
8. Heaven Plate 24 Mountains
9. 64 Yi Jing
10. Degrees

12 Branches

8 of 10 Stems

4 intercardinal Later Heaven Gua

LUOPAN or
FENG SHUI COMPASS
ILLUSTRATING THE RINGS
OR "PLATES" DETAILED IN THIS BOOK

The Eight Evils Yellow Spring plate is used to establish inauspicious directions of water coming towards a dwelling. It relates to visible moving water such as rivers, and paths, gates and doorways. The *Lo Shu* direction of the Sitting position yields the unfavorable 24 Mountain Earthly Branch direction, e.g., a 9 (south) sitting house has unfavorable water in the *Hai* 24 Mountain Earth Plate direction. This is remedied by screening the view or altering the door angle.

JIU XING, 9 STARS

THE NINE STARS of the *Bei Dou* (Big Dipper) constellation are linked with the Nine Palaces of the *Lo Shu*. The Chinese calendar is based on a 180-year cycle, divided into three 60-year *Yuan*. Each Yuan is further divided into three 20-year *Yun* each of which relates to a number 1-9 and a *Gua* (*see table below*). Each year also has a ruling star whose number 1-9 is found by counting backwards where 2013 is 5, 2014 is 4, 2015 is 3, 2016 is 2, 2017 is 1, etc. Construct a Flying Star chart by placing the ruling star number of the current year, *Yun*, or *Yun* of a building's construction in the centre and "flying" the stars forward through the 9 Palaces according to the *Lo Shu* sequence. Or choose one of the nine opposite which has the required central ruling Star number.

In the San Yuan tradition, if the centre number is for example 8, the lucky *Zhen Shen* (Original Spirit) and best Mountain position is in the NE (8 in the *Lo Shu*); the weaker *Ling Shen* (Fragmentary Spirit) and best Water position is opposite in the SW; and the *Zhao Shen* (Illuminated Spirit) and Wealth position (activated by water) is in the east (*Lo Shu 3, Ho Tu pair of 8*).

S

3	8	1
2	4	6
7	9	5

8	4	6
7	9	2
3	5	1

1	6	8
9	2	4
5	7	3

E / **W**

2	7	9
1	3	5
6	8	4

4	9	2
3	5	7
8	1	6

6	2	4
5	7	9
1	3	8

7	3	5
6	8	1
2	4	9

9	5	7
8	1	3
4	6	2

5	1	3
4	6	8
9	2	7

N

The *Mountain Star* (in the *Sitting Palace* i.e., back wall) represents the retaining *Yin Qi* of a building, so health and family harmony; the *Water Star* (in the *Facing Palace*) represents the *Yang Qi* entering a building, and prosperity. These, monthly, and daily Stars can also be centred and "flown" for detailed readings of Star nature, timeliness, and element combinations in each trigram sector.

STAR	1	2	3	4	5	6	7	8	9
Colour	White	Black	Jade	Green	Yellow	White	Red	White	Purple
Star	Tan Lang	Ju Men	Lu Cun	Wen Qu	Lian Zhen	Wu Qu	Po Jun	Zhou Fu	Yu Bi
Translation	Greedy Wolf	Officer at the Gate	Preserver of Rank	Literary Pursuits	Purity in Truth	Military Pursuits	Destroyer of Armies	Left Supporter	Right Supporter
Yin/Yang	o	●	●	o	●	o	●	●	●
Element	Wood	Earth	Earth	Water	Fire	Metal	Metal	Wood	Wood
Gua	Zhen	Gen	Kun	Kan	Li	Qian	Dui	Xun	Xun
Fortune	Ausp.	Inausp.	Varies	Ausp	Power	Ausp	Varies	Ausp	Power
Yun	1864	1884	1904	1924	1944	1964	1984	2004	2024
Portent	Sheng Qi	Tian Yi	Huo Hai	Liu Sha	Wu Gui	Yen Nian	Jue Ming	Fu Wei	Fu Wei
Translation	Fertile Qi	Heaven's Will	Mishap	Six Curses	Five Ghosts	Long Life	Severed Fate	Throne	Throne
Land-Form	⌂	⌂	⌂	⌂	⌂	⌂	⌂	⌂	⌂

8 HOUSE PORTENTS

The Eight Portents, listed below, are derived from the trigram in which the house sits (i.e. the back of the house) to read health, and from the facing trigram to read wealth. Use the chart (right) to identify these two *Lo Shu* numbers, their trigrams, and the grid of Portent directions for each trigram. The Portents define room use, Element cures (controlling or draining to the negative Portent element) and enhancements (nourishing or same element to positive Portents).

To construct a *Ming Gua* (personal Natal trigram) chart: i) Add 1 to the year of birth if born after Winter Solstice. ii) For males, divide the last two digits of the birth year by 9 and note the remainder (if the remainder is 0 read it as 9), then subtract it from 10 (or from 9 if born after 2000) to find the *Ming Gua*. iii) For females add 5 to the last two digits of the birth year (or 6 if born after 2000), divide by 9 and the remainder is the *Ming Gua*. iv) If the *Ming Gua* is 5 it becomes 2 for males, 8 for females. The *Later Heaven Ba Gua* trigram relating to this number via the *Lo Shu* is the *Natal trigram*, and defines which of the eight grids to choose from.

1. SHENG QI is the best portent, energizing, bringing good fortune and prosperity to business and personal life; being in the right place at the right time. A good area and orientation for the front door, bedroom, living room, study, or creative work space.

2. TIAN YI brings spiritual and physical healing, financial regeneration, and cures bad luck and evil influence. Good for a therapy room or sick person's bedroom, and the best direction for the *Fire Mouth*, or door of the kitchen stove to face.

3. HUO HAI is the weakest of the unlucky portents, bringing minor accidents, money loss, legal disputes, contagious diseases, worry and irritability. Best used for kitchen, bathroom or storage.

4. LIU SHA brings accidents, illness, financial & legal problems, lost *Qi* and the death of family members or

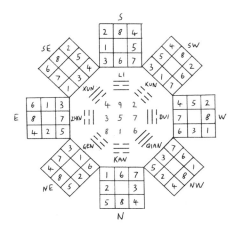

employees. Best for kitchen, toilet, or storage.

5. WU GUI is associated with hauntings, burglary, fires, quarrels, betrayal, loss of employees, legal and financial loss, and injury to the youngest child—best used for kitchen or toilet, though positively aspected good for a shrine or work with spirit guides.

6. YEN NIAN represents longevity & harmonious family relations. Activating this area enables relationships, cures quarrels and infertility, and ensures rich descendants—a good area for family, dining and bedrooms.

7. JUE MING is the worst portent, and can bring redundancy, bankruptcy, divorce, persistent poor health and death, "all descendants die and the family name is lost," if activated by underground, form or astrological *Sha*. Use for toilet or storage.

8. FU WEI represents the throne, one's basic self and personal path, clear thinking, a harmonious and favorable life, and strong protection against bad luck. A good area if well protected for the front door or main bedroom, study, and desk orientation.

Animal Symbolism

TORTOISE: Represents deep spiritual wisdom, longevity and strength. Most auspicious placed in the north of home.

DRAGON: Symbolizes benevolent power, good fortune, the essence of strength, goodness and blessings; best in east.

PHOENIX: Sun and purification, virtue, peace and prosperity; best in the south. A Phoenix and Dragon together symbolize the Empress and Emperor, and are especially auspicious for marriage, as are a pair of fish or mandarin **DUCKS**.

TIGER: Majesty, ferocity, courage. Guards house from evil. Best in the west, facing away from house, lest it eat inhabitants.

FISH: Brings abundance, fertility, wealth and success; best in the north, near front door, or in the living room.

ELEPHANT: Brings strength, sagacity, prosperity and power, and is best in the east.

LION: Majesty and courage. Guards house from evil when placed outside main gate or door in pairs. On the right side (looking out) it is female and may have a foot on a baby lion, for family protection. On the left it is male and may have a foot on a sphere, symbolizing the sun and spiritual protection. Best in the south.

UNICORN: Brings happiness, good fortune, wisdom, goodness and longevity, and is exalted in the west.

SNAKE: Symbolizes wisdom, the deep secrets of life, and is auspicious in the north and centre.

STORK: Signifies longevity, fertility and family harmony and is best in the southeast, south and southwest.

HORSE: Represents speed, strength, high status and good repute and is best in the south.

FROG / TOAD: Calls down moon, rain and money. Best in the SW, W, NW or unobtrusively inside facing front door.

Pronouncing Pinyin

Consonants

Like English, except for:

x like the *s* in *see* + the *sh* in *she*. Smile when you say it!

z like *ds* in *words*.

r like *r* in *raw*, with your tongue curled back.

c like *ts* in *eats*.

q like *ch* in *cheat*.

j like the *dj* in *jam*, with minimal exhalation.

ng like the *ng* in *song*.

zh like *dg* in *sludge*.

sh like the *sh* in *wash*, with tongue curled back.

Single Vowels

a like the *a* in *far*.

o is like *or*.

e like the *e* in *send* or *very*. Except when a single vowel follows a consonant, then more like *ir* in *bird*.

i as in *sit*. Except when preceded by *c, s* or *z*, then like a mosquito ... *ziiiii*.

u like the *oo* in *loop*.

Vowel Combinations

an Like a soft *an* in *ban*.

ang *a* + *ng*.

ao is like *ow* in *cow*.

ei is like *ay* in *bay*.

en like the *en* in *taken*.

eng is like *ung* in *sung*.

er is like *ur* in *purse*.

ia is like *ya*.

iang *y* + *ang*

ie is like a tight *yeh*.

iu is like the *ou* in *you*.

ian like *yen*.

iao like *eow* in *meow*.

in like the *in* in *gin*.

ing like the *ing* in *sing*.

iong is like *eyong*.

ong as in *kong*.

ou is like *ow* in *low*.

ua is like *ua* in *guava*.

uan *u* + *an*.

uang is like *oo* + *ang*.

ui is like *way*.

un is like *wou* in *would* + *n*.

uo is like *war*.

uai is like *why*.

ue is like *oo-eh*.

NB: This is not the complete Pinyin system. It is a guide to aid pronunciation of the Chinese terms in this book.

YI JING

 1. *Qian*. The Creative. Activity and perseverance in what is right brings sublime success.

 2. *Kun*. The Receptive. Following guidance and subtle action brings good fortune.

 3. *Tun*. Sprouting. Fragility at the beginning, furthering through perseverance.

 4. *Meng*. Youthful Folly. Success, though enthusiasm should be tempered with discipline.

 5. *Xu*. Waiting. Good outcome is possible with politeness and circumspection.

 6. *Song*. Dispute. Confidence obstructs, compromise and wise advice bring good fortune.

 7. *Shi*. The Multitude. Guidance by responsible leadership has good fortune.

 8. *Bi*. Union. Timely cooperation from the start is fortunate. Those who are uncertain gradually join.

 9. *Xiao Chu*. A Small Offering. Restraint and attention to necessary details fulfill plans.

 10. *Lu*. Walking. Good conduct brings success and no harm, though treading on the tiger's tail.

 11. *Tai*. Great. Peaceful prosperity, Heaven and Earth unite in harmony. An end to all feuds.

 12. *Pi*. To Close. Stop, inferior people are in ascent, change the obstruction or yourself.

 13. *Tong Ren*. Union of Men. Group effort and participation in projects brings profit.

 14. *Da You*. Great Possessions. Immense wealth, honor the spiritual realms and offer charity.

 15. *Qian*. Modesty. Reverence and offerings can harmonize events.

 16. *Yu*. Pleasure. Easy movement with forethought and prearrangement. Install helpers.

 17. *Sui*. Following. Following form and experience is advantageous. To rule, first learn to serve.

 18. *Gu*. Poison. Preparation and reflection are required to correct deficiencies.

 19. *Lin*. Approach. Advancing brings great success, arrival must be within eight months.

 20. *Guan*. Observation. Sincerity, dignity and spiritual cleansing bring rewards.

 21. *Shi He*. Punishment. Biting and chewing through problems is difficult but rewarding.

 22. *Bi*. Decoration. Small successes and minor goals achieved with outward refinement.

 23. *Bo*. Stripping. Vulnerability. To examine the true skeleton it is best to stay still at home.

 24. *Fu*. Return. Movement is advantageous, return to the Dao without urgency.

 25. *Wu Wang*. Innocence. Movement with ignorance brings misfortune; with correctness good.

 26. *Da Chu*. Great Restraint. Offer large charitable gifts and feast in good company.

 27. *Yi*. Nourishment. Attend to quality and quantity of nourishment for yourself and others.

 28. *Da Guo*. Extraordinary. Calls for measures greatly beyond the ordinary.

 29. *Kan*. Abyss. There is honor in dangerous waters; heart-centred action.

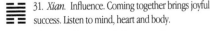 30. *Li*. Brightness. Fiery intelligence and correct action profits. Nurture male & female equally.

 31. *Xian*. Influence. Coming together brings joyful success. Listen to mind, heart and body.

32. *Heng*. Constancy. Endurance and perseverance bring regularity and stability.

33. *Dun*. Hiding. Conceal assets from ascendant dark forces, and virtuous actions with modesty.

34. *Da Zhuang*. Great Strength. Power is only useful with intelligence and timeliness.

35. *Jin*. Advance. Flourishing prosperity, tempered with virtue and caution as all is transient.

36. *Ming Yi*. Brightness Obscured. In adversity, hide your light to take advantage of problems.

37. *Jia Ren*. Family. With family responsibilities and virtue in order, all is well.

38. *Kui*. Strange. Unusual circumstances, but no misfortune in small matters. Discord will not benefit.

39. *Jian*. Difficulty. Pause and seek wise counsel, let events take their course.

40. *Jie*. Loosen. When danger abates, establish a good location and let goals arrive.

41. *Sun*. Decrease. Even with slender means, sincerity and inner offering is substantial.

42. *Yi*. Increase. Every action will bring earthly prosperity and spiritual flowering.

43. *Quai*. Decision. Define goals, strategy and a place to go to establish a stong position.

44. *Gou*. Coupling. Meeting in sexual congress; a female too powerful to marry.

45. *Cui*. Gathering together. Commune with others, spiritual powers, and self through sacrifice.

46. *Sheng*. Ascend. Communicate with Heaven, sacrifice, put one's house in order.

47. *Kun*. Distress. Confinement, fatigue and lost trust demand reverence and wise counsel.

48. *Jing*. The Well. Nature is constant. Human structures require the responsibility of mutual care.

49. *Ge*. Change. Shedding a skin, personal internal transformation, with confidence.

50. *Ding*. Cauldron. Make works of art as human and spiritual gifts, alchemical transformation.

51. *Zhen*. Arousing. Waves of thunder bring fright and laughter, sacrifice and ritual maintain calm.

52. *Gen*. Stillness. Meditation and transcendant consciousness. Power comes from being still.

53. *Jian*. Development. Move gradually when performing actions of bonding.

54. *Gui Mei*. Marrying Maiden. Imposition of service, undertakings bring misfortune.

55. *Feng*. Abundance. Paranormal spiritual vision brings rewards of future prosperity.

56. *Lu*. Traveller. Pay respects to the spirits for a safe journey and good fortune. Do not be overbearing.

57. *Xun*. Gentle. Wise counsel, a small offering, and discipline bring gradual rewards.

58. *Dui*. Joyful. Take pleasure and profit in the moment, rejoice in giving and receiving

59. *Huan*. Disperse. Expand into new territory for gain, protection and insight. Dissolve egotism.

60. *Jie*. Regulations. Ensure rules are not too restrictive, but are in accord with the Dao.

61. *Zhong Fu*. Inner Sincerity. Success in major actions, maintain inner centredness.

62. *Xiao Guo*. Small and Extraordinary. If small details are supported, great fortune will follow.

63. *Ji Ji*. Already Completed. Small actions bring good fortune if timely, disorder if late.

64. *Wei Ji*. Not Yet Completed. No profit until the end, yet no event is ever truly complete.

Sixth *Yao*, uppermost stroke: Gods, Ancestors
Fifth *Yao*, middle of top trigram: Emperor
Fourth *Yao*, fourth stroke: Mandarin, Noble

Third *Yao*, top of lower trigram: Magistrate
Second *Yao*, second stroke: Official
First *Yao*, lowest line: Layman

WESTERN DIVINATORY GEOMANCY

The oracular divinatory tradition of Geomancy has been in use for millennia across Africa, Arabia, Europe and Asia. The earliest styles of divination involved reading cracks in the ground, throwing handfuls of earth onto the ground, striking the sand with a stick to create random patterns, or randomly drawing a number of stones, seeds, or roots, and recording the odd or even numbers of dots generated as a single or two points respectively. Performing this four times generates one of sixteen binary tetragrams, the geomantic tableaux, each with associated meanings and astrological correspondences. The top line of one or two points is the *head*, the fire element, the second line the *neck*, air element, the third line the *body, or* water element, and the bottom line is the *feet, or* earth element.

Dice or coins can be used to generate the figures, so *even, even, odd, odd* gives the figure of *Fortuna Major*.

THE 16 GEOMANTIC TABLEAUX
Names in Latin, English, *Arabic*, Later Norse Futhark, English; Ascriptions: quality, planet, sign, element.

 1 **VIA, The Way,** *Tariq,* Rait
Path, journey, direction, ways and means, solitude, movement, action, change of fortune, neutral, favourable for travel. Mobile, Moon, Cancer, Water.

 2 **ACQUISITIO, Gain,** *Djama'a,* Ur
The primal ox, gain through strength, interior comprehension, wit, promotion, pain, legal success, profit, very favourable. Stable, Jupiter, Sagittarius, Fire.

 3 **PUELLA, Girl,** *Naky al-khad,* Bria
Goddess's tree, birch, purity, happiness, riches, love, land, music, arts, healing, fickleness, gracious cheeks, nearly always favourable. Stable, Venus, Libra, Air.

 4 **CONJUNCTIO, Conjunction,** *Idjima'a,* Lagu
Flow and growth, connection, attraction, love, friendship, reunion, recovery, communion, contracts, weights and measures, neutral to favourable. Mobile, Mercury, Virgo, Earth.

 5 **TRISTITIA, Sorrow,** *Ankis,* Iss
Ice, stasis, sorrow, spouse, stubbornness, suffering, poverty, cross purposes, reversed, change for the worse, secret kept, unfavourable except for Earth and building plans. Stable, Saturn, Aquarius, Air.

 6 **ALBUS, White,** *Bayad,* Sol
The Sun, the diviner, dazzling beauty, peace, sleep, wisdom, heartbreak, purity, patience, moderation, favourable for beginnings and business ventures. Stable, Mercury, Gemini, Air.

 7 **CAPUT DRACONIS, Dragon's Head,** *Al-'ataba al dakhil,* Thuris
The giant, flag of joy, interior threshold, ascending node of the moon, doorway to the upperworld, children, innocence, alertness, wars, arguments, favourable for beginnings and gain, good with good and evil with evil. Stable, Jupiter, Venus, Earth.

 8 **FORTUNA MAJOR, Greater Fortune,** *Al-nusrat al-dakhil,* Feu
The creator, sacred fire, power, wealth, good fortune, good position, safe property, success, inner victory, very favourable. Stable, Sun, Leo, Fire.

9 **FORTUNA MINOR, Lesser Fortune,** *Al-nusrat al-kharidj,* Ar

The god rune, chiefs, elders, external protection, outward victory, pride, domination, assistance from others, good for proceeding quickly. Mobile, Sun, Leo, Fire.

10 **CAUDA DRACONIS, Dragon's Tail** *Al-'ataba al-kharidj,* Yr

The ending, death rune, yew tree, exterior threshold, the descending node of the moon, the underworld, exit, possible problems, cold words, fraud, slaves, unfavourable in most questions, brings good with evil and evil with good. Mobile, Saturn, Mars, Scorpio, Fire.

11 **RUBEUS, Red,** *Hamrah,* Chaion

The wound, hot burn, passion, vice, temper, joy, jewels, destructive fire, ghost, danger, caution, stop, very unfavourable, evil in good and good in evil. Mobile, Mars, Scorpio, Water.

12 **LAETITIA, Joy,** *Al-lahyan,* Os

The mouth, speech, laughter, full beard, king, happiness, delight, grace, women, sanity, balance, good health, secret revealed, very propitious for marriage and house foundation. Mobile, Jupiter, Pisces, Water.

13 **CARCER, Prison,** *'Uklah,* Naut

Need, constraint, closed circle, link, delay, limitation, confinement, servitude, house, food, usually unfavourable. Stable, Saturn, Capricorn, Earth.

14 **PUER, Boy,** *Djaudala,* Tiu

The sword, the warrior, downy beard, erect phallus, rashness, initiative, combativeness, violence, robbers, workers, unfavourable except in combat or love. Mobile, Mars, Aries, Fire.

15 **AMISSIO, Loss,** *Al-kabd al-kharidj,* Hagal

Hailstone, transformation, exterior comprehension, transience and loss, tears, things outside one's grasp, loss by illness or theft, unfavourable for material matters. Mobile, Venus, Taurus, Earth.

16 **POPULUS, Man,** *Djama'a*

Multitude, humanity, meeting, congregation, news, abundance, common freedom, union, good with good, evil with evil. Stable, Moon, Cancer, Water.

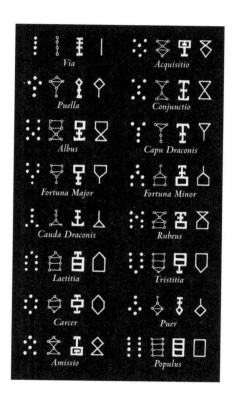

WESTERN DIVINATORY GEOMANCY (CONT.)

FOUR MOTHERS are made from sixteen throws of a dice or coin (*see technique on previous page*). These are known in order as the south, east, north and west figures and are placed at the top of the shield from right to left (*see opposite*).

FOUR DAUGHTERS are then created by taking the top line or head of the first mother to become the head of the first daughter, then the heads of the second, third and fourth mothers to become the neck, body and feet of the first daughter, then the necks of the four mothers become the second daughter, and so on.

FOUR NIECES figures are then generated: the first by adding the heads, necks, bodies and feet of the 1st and 2nd mothers to produce either odd (one dot) or even (two dot) results; the second by adding the 3rd and 4th mothers; the third by adding the 1st and 2nd daughters and the fourth by adding the 3rd and 4th daughters.

TWO WITNESSES are erected by adding the 1st and 2nd nieces to make a right witness and adding the 3rd and 4th nieces to make a left witness. The right witness is the 'father of the judge' and reveals 'past testimony', and the second, left witness is the 'mother of the judge' and reveals 'future testimony'.

THE JUDGE is made by adding together the two witnesses: the judge gives the answer to the question posed at the beginnning of the divination. Only one of eight figures will ever end up as the Judge: Acquisitio, Amissio, Conjunctio, Carcer, Fortuna Major, Fortuna Minor, Populus and Via.

A RECONCILER may also be formed by adding the judge to the first mother, in order to clarify the judgement.

INTERPRETATION of the shield includes the witnesses. Thus a bad judge with good witnesses suggests no enduring success, while a good judge

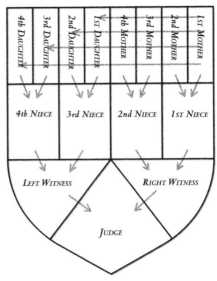

The geomantic shield, the classic European method of displaying the figures erected in a geomantic divination.

and bad first witness suggests success after delays, and bad second witness no assurance of success. The 'triplicities' also carry meaning: the first triplicity of first niece and first two mothers represents the querent's circumstances, health, habits and character; the second shows the events shaping the querent's life at the time of reading; the third stands for the querent's home, family and workmates; and the fourth the querent's friends, associates and authorities.

ASTROLOGICAL INTERPRETATION of the chart may be made by placing the mothers (10,1,4,7), daughters (11,2,5,8,) and nieces (12,3,6,9) inside the medieval square medieval (or modern circular) astrology chart of 12 houses (*see diagram to right*).

In astrological theory the virtues of the planets act upon human beings, the zodiac signs affect their modes of action, and the houses are the location in which their action is experienced. The 16 geomantic figures, related to the planets and their tutelary spirits, are interpreted within the houses as the planets would be, for example by examining the 'dignities' (own house, exaltation, fall, or detriment) and 'aspects' (opposition, square, trine or sextile). The house that most closely reflects the question is the key to the interpretation.

THE HOUSES

1st House, **VITA**, **Life**, The querent: life, health, habits, character, behaviour.

2nd House, **LUCRUM**, **Riches**, Property, money, wealth, personal worth, self esteem, gain and loss.

3rd House, **FRATRES**, **Brothers**, Siblings, relatives, communication, news, early education, short journeys.

4th House, **GENITOR**, **Father**, Home, male forebears, property, inheritance, possession, conclusion, an important indicator of outcome.

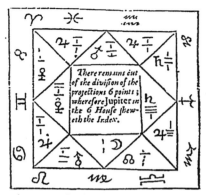

Above: A typical medieval astrological geomantic chart.

5th House, **NATI**, **Sons**, Reproduction, children, women, luxury, entertainment, feasting, speculation.

6th House, **VALETUDO**, **Health**, Aunts and uncles, employees, domestic animals, utensils, illness, daily work.

7th House, **UXOR**, **Wife**, Love, marriage, partnerships, lovers, conflict, theft, dishonour.

8th House, **MORS**, **Death**, Death, pain, anxiety, legacies, shared resources, investigations, poverty.

9th House, **ITINERIS, Journeys**, Long journeys, pilgrimage, religion, philosophy, the arts, divination.

10th House, **REGNUM**, **Kingdom**, Mother, status, reputation, authority, worldly position, environment.

11th House, **BENEFACTA**, **Good Fortune**, Friends, supporters, patrons, charity, dependency, hopes and wishes.

12th House, **CARCER**, **Prison**, Fear, grief, punishment, imprisonment, secret enemies, hidden dangers.

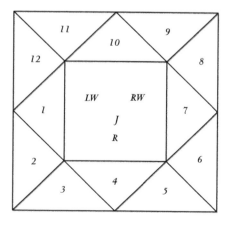

NOTABLE BRITISH LEYS

'OSLS' refers to the 1:50 000 Ordinance Survey Landranger Sheet No.

A Cornish Spirit Path (OSLS 203). St Mary's church, Penzance, Cornwall - Chapel Street, Penzance - Madron church and holy well - section of straight track - cross - Lanyon Quiot dolmen - straight section of road to Trevowhan.

A Supernatural Highway in the Mendips (OSLS 172). Cross Keys Inn, Bedminster Down (site of gibbet and appearance of spectral horse) - the haunted driveway to Bishopworth manor house - a haunted stretch of road over Dundry Hill - the ancient spring of Wriggleswell - Pagan Hill (site of Roman temple and votive well) - Pilgrim's Way burial path at Chew Stoke - St Andrew's church - site of a stone circle and holy well - Moreton Cross and St Mary's well - White Cross (suicide burial site) - Harptree parish boundary.

Two Glastonbury Leys (OSLS 182, 172).

Glastonbury Ley 1: St Benedict's church, Glastonbury - Glastonbury Abbey (axis of abbey is on the ley) - the line of Dod Lane - St Michael's church on Gare Hill - Stonehenge.

Glastonbury Ley 2: St Nicholas' church, Brockley (tunnel legend) - Holy Trinity church, Burrington - Gorsey Bigsbury henge - Westbury Beacon camp, Mendips - crossroads and mark stone at Yarley - St. Michael's church tower, Glastonbury Tor - St Leonard's church, Butleigh (centre of the Glastonbury Zodiac).

The First Ley discovered by Alfred Watkins in Herefordshire (OSLR 149). Croft Ambrey Iron Age hill fort - the line of Croft Lane (1.5 miles long) - mark stone at crossroads at Blackwardine - Risbury Camp - high point at Stretton Grandison (site of a Roman station). Burial Lane at Feckenham, Worcestershire. (OSLR 150). Ham Green hamlet - derelict chapel at Cruise Hill - Burial Lane (street name) - bridleway - iron gate across path - ford and footbridge - road - Feckenham church

Cerne Abbas Ley, Dorset (OSLR 194). St Lawrence's church, Holwell in Dorset - tumulus - prehistoric settlement site - The Trendle earthwork enclosure on Giant's Hill - Cerne Abbas abbey ruins - holy well (site of a vision by St Augustine) - St Mary's church, Cerne Abbas.

Church Path at Gotherington, Gloucs. (OSLR 163). Shutter Lane, Gotherington -'Church Walk' footpath - green lane and path through fields - St Michael's, Bishop's Cleeve.

Coldrum Ley, Kent (OSLR 188). St. Peter and Paul's, Trosley (large stones set into foundations, axis of church on ley) - Coldrum long barrow (tunnel legend links Trosley church and Coldrum barrow) - old track crossing - All Saint's, Snodland (Pilgrim's Way skirts the churchyard) - lost paved ford across the River Medway - St Mary's, Burnham Court - Blue Bell Hill.

The Devil's Arrows, Yorkshire (OSLR 99). Ley 1: Thornborough henges - Nunwick henge - central Devil's Arrow, Boroughbridge. Ley 2: Central and southernmost Devil's Arrows standing stones, Boroughbridge - Cana henge - tumulus at Low Barn - Hutton Moor henge.

Knowlton Henge Ley, Dorset (OSLR 195). Bronze Age tumulus - Bronze Age tumulus - Bronze Age tumulus - Knowlton henge (ruined medieval church) - summer solstice sunrise.

Loanhead of Daviot, Aberdeenshire (OSLR 38). Loanhead of Daviot recumbent stone circle - stone circle in Daviot churchyard (removed) - New Craig recumbent stone circle.

London Leys (OSLR 176).

London Ley 1: St. Martins-in-the-Fields - St. Mary-le-Strand - St. Clement Danes (pre-conquest and once held by the Knight's Templar) - St. Dunstan's, Fleet Street - site of an ancient mound approximately at Arnold's Circus in Shoreditch (parts of Pall Mall and The Strand fall on the alignment).

London Ley 2: St. Paul's, Covent Garden - The Temple church (a Knight's Templar round church) - St Bride's, Fleet Street - church on Ludgate Hill - church near the Guildhall - St. Stephen's, Coleman Street - St. Botolph's, Bishopsgate (the Temple church and St Bride's are oriented on the ley).

London Ley 3: Temple church - St. Paul's Cathedral (built on Ludgate Hill) - St Helen's Bishopsgate - St. Dunstan's, Stepney - St. Clement Dane's (St Paul's, St Helen's and St Dunstan's all orient closely on the same angle as the ley).

May Hill Ley, Gloucestershire (OSLR 163). Giant's Stone long barrow - Wittantree (Saxon moot place) - Bull's Cross (site of appearance of phantom coach and horses) - Painswick church (site of annual 'clipping' ceremony) - May Hill.

Old Sarum Ley, Wiltshire (OSLR 184). Stonehenge - Old Sarum (Iron Age earthwork and later medieval cathedral site) - Salisbury Cathedral - Clearbury Ring (Iron Age hill fort) - Frankenbury Camp (Iron Age hill fort) - tumulus on Durrington Down.

Saintbury Ley and Funeral Path, Gloucestershire (OSLR 150). Cross and crossroads - straight section of road (once a funeral path) - St. Nicholas church, Saintbury - Bronze Age round barrow - Neolithic long barrow - a pagan Saxon cemetery - Seven Wells farm (a place locally associated with medieval witchcraft).

Silbury Hill Ley, Wiltshire (OSLR 173). Bincknoll Castle - a Norman motte and bailey - an ancient well, Broad Hinton - churchyard of St Peter's, Broad Hinton (via the lych gate) - Avebury Henge - Silbury Hill - site of a lost stone circle (noted by Stukeley) - Tan Hill (site of a former fair) - the crossing of an earthwork ditch and the Wansdyke (a post-Roman boundary bank and ditch, phantom funerals have been seen at this point) - Marden henge.

Stanton Drew Leys, Somerset (OSLR 172).

Alignment 1: Centre of the SW circle - centre of the Great Circle - Hautville's Quoit - midsummer sunrise point (2000BC).

Alignment 2: Centre of the NE circle - centre of the Great Circle - The Cove (Neolithic portal dolmen) - midwinter sunset point on the horizon (2000BC).

Sutton Walls Ley, Herefordshire (OSLR 149). Wellington church - Marden church - Sutton Walls Iron Age hill fort (through sighting notch in ramparts) - churchyard cross at Sutton St. Nicholas church - Western Beggard church.

Funeral Path at Wick, Worcestershire (OSLR 150). The old road west out of the village (as existing public footpaths) - crossing over River Avon - field path (pointing directly at Pershore Abbey) - a stile and hollow way - the line of Church Street (formerly Lyce (or corpse) Street) - Pershore Abbey.

Uffington Ley, Oxfordshire/Berkshire (OSLR 174). St. Mary's, Uffington - Dragon Hill (conical hill and site of dragon legend) - Bronze Age barrow - Uffington Castle Iron Age hill fort (above the White Horse) - tumulus at Parkfarm Down - linear earthwork at Near Down - linear earthwork at Farncombe Down - tumulus east of Preston.

Winchester Ley, Hampshire (OSLR 185). Tidbury Ring Iron Age hill fort - remains of a Neolithic long barrow, South Wonston - St. Batholemew's church, Winchester - Hyde Gate (site of Hyde Abbey, burial place of Alfred the Great) - Winchester Cathedral - St. Catherine's Hill (Iron Age hill fort and site of turf labyrinth called the Mizmaze).

Yazor Ley, Herefordshire, Monmouthshire (OSLR 149). A mark stone on the highway at Yazor church, Herefordshire - the ruined tower of Yazor Old Church - a mark stone in a clump of trees at Mansel Gamage - Monnington Court - a mark stone on the highway at Wilmarston - a hill fort near Whitehouse Farm - a churchyard cross at Capel-y-Ffin, Monmouthshire - a bridle pass over Taren-yr-Esgob - mountain peak of Pen-y-Gader, Black Mountains.

Hereford Church Ley (OSLR 149). Aligned section of Portland Street - All Saint's church - Site of St. Owen's church - St. Owen Street - St. Giles' chapel - Eign Road - The Crozen (house on a mound) - site of Saxon burial ground).

Ley Line Cross, Forest of Dean, Gloucestershire (OS Outdoor Leisure Map 14).

Ley 1: Sedbury Stone on Offa's Tump - Coomsbury Wood (high point) - Coldharbour Piece, St. Briavels (circular field with radial field boundaries) - clump of Scots Pines at Cauldwell Farm, Stowe - Staunton Longstone - Longstone, Symond's Yat (natural feature) - Queen Stone, Huntsham (peninsula in the River Wye).

Ley 2: Butt Acre, Monmouth (town centre, possible stone or temple site) - Kymin, near Monmouth (high point, earthworks) - Buckstone, Staunton (logan or rocking stone) - Staunton Longstone - Berry Hill crossroads - Cannop crossroads - Hungry Croft, Ruddle - Barrow Hill, Arlingham (on the peninsula in the River Severn horseshoe bend).

CHINESE DRAGONS

NINE CLASSICAL DRAGON TYPES:

(Chinese dragons are thought of as male, or 'yang', and are generally benevolent, holy and auspicious).

Tianlong, The Celestial Dragon

Shenlong, the Spiritual Dragon

Fucanglong, the Dragon of Hidden Treasures

Dilong, the Underground Dragon

Yinglong, the Winged Dragon

Jiaolong, the Horned Dragon

Panlong, the Coiling Dragon: lives in water

Huanglong, Yellow Dragon, emerged from the River Luo to show Fuxi how to write

Dragon King, one for each of the four directions

DRAGON CHILDREN:
(normally nine, but more are known, found in architectural and monumental decorations)

Baxia, sometimes Bixi, (Genbu in Japan), the first son, looks like a giant tortoise. He represents the element of rock and earth, is very strong and is often found as the carved stone base of monumental tablets.

Chiwen (the phoenix Suzaku in Japan), the second son, is a dragon who can see a long way and generally decorates the corners of rooftops. Sometimes called Chaofeng, while Chiwen becomes the Ridge-Swallowing beast, who rules rainfall and safeguards buildings from fire.

Pulao (Seiryuu in Japan), the third son, resembles a small blue dragon. He represents the elements of water and wind, likes to roar and is always found on musical instruments and bells.

Bi'an (Byakko in Japan), the fourth son, looks like a white tiger. Incredibly powerful, he tells good from bad and is found at court and on prison doors. He represents the metal element.

Taotie, the fifth son, loves eating and is found on food-related wares. He is often swapped for *Qiuniu,* a dragon who is fond of music and decorates the bridge of stringed instruments, or Fuxi, who loves literature and is carved on the sides of inscribed stone tablets.

Gongfu, the sixth son, likes to be in water. His dragon's head is found on bridges.

Yazi, the seventh son, loves fighting and is found on sword and knife hilts and battle axes.

Suanmi, the eighth son, looks like a lion and is fond of smoke and fire. He is guards the main door and is often found on incense burners.

Jiaotu, the youngest son, looks like a conch or clam and is tight-lipped, and does not like to be disturbed. He appears on the front door, the door knocker or the doorstep.

There are also two inferior, malevolent (rare for Chinese dragons) and hornless dragon species, the jiao and the li. The jiao are female dragons and the li are yellow jiao.

Bench End from Crowcombe Church, UK.

GAZETTEER OF EUROPEAN DRAGON SITES

AUSTRIA

THE BRAND DRAGON. Brand, Western Austria. A fierce dragon once haunted the mountains near the remote village of Brand, regularly eating the cattle and peasants. A travelling scholar defeated the dragon by means of a huge thunderstorm which collapsed the whole hillside and killed the dragon in a great flash.

THE KLAGENFURT LINDWURM, Carinthia. A 13th century tale speaks of a winged "lindwurm" that lived in the moors by the lake near Klagenfurt and fed on virgins and caused floods. A Duke offered a reward for anyone who could capture it, so some young men tied a fat bull to a chain, and when the lindwurm swallowed the bull, it was hooked like a fish and then killed.

THE TATZELWURM, Austrian/Bavarian/Italian/Swiss Alps. A stubby, lizard-like creature of Alpine folklore. A cat at the front and a serpent at the rear. Regional names include *stollenwurm, springwurm, arassas* and *praatzelwurm*. In 1934 a Swiss photographer named Balkin allegedly saw a strange creature near a log and photographed it. The resulting interest inspired the *Berliner Illustrierte* to sponsor an  expedition in search of the Tatzelwurm, but the expedition was a failure and interest quickly faded.

ENGLAND

THE FLYING SERPENT. *Aller, Somerset.* This giant winged serpent lived in a den on Round Hill until it was slain by the Lord of Aller with the help of several of his labourers. In Aller church there is an effigy of the knight while at nearby Low Ham Church is a spear said to be the one that killed the dragon.

THE DRAKE. *Anwick, Lincolnshire.* A field known as *Drake Stone Close* was said to be the home of a treasure-guarding dragon. A boulder in the field, now broken, is known as the 'Drake Stone'. 'Drake', an old name for a dragon, was forgotten when the story was retold as the creature described, rising out of the ground, later became a quacking duck.

THE LAIDLY WORM OF SPINDLESTONE HEUGH. *Bamburgh, Northumberland.* The legend can be seen displayed at Bamburgh Castle; the Spindlestone, sometimes known as the Bridlestone, where the Worm coiled herself, can be seen nearby at Spindlestone Heugh.

THE FIERY DRAGON OF BISTERN. *Bisterne Park, Hampshire*. Sir Maurice de Berkeley slew a fire breathing dragon in an area called Dragon Field. His two dogs died in the battle, Sir Maurice died later. At Bisterne Park there is a carved dragon over the main entrance and statues of two dogs in the grounds.

THE BRENT PELHAM DRAGON. *Brent Pelham, Herts.* The Brent Pelham dragon dwelt in a cave under the roots of an old yew tree that stood on the boundary of Great and little Peppersall Fields. The local church contains the tomb of Piers Shonks who killed the savage Brent Pelham dragon by thrusting his spear down its throat at nearby Peppsall Field.

ST GEORGE'S DRAGON. *Brinsop, Hereford & Worcester*. The church at Brinsop is dedicated to St George and has a fine tympanum showing the saint spearing a worm-like dragon. The dragon lived in Dragon's Well in Duck's Pool meadow to the south of the church and the bare patch in Lower Stanks field is said to be the place where the dying dragon's blood poisoned the earth. Close by is Wormsley village.

THE GURT VURM OF SHERVAGE WOOD. *Crowcombe, Somerset.* Crowcombe Church contains bench end carvings of men and dragons fighting and dragons with foliage issuing from their mouths. When the Vurm was cut in two by a woodsman, one end went to Bilbrook where a dragon can be seen on a wall painting in Cleeve Abbey, there is also a hotel in Bilbrook called 'The Dragon House' and Dragon Cross is nearby. The other half of the Vurm went to Kingston St. Mary where there is another dragon killing legend, perhaps it was the other half of the Vurm.

THE DEERHURST DRAGON. *Deerhurst, Gloucestershire.* The Deerhurst Dragon. A labourer, John Smith won an estate on Walton Hill by killing a dragon. He fed it with milk until it relaxed and went to sleep, Then he took his axe and chopped off its head. The church has a number of stone heads said to be dragon's heads; over the outer doors, the inner doors, a window and the chancel arch.

THE HANDALE WORM. *Handale, Yorkshire.* A gallant youth named Scaw slew the Handale Worm, rescued an earl's daughter and married her. In the now demolished Benedictine Handale Priory a stone coffin was found which contained an Elizabethan sword, said to be that of the dragon slayer. Scaw Wood, a wood bearing the name of the dragon killer is nearby.

THE DRAGON OF ST.LEONARD'S FOREST. *Horsham, Sussex.* In St Leonard's forest with it's great old trees and hammer ponds is Dragon Inn, beds of lilly-of-the-valley mark the place where St Leonard's blood is said to have flowed and changed into these flowers as he fought the dragon; lilly-of-the-valley is one of the symbols of the coming of Christ.

THE SERPENT OF KELLINGTON. *Kellington, West Yorkshire.* The surrounding woodlands harboured a giant serpent who devoured all the sheep in the area. A shepherd aided by his dog and wielding a crook eventually killed the monster although both shepherd and dog died. Kellington Church contains the Serpent Stone, a monument carved with a cross and a weathered serpent on one side.

ST. CARANTOC'S SERPENT. *Ker Moor, Somerset.* A terrible serpent devastated the landscape around Ker Moor. St. Carantoc approached the serpent who meekly allowed the saint to put his stole around its neck. Carantoc brought it to King Arthur's stronghold but would not let it be killed. He ordered it to go away and never return and this it did. King Arthur's stronghold is said to be Dunster Castle and Ker Moor where the serpent dwelt.

THE INVISIBLE DRAGON. *Longwitton, Thurston, Northumberland.* The people of Longwitton were unable to use their three wells because they sensed the

presence of an invisible dragon. The legendary hero Guy of Warwick was passing by and agreed to fight the dragon as he had a magic eye ointment that enabled him to see his adversary.
Guy killed the dragon and the locals were able to use the healing wells again.

THE KNUCKLER. *Lyminster, Sussex.* The Knuckler lived in an almost bottomless pool called The Knuckler Hole which can be seen northwest of Lyminster near the church which contains a Norman coffin lid called the Slayer's Stone said to belong to the Knuckler's killer.

THE MOSTON DRAGON. *Middlewich, Cheshire.* Sir Thomas Venables shot a dragon in the eye at Bache Pool at Moston just as it was about to eat a small child. The family crest is a dragon with a child in its mouth.

THE MORDIFORD DRAGON. *Mordiford, Hereford & Worcester.* The dragon was killed by a villain called Garston as it slithered down Serpent Lane to the River Lugg. Garston hid in an iron spiked barrel and persuaded the dragon to attack him; it was cut to pieces on the spikes. A painting of the dragon on the church wall was destroyed in 1810.

THE DRAGON OF LOSCHY HILL. *Nunnington, Yorkshire.* Peter Loschy slew a dragon on a hill by wearing a suit of armour studded with sharp blades which cut the dragon to pieces when it tried to crush him. Both Peter and his dog died when they touched the dragon's poisonous blood. The place of the battle is now named Loschy Hill. Nearby Nunnington Church contains a tomb of a knight with his feet partly destroyed resting on what could be the remains of a dog or lion.

THE LAMBTON WORM. *Penshaw, Durham.* Worm Hill around which the Worm coiled can be seen in North Biddick on the bank of the Wear River. There is a replica of the well where the worm spent its formative years; and 'growed and growed, and growed to an awful size.'

THE RENWICK COCKATRICE, *Renwick, Cumberland.* This strange creature escaped from the foundations of the local church when it was demolished.

John Tallantine killed the dragon using the branch of the rowan tree which is reputed to have magical powers.

THE LONG SLINGSBY SERPENT. *Slingsby, Yorkshire.* A local hero, Wyvill, and his dog slew the dragon which was documented as being either one mile or eighteen yards long but both perished in the attempt. The coat of arms of the Wyvilles has a Wyvern upon it. The serpent dwelt in a large hole, probably a disused limestone quarry, which looked like a cup-like hollow, half a mile from the town.

THE SOCKBURN WORM. *Sockburn, County Durham.* One of the oldest legends in the country. Sir John Conyers killed the Worm/ dragon/ wyvern with a weapon called a Conyer's Falchion which is still used in the inauguration rites of the bishops of Durham. The falchion can be seen in Durham Cathedral Treasury. In the grounds of Sockburn Hall is the remains of a church containing an effigy of a knight in armour with a lion fighting a dragon at its feet. A manuscript in the British Museum recounts the legend.

THE UFFINGTON DRAGON. *Uffington, Oxfordshire.* Below the chalk-hill figure of the White Horse of Uffington in the White Horse Vale is Dragon Hill where, again, there is a bald patch of ground where the dragon's dying blood is said to have poisoned the earth. In Saxon times King Certic's warriors were said to have slain the Pendragon Naud and his army here, perhaps that is how it got its name. It has been suggested that the ancient chalk carving here is a dragon and not a horse.

THE DRAGON OF WANTLEY. *Wantley, Yorkshire.* A 17th century ballad recounts the story. A dragon with forty four iron teeth, long claws, a sting in his tail, a tough hide and two wings, lived in Yorkshire near Rotherham. The people thereabouts begged More of More Hall to kill

it. He agreed in exchange for a fair maid of sixteen and armed with the traditional spiked armour he fought the beast for two days and two nights. Eventually More kicked the dragon in a vulnerable place, his arsehole, which ended the creature's life. The scene of the ballad is a place called Warncliffe Lodge, generally known as Wantley, a mile from the village called Wortley. The More coat of arms bears a green dragon.

THE WHERWELL COCKATRICE. *Wherwell, Hampshire.* This monster, hatched by a toad incubating a duck's egg, lived in a crypt beneath Werwell Priory and caused much devastation in the surrounding area. A man called Green destroyed the cockatrice by lowering a polished metal mirror into its den. The cockatrice fiercely attacked its own reflection in the mirror with such vigour that it killed itself. There is an area called Green's acre at Wherwell.

FRANCE

THE TARASQUE OF NERLUC. *Nerluc, Provence.* Originally from Galatia, home of the Onachus, this was a scaly, bison-like beast which burned everything it touched (similar to the Bonnacon). The king of Nerluc had attacked the Tarasque with knights and catapults with no success. But Saint Martha found the beast and charmed it with hymns and prayers, and led it back tamed to the city. The people, terrified by the monster, attacked it when it drew nigh. The monster offered no resistance and died there. Martha preached to the people and converted many to Christianity. Sorry for what they had done, the townspeople changed the town's name to Tarascon.

THE GARGOUILLE. *River Seine, Rouen.* The gargouille was a water-spouting dragon with four legs and wings that appeared in the Seine River in France. It terrorised boats and caused flooding of the land. Saint Romain, the archbishop of Rouen, lured the monster to shore using a convict, and then made a cross with his fingers which tamed it before leading it into town where it was burned to death. Neither the monster's head or neck would burn, so they were mounted on the town's cathedral to display God's power. The creature was then carved onto buildings to be used as a water drainage, thereby creating the modern gargoyle.

THE PELUDA. *La Ferté-Bernard, Pays de la Loire.* This shaggy or hairy dragon (La Velue) terrorised La

Ferté-Bernard, France, in medieval times. It lived in a cave near the river Huisne close to the town. It had an ox-sized porcupine-like body covered with green hair-like stinger-tipped tentacles which erected into quills which it could shoot off its body.
It rampaged across the countryside, wilting crops with its breath and devouring both livestock and humans before it was finally defeated after it killed a man's fiancée.

Furious, he tracked it down and cut off its tail (the dragon's only vulnerable point) whereupon it died immediately.

GERMANY

THE KÖNIGSWINTER DRAGON. *Rhien-Sieg, North Rhine-Westphalia*. A dragon used to live in a cave in the mountain above the medieval Schloss Drachenburg palace (a castle which stands on a wooded hill high above the Rhine River) near the sleepy town of Königswinter. According to German folklore, it was slayed by Siegfried.

THE FURTH IM WALD DRAGON, Bavarian Forest. The *Drachenstich* (Slaying of the Dragon) is the oldest traditional folk spectacle in Germany, held in Furth Im Wald (City of Dragons) in Bavaria. Dating back 500 years, the event includes a re-enactment of the slaying of a dragon which threatened the town in the Middle Ages.

FÁFNIR. Worms, Rhineland. The dragon Fáfnir from the Norse Völsunga saga appears in the German Nibelungenlied as a lindworm that lived near Worms and which was killed by Siegfried. The hero reputedly drank the dragon's blood to gain wisdom.

ITALY

THE FORLÌ DRAGON. The first bishop of the city of Forlì, named Saint Mercurialis, was said to have killed a dragon.

THE FORNOLE DRAGON. *Terni, Umbria*. Pope Saint Sylvester freed the people of Fornole from a huge and ferocious dragon which had been terrorising the locals and their livestock, by taming it and thus making it into a gentle creature. In gratitude, the locals built a little church dedicated to the saint on the top of the mountain, near the dragon's lair.

THE THYRUS WYVERN. *Terni*. This dangerous wyvern besieged Terni in the Middle Ages. It was eventually killed by a brave knight, tired of witnessing the death of his fellow citizens and depopulation of Terni.

THE SCULTONE. *Baunei, Sardinia*. This basilisk lived in the middle of Sardinia on a natural plateau near the country church of San Pietro, in Supramonte Baunei, beside the "su golgu" (the gorge) sinkhole canyon, the deepest chasm in Europe. It could kill humans beings with a single look. To get rid of it, the people called on Peter the Apostle, who despatched the dragon with ease by making the dragon look into a mirror, whereupon, seeing it's own reflection, it was destroyed.

POLAND

THE WAWEL DRAGON. *Kraków.* Smok Wawelski, the Dragon of Wawel Hill, terrorised ancient Kraków and lived in caves on the Vistula river bank below the Wawel castle. The townspeople appeased it by feeding it young maidens. The king offered his daughter's hand in marriage to whoever could kill it and eventually a cobbler's apprentice called Skuba offered it a sheepskin filled with sulphur and tar. After devouring this, the dragon became extremely thirsty

and drank and drank the river water until it finally exploded.

SCANDINAVIA

THE LINDORM. *Småland, Blekinge and Skane.* Tales of the lindorm, or "lime tree serpent", named for its habit of laying its eggs under the bark of the lime tree, are common all over Southern Sweden but particularly in these counties. 19th century Swedish folklorist Gunnar Olof Hyltén-Cavallius collected many stories of these creatures and in 1884 set up a big reward for a captured specimen, dead or alive.

THE KARLSKRONA/BLEKINGE LINDORM. Two lindorms escaped from a ship anchored in the harbour. After causing some distress to the townspeople, the serpents disappeared out into the sea and were later each spotted at different locations along the coastline, basking on rocks in the sunshine. Both these locations are named after the lindorms.

THE LAKE LÄEN SERPENT. *Småland.* On a small island in Lake Läen eyewitness Johan Sedig reported seeing a serpent "12ft long and a horror to behold. The eyes were shiny, like those of the asp, and about the size of hazelnuts. Its stare was sharp and terrible. There was much talk amongst people about our adventure, so I can truthfully declare that this type of snake or dragon has been much discussed in our watery woodland and that people have claimed to have seen specimens with a long, dark mane along its neck, and reaching lengths up to 18–20 feet."

THE SIRK ISLAND LINDORM, *Lake Åsnen, Småland* - In 1844, a lindorm was said to have scared off a group of carpenters working on Sirk Island in Lake Åsnen. The following day, the men returned, but could find no trace of the serpent.

SKÅNE COUNTY LINDORMS. One Whit Sunday in the early 1850s, maid Elna Olsdotter was on her way to church. She stopped to rest for a moment under a big lime tree when a huge lindorm appeared from within the tree and gobbled her up whole. The monster left only two items: Elna's silk scarf and her hymnbook. In another part of Skåne, a little girl and her mother were picking berries near the stump of an old lime tree. The girl discovered a huge snake lying within the tree, and despite warnings from her mother that the snake was nothing less than a lindorm, the girl reached in her hand to touch it and was promptly grabbed and devoured.

SCOTLAND

THE WHITE SERPENT. *Dalry, Dumfries and Galloway.* The lord of Galloway offered a reward to whomsoever would kill a corpse eating giant serpent that lived in Dalray coiled around Mote Hill. A blacksmith gained the reward by covering himself with spikes and goading the serpent into swallowing him. The spikes tore the serpent to pieces and for three days the waters of the Ken ran red with blood.

THE WYRM OF WYRMISTON. *Linton, Roxburghshire, Scotland.* This Wyrm was killed by Norman Somerville, Laird of Larriston who thrust a lance, tipped with a lump of peat dipped in scalding tar, down its throat. This is a

similar technique to the slaying of the Cnoc-na-Cnoimh Worm. The contractions of the dying Wyrm coiled round Wormington Hill marked the hill with vermicular traces. Somerville was created Baron of Linton and given the post of Royal Falconer. In Linton Church there is a carving of a man, with a creature that could be a falcon, slaying a dragon.

THE WORM OF CNOC-NA CNOIMH. *Cnoc-na-Cnoimh, Dumfries and Galloway.* A farmer, Hector Gunn, killed the Worm because he could not stand its

poisonous breath. He used a spear on the tip of which was a lump of peat soaked in boiling pitch which he thrust down the worm's throat. The hillside, Cnoc-na-Cnoimh means wormhill, is ringed by spiral undulations said to have been caused by the worm in its death throes.

MARTIN'S DRAGON. *Kirkton of Strathmartin, Angus.* The Legend of the Nine Tempting Maidens. Martin's Stone where Martin killed a dragon after it had eaten nine maidens when they went to a well at Pitempton, can be seen in a field to the north of Baldragon Wood (below). The dying dragon uttered these words:-

"I was tempit at Pitempton,
Draiglet [dragged] at Baldragon,
Striken at Strikemartin,
And killed at Martinstane."

These are all place names in the surrounding area. Nine Maiden's well has been filled in and can no longer be seen.

SLAVIC

THE BRNO DRAGON, Czech Republic. A legend tells of a huge dragon which ate poultry and strangled lambs. A reward was announced for the killing of the dragon. One day, a travelling butcher sewed up burnt lime into an ox skin, and hid it in long grass. The dragon sniffed it out and ate it, which made him very thirsty, so he went to the river and drank and drank until his stomach burst out. The dragon was taken into the city, and was stuffed and then hung in the Old Town Hall passage.

THE BILÄR DRAGON, *Bilär, Bulgaria*. A big snake used to live in the medieval city of Bilar, in Volga Bulgaria. When the locals decided to kill it, the snake begged for peace and asked Allah to give her wings. Allah obliged and the snake flew away from Bilär and was not seen again.

SPAIN

THE CAUCHADOR REAL, *Almeria*. These large orange dragons used to roam the barren deserts of southeast Spain. In the wild they grew to 10-12 tons, but when kept in captivity for fighting purposes they were said to grow to 25 tons.

THE CUÉLEBRE SERPENT. Asturias and Cantabria. This is a giant winged serpent which lives in a cave, guards treasures and imprisons beautiful nymphs. They grow old despite being immortal, and can be tricked if youo know what you are doing, especially on certain days.

THE FLECHA-DEL-FUEGO DRAGON. *South-western Spain & Portugal*. A small dragon, only 7-8m, it has large, light, strong wings which make it a supreme flyer, unlike many other dragons. The males have long curled horns and neck frills.

THE HERENSUGE DRAGON. *Basque Country*. Supposedly the "last serpent" the Basques tell of St. Michael descending from Heaven to kill it but only once God had agreed to accompany him in person. The ancient Basque male god Sugaar "male serpent" is often associated with the serpent or dragon but able to take other forms as well.

THE PEÑA URUEL DRAGON. *Jaca*. A dragon once lived in a cave in the Peña Uruel mountain near Jaca which could mesmerize people with its glance. A young man equipped with a shiny shield, so that the dragon's glance would be reflected, killed it easily as the dragon mesmerised itself.

WALES

THE RED AND WHITE FIGHTING DRAGONS. *Dinas*

Emrys, Snowdonia, Wales. [See *Dragons in Heraldry*]. Remains of an Iron age hill fort can be seen on the top of Dinas Emrys.

THE WISTON COCKATRICE. *Pembrokeshire*. Centuries ago, there were several claimants to the estate of Castle Gwys, now known as Wiston. It was agreed by the family that anyone of them who could observe a multi-eyed cockatrice who lived in a hole in a bank near the castle without it seeing him would gain the estate. One wily claimant devised a plan; he secured himself in a barrel and peered at the cockatrice through its bunghole as the barrel rolled down the hill past the cockatrice's lair. This stratagem won him the estate.

THE WYVERN OF CYNWCH LAKE. *Dolgellau, Gwynedd*. The Wyvern lived in the lake until it was killed by a shepherd lad with the help of the inhabitants of the Monastery of the Standard.

THE DRAGON IN THE TOWER. *Llandeilo Graham, Powys*. The local church tower was the roosting place of a terror-inspiring dragon. A cunning ploughboy made a dummy of a dragon with knives and hooks sticking out of it and placed it in the tower when the dragon was away. The dragon returned, attacked the dummy and was impaled upon its spikes. It is thought that this legend was inspired by a draconian weather vane that used to be on the church tower.

INDEX

QUADRIVIUM

THE FOUR CLASSICAL LIBERAL ARTS OF
NUMBER, GEOMETRY, MUSIC, & COSMOLOGY

TRIVIUM

THE CLASSICAL LIBERAL ARTS OF
GRAMMAR, LOGIC, & RHETORIC

NOUN
Verb
Adjective ADVERB

LOGOS
ETHOS
pathos

and
or
not

deduction
induction
analogy

PROOF
fallacy
paradox

REPETITION
rhythm
RHYME

trochee
iamb dactyl
amphibrach
anapest

IRONY
METAPHOR
enthymeme

VIRTUE
dilemma
JUSTICE

TRUE

tetra-
penta-
hexameter

ballad
sonnet ode

GOOD